Partnership in Higher Education

African Higher Education

DEVELOPMENTS AND PERSPECTIVES

Series Editors

Michael Cross (*University of Johannesburg, South Africa*)
Jane Knight (*University of Toronto, Canada*)

Editorial Assistants

Marlene de Beer (*University of Johannesburg, South Africa*)
Amasa Ndofirepi (*University of Johannesburg, South Africa*)

Advisory Board

N'Dri Therese Assie-Lumumba (*Cornell University, USA*)
Akilagpa Sawyerr (*Ghana Academy of Arts, Ghana*)
Paul Tiyambe Zeleza (*United States International University, Kenya*)

Editorial Board

Saleem Badat (*Andrew Mellon Foundation, South Africa*)
James Otieno Jowi (*Moi University, Kenya*)
Goolam Mohamedbhai (*Formerly University of Mauritius, Mauritius*)
Teboho Moja (*New York University, USA*)
Reitumetse Obakeng Mabokela (*University of Illinois Urbana–Champaign, USA*)
Adebayo Olukoshi (*International IDEA, Ethiopia*)
Chika Sehoole (*University of Pretoria, South Africa*)

VOLUME 4

The titles published in this series are listed at *brill.com/afhe*

Partnership in Higher Education

Trends between African and European Institutions

Edited by

Emnet Tadesse Woldegiorgis and Christine Scherer

BRILL
SENSE

LEIDEN | BOSTON

All chapters in this book have undergone peer review.

Library of Congress Cataloging-in-Publication Data

Names: Woldegiorgis, Emnet Tadesse, editor. | Scherer, Christine, editor.
Title: Partnership in Higher Education : Trends Between African and
   European Institutions / Edited by Emnet Tadesse Woldegiorgis and
   Christine Scherer.
Description: Leiden ; Boston : Brill Sense, [2019] | Series: African Higher
   Education: Developments and Perspectives, 26662663 ; Volume 4 | Includes
   bibliographical references and index.
Identifiers: LCCN 2019032192 (print) | LCCN 2019032193 (ebook) | ISBN
   9789004411869 (hardback) | ISBN 9789004411852 (paperback) | ISBN
   9789004411876 (ebook)
Subjects: LCSH: University cooperation--Africa. | University
   cooperation--Europe. | Education, Higher--Africa. | Education,
   Higher--Europe. | Educational change--Africa. | Educational
   change--Europe.
Classification: LCC LB2331.5 .P367 2019 (print) | LCC LB2331.5 (ebook) |
   DDC 378.1/04--dc23
LC record available at https://lccn.loc.gov/2019032192
LC ebook record available at https://lccn.loc.gov/2019032193

Typeface for the Latin, Greek, and Cyrillic scripts: "Brill". See and download: brill.com/brill-typeface.

ISSN 2666-2663
ISBN 978-90-04-41185-2 (paperback)
ISBN 978-90-04-41186-9 (hardback)
ISBN 978-90-04-41187-6 (e-book)

Copyright 2019 by Koninklijke Brill NV, Leiden, The Netherlands.
Koninklijke Brill NV incorporates the imprints Brill, Brill Hes & De Graaf, Brill Nijhoff, Brill Rodopi,
Brill Sense, Hotei Publishing, mentis Verlag, Verlag Ferdinand Schöningh and Wilhelm Fink Verlag.
All rights reserved. No part of this publication may be reproduced, translated, stored in a retrieval system,
or transmitted in any form or by any means, electronic, mechanical, photocopying, recording or otherwise,
without prior written permission from the publisher.
Authorization to photocopy items for internal or personal use is granted by Koninklijke Brill NV provided
that the appropriate fees are paid directly to The Copyright Clearance Center, 222 Rosewood Drive, Suite
910, Danvers, MA 01923, USA. Fees are subject to change.

This book is printed on acid-free paper and produced in a sustainable manner.

Contents

Acknowledgments   VII
List of Figures and Tables   VIII
List of Abbreviations   X
Notes on Contributors   XIII

Introduction   1
   Emnet Tadesse Woldegiorgis and Christine Scherer

1   Higher Education Partnership in Africa: The Case of the Pan-African University Network and the Mwalimu Nyerere Mobility Programme   12
   Emnet Tadesse Woldegiorgis

2   A Critical Assessment of the Internationalization of Higher Education: The Case of Sub-Saharan Africa   29
   Sintayehu Kassaye Alemu

3   Reflections on the Role of Africa in Research for Development: A Plea for Collaboration   62
   Brook Lemma

4   Relational Policies in Higher Education Partnership and Collaboration: Europe's Approach to Africa and the Special Case of Germany   76
   Christine Scherer

5   Higher Education Partnership between Maghreb and European Higher Education Institutions during the 2002–2013 Decade   103
   Baghdad Benstaali

6   Developing International Quality Assurance Standards in Africa: Reference to the Pan-African University as Institutional Partnership in the Framework of Bologna   120
   Abbes Sebihi and Leonie Schoelen

7   Internationalizing Higher Education through Service Learning: The Case of the University for Development Studies, Ghana   138
   Lydia Kwoyiga and Agnes Atia Apusigah

8   Prospects and Challenges in North-South Curriculum Development
     Partnerships: The Case of a Finnish-Cameroonian University Project in
     Higher Education Studies   163
         Pascal Doh

9   Prospects, Challenges, and Opportunities of International Exchange
     Programmes: The Case of a Double Degree Master's Programme   185
         Thomas Asante and Agnes Atia Apusigah

10   Challenges and Prospects for Higher Education Partnership in Africa:
     Concluding Remarks   203
         Emnet Tadesse Woldegiorgis and Christine Scherer

     Index   213

Acknowledgments

It is our great pleasure to extend our heartfelt appreciation and gratitude to the scholars who contributed the chapters of this book. The book could not have been realized without their valuable expertise. Each chapter has passed through a thorough peer-review and editorial process, which took more time than expected, and we are very grateful for the enduring patience of all the authors.

Our appreciation and recognition go to Bayreuth International Graduate School of African Studies (BIGSAS), University of Bayreuth for their financial support and key role in the conference that was the base for this publication. We also extend our gratitude to the entire network of BIGSAS as the idea was further enriched by the impact of partner institutions. We would like to highlight that BIGSAS is supported by the German Research Foundation (DFG) and founded in the frame of the Excellence Initiative (2005–2019) aimed to promote top-level research and to improve the quality of German universities and research institutions.

We are also grateful to Miriam Straßer, project support at BIGSAS, for her technical support in the process of formatting the book.

The book is meant to stimulate a new generation of scholars, who are inspired to work on and understand the paradigms of higher education partnerships within an ever-changing changing international and global context.

Figures and Tables

Figures

2.1   Network of internal research collaboration (from Adams et al., 2010).   48
2.2   Trends in African research article output in the international journal literature, 1980–2004 (from Tijssen, 2007, p. 308).   50
2.3   Regional research production, 1999–2008 (adapted from Adams et al., 2010).   51
3.1   The push-pull (supply-demand) model of research (developed after Godin & Lane, 2005).   66
3.2   International flows of scientific authors (researcher mobility) from 1996 to 2011: Largest bilateral flows (Appelt et al., 2015; see also OECD, 2013; Hulten, 2013).   67
3.3   Model of the research process in neo-liberal times (Taylor, 2006; Knight, 2007; Meek & Davis, 2009; Jacob & Meek, 2012).   68
3.4   Investments in basic research for 2011 (from OECD, 2012, 2013a, 2013b; Hulten, 2013).   68
4.1   Participations of African R & D institutions in FP 7 (Source: Cordis FP 7 Organizations).   87
4.2   Participating nations (Source: Cordis FP 7 Organizations).   87
4.3   Funding development of German research and research funding institutions (2005–2013) (Source: Internationales Büro (DLR), May 2014).   94
4.4   Germany's regional funding of science and technology programmes and projects (Source: International Office, May 2014).   95
5.1   Partnership relationship to the priority themes (Benstaali, 2014).   109
5.2   Contribution of South Mediterranean HEIs with Algerian counterparts to Tempus projects (Benstaali, 2014).   110
5.3   Partnership with European partners (Benstaali, 2014).   112
5.4   European universities' participation to Erasmus Mundus partnerships (Benstaali, 2014).   113

Tables

1.1   Thematic areas of the Pan-African University.   21
2.1   A compiled data on brain drain: Sub-Saharan Africa (SSA).   39
2.2   Regional comparison of scientific publications and patent applications in 2007.   52
2.3   Percentage of collaborative scientific paper production.   53
4.1   Overview of the Africa-EU summits since the year 2000.   84

FIGURES AND TABLES

4.2 Overview of the FPs. 86
5.1 Maghreb HEIs network (as of July 2012). 107
5.2 Tempus programme partnerships for SM countries 2002–2012 (the main achievements of the Tempus programme in the Southern Mediterranean 2002–2013, 2013). 111
5.3 Rate of involvement of HEIs in partnerships (as of July 2012). 111
5.4 Combined mobility for SM Nationals Action 1 & Action 2 (Erasmus Mundus in the Southern Mediterranean, 2013). 114
5.5 North-South student mobility within selected partnerships between 2007–2010. 115
8.1 The curriculum development seminars for the master's programme in higher education management in Cameroon. 171
8.2 Courses of the Cameroon master's programme in higher education management. 173

Abbreviations

AAU	Association of African Universities
ACP	African, Caribbean and Pacific Group of States
AECID	Spanish Agency for International Cooperation
AFD	Agence Française de Développement/French Development Agency
AfDB	African Development Bank
AfriQAN	Africa Quality Assurance Network
AMCOST	African Ministerial Council on Science and Technology
ARA	African Research Area
AU	African Union
AUC	African Union Commission
AUF	Agence Universitaire de la Francophonie/Francophone University Association
AU-HEP	African Union's Strategy for the Harmonization of Higher Education Programmes
APPEAR	Austrian Partnership Programme in Higher Education and Research for Development
APSA	African Peace and Security Architecture
BMBF	Bundesministerium für Bildung und Forschung/Federal Ministry of Education and Research
BMZ	Bundesministerium für wirtschaftliche Zusammenarbeit und Entwicklung/Federal Ministry for Economic Cooperation and Development
CAAST-Net	Network for the Coordination and Advancement of Sub-Saharan Africa-EU Science and Technology Cooperation
CAMES	Conseil Africain et Malgache pour l'Enseignement Supérieur (African and Malagasy Council for Higher Education)
CATS	Credit Accumulation and Transfer System
CENSUDI	Centre for Sustainable Development Initiatives
CODESRIA	Council for the Development of Social Science Research in Africa
COMEDAF	Conference of Ministers of Education of the African Union
COMESA	Common Market for Eastern and Southern Africa
CoP	Community of Practice
CPA	Africa's Science and Technology Consolidated Plan of Action
DAAD	German Academic Exchange Service
DfID	Department for International Development
DIES	Dialogue on Innovative Higher Education Strategies
EACEA	Education, Audiovisual and Culture Executive Agency of the European Commission

ECTS	European Credit Transfer System
EDF	European Development Fund
ENPI	European Neighbourhood and Partnership Instrument
EQF	European Qualification Framework
ERA	European Research Area
EU	European Union
EUC	European Union Commission
FPs	European Framework Programmes
GIZ	Deutsche Gesellschaft für Internationale Zusammenarbeit/German Society for International Cooperation
GTZ	Deutsche Gesellschaft für Technische Zusammenarbeit/The German Organization for Technical Cooperation
HEG	Higher Education Group
HEI-ICI	Higher Education Institutions Institutional Cooperation Instrument
HLPD	High-Level Policy Dialogue
IAEPS	International Academic Exchange Programmes
IAU	International Association of Universities
ICT	Information and Communication Technology
JAES	Joint Africa-Europe Strategy
JICA	Japan International Cooperation Agency
IEPS	International Exchange Programmes
LMD	Licence-Master-Doctorat/Bachelor's Master's Doctorate System
LMS	Learning Management System
NASAC	Network of African Science Academies
NEPAD	New Partnership for Africa's Development
NICHE	Netherlands Initiative for Capacity Development in Higher Education
NORHED	Norwegian Programme for Capacity Development in Higher Education and Research for Development
Nuffic	Dutch Organization for Internationalization in Education
OAU	Organization of the African Unity
ODA	Official Development Assistance
OECD	Organization for Economic Cooperation and Development
PAU	Pan African University
PAUGHSS	PAU Institute for Governance, Humanities and Social Sciences
PAULESI	Pan African University for Life and Earth Sciences Institutes
PAUSS	PAU Institute for Space Sciences
PAUSTI	PAU Institute of Basic Sciences, Technology, and Innovation
PAUWES	Pan-African University Institute of Water and Energy Sciences (including Climate Change)
RECP	Africa-EU Renewable Energy Cooperation Programme
PHEA	Partnership for Higher Education in Africa

RQF	Regional Qualification Framework
SIDA	Swedish International Development Cooperation Agency
SL	Service Learning
SM	Southern Mediterranean
SEVIS	Student and Exchange Visitor Information System
STI	Science, Technology and Innovation
UASD	University of Applied Sciences Düsseldorf
UDS	University for Development Studies
UEMOA	West African Economic and Monetary Union
UIS	UNESCO Institute for Statistics
UN	United Nations
UNECA	United Nations Economic Commission for Africa
UNESCO	United Nations Educational, Scientific and Cultural Organization
UNDP	United Nations Development Programme
UNICEF	United Nations International Children's Emergency Fund
UNU-EHS	United Nations University Institute for Environment and Human Security
USAID	US Agency for International Development
ZEF	Zentrum für Entwicklungsforschung/Center for Development Research

Notes on Contributors

Sintayehu Kassaye Alemu
has studied his BA and MA in History at Addis Ababa University, Ethiopia, in an Erasmus Mundus European Master programme, and got his Master Degree in Higher Education from the Universities of Oslo (Norway), Tampere (Finland), and Aveiro (Portugal). The University of Tampere has also awarded him a Master Degree in Administrative Sciences. Sintayehu conducted his Ph.D. (2013–2016) within the project "Universities in the Knowledge Economy" (UNIKE) which is funded by the European Commission. The project included six European Universities namely, Aarhus University (Denmark), University of Bristol (UK), Roehampton University (UK), University of Porto (Portugal), University of Ljubljana (Slovenia), and École normale supérieure de Lyon (ENS de Lyon) (France). At present, Dr. Sintayehu Kassaye is working as a lecturer and researcher at Mekelle University.

Agnes Atia Apusigah
is an Associate Professor of Cultural analysis and Gender studies in the University for Development Studies (UDS), Tamale, Ghana. She has worked in the UDS since the completion of her doctoral thesis in Cultural studies and Curriculum Studies from Queen's University, Kingston, Ontario, Canada, in 2002. Her research interests are in the areas of the political economy of African development, educational reform and development, indigenous knowledge and gender equality and women's rights and development. Her most recent works are: *Bridging Worlds: Interfacing Indigenous and Conventional Knowledges for Ghana's Development, Women's Rights Organizations and Funding Regimes in Ghana, Teacher Professionalism and Educational Quality*, and *Community-Based Ecotourism for Sustainable Development in Ghana: The Place of Indigenous Knowledge*. She is currently the Dean of the Faculty of Education of the University for Development Studies.

Thomas Asante
is from Ghana. He was ordained to the Catholic priesthood on 18th July 1992. In 1996, he went to the United States of America for further studies. He holds a Master of Arts degree in Theology from the University of Scranton, Pennsylvania, and Ph.D. in Educational administration from Marywood University, Scranton, Pennsylvania. He is currently a lecturer at the Faculty of Education, University for Development Studies, Tamale, Northern Region, Ghana.

Baghdad Benstaali

is an Expert in Quality Assurance and Accreditation in Higher Education. He assists higher education institutions to implement quality standards and self-assessment for international accreditation. He is the former Director of Tempus/Erasmus+ programmes in Algeria. His main role was to improve the participation of national HEIs to South Mediterranean – European partnerships investigated in a Tempus study "The Tempus programme in Algeria 2002–2013" published in 2014. He is also a programme evaluator with the American Accreditation Board for Engineering and Technology. He is an alumnus of the University of East Anglia in the United Kingdom.

Pascal Doh

is a Cameroonian scholar, consultant and lecturer of Higher Education (HE) resident in Finland. He holds a Ph.D. in Higher Education Management from the University of Tampere, Finland (UTA), an MPhil/Master in HE policies from the Universities of Oslo (Norway), Tampere (Finland) and Aveiro (Portugal) under the Erasmus Mundus Programme by the European Commission (2007). Pascal Doh has been involved for more than a decade in HE studies, teaching, research and consultancy with several publications. He has participated in over 50 higher education conferences including with UNESCO, OECD, EC, EUA, AAU, CUD-Belgium, ADEA, Finnish and African institutions. He is the coordinator of an international network of HE management and policy consultants between Africa and Europe, HECADEV Consulting in Turku, Finland, a part-time lecturer of HE Management at the University Tampere, Finland, and visiting lecturer to many African Universities. He has been involved in several HE capacity-building projects between Europe and Africa. Doh works in the languages English, French, and Finnish.

Lydia Kwoyiga

is a lecturer at the Faculty of Education since completing her two Master degree studies from the University of Oslo and the Norwegian University of Life Sciences in 2013. Her research interest includes institutions and the environment, climate change adaptation and natural resources use, education and development and local knowledge and sustainable development. She was the Faculty coordinator for the Third Trimester Field Practical Programme (TTFPP) of the University for Development Studies (USD), Ghana. She is currently a Ph.D. student at the Faculty of Environmental Sciences, Technische Universität Dresden (Technical University Dresden).

Brook Lemma

is the Director of Research Programmes and the Coordinator of the Grants' Office of Addis Ababa University, Ethiopia, and President of the Ethiopian

Fisheries Association (EFASA). He did his Ph.D. at Technische Universität Dresden (Technical University Dresden), Germany. He has been working at both Haramaya University and Addis Ababa University in different leadership capacities including the function of the Assistant Secretary to the Dean, Academic Programme Officer, Coordinator of Continuing Education, University Registrar, Dean of the Faculty of Education, and President of Ethiopian Higher Education Institutes Sports Association at Haramaya (Alemaya) University, Eastern Ethiopia. He continued providing university and social services as Head of Department of Biology Education, Director Research Programmes, Coordinator of Grants' of Addis Ababa University, and President of the Ethiopian Fisheries Association (EFASA) as part of social service.

Christine Scherer

is an expert in science management and science communication. She is a print-media journalist and worked for science broadcasting and media during her studies of administrative sciences (University of Konstanz), anthropology, political sciences and romance studies (University of Bayreuth). She holds a Ph.D. in social anthropology that she accomplished as a member of the Collaborative Research Centre 'Local Agency in Africa in the context of Global Influences' (2007). Recently, she initiated a range of projects and international conferences on higher education and opened the research direction on higher education in Africa at the University of Bayreuth including a lecture series titled "Developments in Higher Education in Africa" and a related workgroup. As the former coordinator of the Bayreuth International Graduate School of African Studies, BIGSAS, Christine Scherer has been involved in the organizational development of the doctoral research and training institution and implementing the intercontinental collaboration with six Universities in Africa.

Leonie Schoelen

is currently a Ph.D. candidate in Education Sciences and Sociology. Her dissertation is about the transformation of the Algerian higher education system (1962–2017). She receives a full doctoral scholarship by Cusanuswerk, Germany. Prior to that, she got her B.A. in English Studies, Politics and Society, University of Bonn, Germany, and M.A. Peace and Conflict Studies, University of St Andrews, Scotland/UK. She is also a former *Deutsche Gesellschaft für Internationale Zusammenarbeit* (GIZ GmbH – German Development Cooperation) consultant in Algeria and United Nations University Institute for Environment and Human Security (UNU-EHS) and *Zentrum für Entwicklungsforschung* (ZEF – Centre for Development Research) Associate after working in India and Benin.

Abbes Sebihi
is senior education and training specialist and expert in the field of international higher and vocational education, technology-mediated learning, pedagogies and capacity/institutional development. He is currently working at Centre for International Migration and Development (CIM) seconded expert to Southeast Asian Ministers of Education Organization Regional Centre for Vocational and Technical Education and Training (SEAMEO VOCTECH), Brunei Darussalam. With 20 years of project management experience from a technical and strategic management background on four continents, he has worked as an IT expert for several companies including Bosch, Volkswagen, TÜV Nord, ABB, and IBM Global Services. His contribution has proven to be invaluable in the framework of several projects involving European, Middle Eastern and African stakeholders, such as the Pan-African University (African Union) and the Technical and Vocational Training Corporation (TVTC), Saudi Arabia.

Emnet Tadesse Woldegiorgis
is a political scientist researching on higher education issues since 2006. He did his Ph.D. in Political science focussing on the topic of harmonization of Higher education systems in Africa. He has been a post-doctoral researcher at Bayreuth University, Germany. His research focuses on regionalization and internationalization of higher education in Africa. He did his joint Master's Degree in Higher Education Studies at Oslo University in Norway, Tampere University in Finland and Aveiro University in Portugal. Prior to his position at Bayreuth University, he has been working as Head of Quality Assurance Officer, Department Head and team leader at Mekelle University, Ethiopia, for four years. He has published a number of articles and book chapters on higher education issues particularly, theories of regionalization, student mobility, cost-sharing, and harmonization of higher education systems in Africa.

Introduction

Emnet Tadesse Woldegiorgis and Christine Scherer

Globally, there is an increasing understanding of the significance of close cooperation among institutions, countries, sub-regions, and continents. Collaboration is done through sharing resources and technologies, addressing common problems, and exploring opportunities for effective and efficient development endeavours, in the era of globalization. Moreover, the nature of production of goods and services in the 21st century has begun utilizing knowledge facilities and has significantly shifted the economy from the classical assumptions of the industrial revolution, which took labour and capital as the only means of production, to an increasingly significant and new role of knowledge and information in the economy (Bloom, David, & Chan, 2005). As knowledge has become increasingly significant in the process of production and dissemination of goods and services, so have higher education institutions, which have put higher education at the centre of global transformations, moving from industrially-based to knowledge-based societies. Thus, the quality and competitiveness of higher education institutions have become important factors within the so-called global knowledge economy, seeking 'excellence' and 'relevance' in a competitive environment.

Relevance and competitiveness in higher education research is understood as the capacity of institutions to generate and create, refine and develop, mediate consume and disseminate new knowledge within the global environment. In this regard, we are witnessing universities worldwide as central actors in a field that is aspiring to be connected to an international knowledge system, establishing themselves as acknowledged and relevant actors of knowledge production and dissemination. Higher education institutions in Africa have also been aligning their missions, visions and academic environments to meet certain international standards, in order to be relevant and competitive on both national and international levels. Moreover, national governments, development cooperation agencies, and international funding institutions also tend to correlate the quality of higher education provided as an important factor for the economic growth of nations. In the 'Higher Education and Society' document published in the year 2000, the World Bank stated that "the quality of knowledge generated within higher education institutions and its availability to the wider economy is becoming increasingly critical to national competitiveness" (World Bank, 2000, p. 15).

To this particular end, collaboration and partnership have become among the most important policy directions that are being used as instruments to achieve capacity building for academic institutions. Collaboration and international partnership are believed to foster the quality of teaching, learning, and research. In this regard, partnerships in higher education have been used not only as instruments for institutional development through a wide range of strategic alliances but also as essential ways for introducing new voices into the operations of universities, initiating new paradigms that bring new perspectives and bear competitive advantage on the partners. In the era of globalization, most graduates of higher education are trained in a way that enables them to work across different national boundaries and deal with various multicultural spaces. In this regard, academic alliances and cooperation across boundaries enable, not only students but also higher education institutions, to gain international exposure and to offer credentials for becoming more competitive in the labour market. Thus, higher education partnership is also an important instrument for striking strategic alliances that can compete in the market of global and mass higher education.

Over the past three decades, trends in institutional partnership in higher education have shown tremendous growth. These trends in higher education are manifested through growing initiatives of joint programmes that promote student and staff mobility, joint curriculum development and course delivery, research collaboration, joint bidding for research projects, and benchmarking. As the trend of partnership in higher education has grown, scholars in higher education have also engaged in conceptualizing higher education partnerships from academic ventures, providing perspectives, analysing trends, and developing models for higher education collaborations.

Partnership and/or collaboration has been defined in a number of ways and has been studied across a host of disciplines, from Political Science and Sociology to Organizational or Educational studies. The core defining denominator, however, has always been the same; a collaboration, among different parties, to achieve commonly defined objectives. It refers to the interests of partners who are involved in the collaboration, with a common purpose and shared rules or norms. In their analysis of institutional collaboration, Wood and Gray (1991), have developed the following definition: "a process in which a group of autonomous stakeholders of an issue domain engages in an interactive process, using shared rules, norms, and structures to act or decide on issues related to that domain" (p. 43).

Within the framework sketched above, partnership in higher education can be broadly understood as "the highest stage of working relationship between different [parties-individuals/institutions] brought together by a commitment to common objectives, bonded by long experience of working together, and sustained by subscription to common visions" (Mohiddin, 1998, p. 5). This explanation implies the processual importance of long-term and sustained collaboration among institutions, bound by agreed-upon principles for a shared vision and goal. Many scholars from the business world have also come up with different models of partnership, advocating the principle of mutuality, trust, transparency, and reciprocity in partnership (Tuten & Urban, 2001; Kedia & Lahiri, 2007; Wood, 2002).

There are also many pressing questions regarding the practical aspects of partnership, including: what are the models and approaches for successful higher education partnership? Under what circumstances are institutional linkages most likely to succeed or fail? What are some of the strategies involved? What kinds of organizational structures are needed or have to be complimented? As clearly stated by de Wit (1998), forming a network among institutions might be easy at first, but establishing a successful partnership scheme demands a comprehensive understanding of success factors. Among others, having a shared mission and objective among the parties involved in the partnership processes is one of the most important success factors. Mission and objectives should, however, be feasible, achievable, and appropriate for all institutions involved in the partnership processes. It is also important to acknowledge that networks are sometimes too large to be able to represent the interests of all members. Thus, the number of partner institutions has to be kept at a manageable level.

One of the biggest challenges of higher education partnership among African and European institutions is the question of sustainability. In many cases, the very process of partnership is often introduced through the provision of funds, and partnerships sometimes collapse as soon as funds dry up. Hence the sustainability of having the required resources to maintain the continuity of partnership over time and achieve different objectives has always been a challenge. Researchers have tried to explore and discuss the major success factors of institutional partnership (see, for example, Prichard, 1996; de Wit, 1998; van Ginkel, 1998). Despite these attempts, scholars in higher education have not fully explored compressive models of partnership in higher education yet. One of the reasons for this challenge could be the fact that the dynamics of higher education partnership have always been changing and incorporating new processes, players, and structures. Thus, it is of paramount importance to constantly look into new developments and various case studies, across different national boundaries.

This book is not in a position to develop a new partnership model but aims at understanding current issues and trends in Africa, and analysing the patterns of partnership processes among African and European higher education institutions. Understanding African and European higher education partnership trends are believed to be a significant condition for establishing working models of partnership among institutions. This book, therefore, intends to address the current trends and debates on internationalization and partnership strategies between African and European stakeholders, and mainly between universities.

The book draws its insights from various case studies of higher education partnership schemes and projects in and with Africa. The cases analyzed in this book cover a broad spectrum of issues, ranging from issues of student mobility, quality assurance initiatives, cases of joint degree programmes and curriculum developments, doctoral training and university networks as excellence initiatives.

The aim of this book is to contribute to an ongoing discussion on trends and key issues in higher education cooperation or partnership between European and African higher education institutions, pointing to the important policy and practical issues within these processes. It addresses a broad spectrum of issues, including trends in higher education partnership, policy, and practical issues in joint programmes, student and staff mobility and research collaborations, strategies in higher education partnership and internationalization, and includes case studies and practical challenges and opportunities in higher education collaboration among African and European universities

1   Outline of the Book

The book is organized in such a way that it is possible to navigate through the questions of higher education partnership from a more general perspective to more specific case studies. Each chapter is complementary, offering insights into new developments in higher education partnerships between African and European institutions. The book consists of ten chapters, each reflecting different case studies of higher education partnership and also scrutinizing aspects of internationalization within and among African institutions. This outline of the book comprises the main summary and themes of each chapter.

1.1   *Higher Education Partnership in Africa: The Case of the Pan-African University Network and the Mwalimu Nyerere Mobility Programme*

Due to the complexity and dynamics of actors involved, conceptualizing higher education partnership has always been a challenge. Partnership as a concept has mostly evolved in the business and management fields, rather than in the field of higher education, and the business model is generally based on the motive of maximizing profit. Applying business model to higher education is challenging due to fact that the main motive behind higher education partnership is the social responsibility that embraces the universal character and mission of universities to generate and disseminate knowledge for the advancement of the global community. This chapter discusses higher education partnership at a conceptual level and provides practical insight from the analysis of Pan-African university network and the Mwalimu Nyerere mobility programme in Africa. This chapter explores the operationalization of these cases of higher education partnership schemes and critically examines the challenges and opportunities within these processes, which can be tapped into in the future.

1.2   *A Critical Assessment of the Internationalization of Higher Education: The Case of Sub-Saharan Africa*

By considering internationalization as a transformative strategy, universities have engaged in the process of internationalization and have constituted international dimensions to their policy documents and mission statements. Higher education institutions in the global south have been inexorably drawn into the competitive environment of internationalization. However, the global resonance of internationalization is both exciting and worrisome. An unequal environment and context underneath the internationalization processes of higher education have posed serious challenges, particularly for developing regions, like the ones in Africa. Countries and institutions with better resources tend to benefit and exploit more from opportunities offered by internationalization, which often occurs at the expense of the developing world. The latter has become needier and more dependent on the more well-established and higher quality centres of higher education institutions and systems in the West. The colonial foundation of higher education institutions, the donor-recipient relationships, and unfavourable internal socioeconomic and political environments have placed African higher education in a more marginalized and periphery position in the process of internationalization. The challenges of internationalization of higher education in sub-Saharan Africa are not well articulated in the literature. Through a review of the related literature, this chapter makes an appraisal of the challenges inherent to the internationalization processes of higher education in sub-Saharan Africa, focusing in particular on the aspects of research and academic mobility.

1.3 Reflections on the Role of Africa in Research for Development: A Plea for Collaboration

This chapter discusses the role of research and development in the context of African higher education. It argued that collaboration among researchers is paramount for quality research in the region. Research is a systematic and organized way of thinking and acting in order to find answers to problems, and it should not be curbed. By nature, research is also unpredictable in some cases, moving in unforeseen directions, with unexpected consequences. The outcomes of research produce knowledge that humans use to guide their competitiveness in this world. To collaborate in the course of addressing common challenges through research makes the outcome of research more comprehensive.

Over the past few years, there has been increasing interest, among researchers and within science policy circles, in the notion of research collaboration in Africa. It is widely assumed that, in higher education, collaboration in research is a desideratum that researchers should be trained in. This particular chapter highlights the general field of research and development in Africa, which has strengthened research on a policy level. Assuming that research highlights human beings strive to improve their living conditions, this chapter offers a model for how to complement basic research with innovative private-public partnerships.

1.4 Relational Policies in Higher Education Partnership and Collaboration: Europe's Approach to Africa and the Special Case of Germany

Germany's history of collaborative engagement with Africa in the higher education sector is less than two decades old. Even though expedient programmes and policy concepts have been developed over a short period of time, by distinct institutions, on the federal government level, Africa has actually long played a marginal role in Germany's national science policies, which have been characterized by an erratic oscillation between development aid and claims of mutual benefits from partnerships. This chapter examines the development and status quo of Germany's approach to partnerships in Africa in higher education since the 1980s, embedding the analysis in the regional European context of international research and science-policy in the making. It discusses institutional agendas on a policy level that supersedes and sometimes compete with each other. Furthermore, it describes and explains the rude awakening of different stakeholders, who are developing and negotiating current higher education policies in Africa, in the context of African migration. The chapter concludes offering an outline of German science and research policies towards the African continent that has tardily started to understand the challenges but also the potential benefits of diversity within Africa, for the development and internationalization of higher education in Germany.

1.5 Higher Education Partnership between the Maghreb and European Higher Education Institutions during the 2002–2013 Decade

Multi-country partnerships have become very popular, representing 52% of the total number of projects in the Southern Mediterranean (SM) region. Partnerships support capacity building of academic, administrative and technical staff and students involved in projects. They encourage knowledge transfer, reinforcing skills, developing expertise and sharing good practices and experiences among Higher Education Institutions (HEIs) and socio-economic partners. In the Southern Mediterranean, preferred partnerships frequently involve countries in the Maghreb, such as Algeria, Morocco, Tunisia, as well as Lebanon, and they are less present in other Middle Eastern countries, such as Egypt, Jordan, Syria, Libya and the Palestinian State. Institutional partnerships between HEIS implemented through Tempus and Erasmus Mundus programmes, have tremendously increased in the last decade from 24 (Tempus III) to 32 (Tempus IV) projects involving Algerian HEIs. Maghreb and Mashriq countries often seem to favour projects that respond to common objectives and specific needs of their sub-regions. Solid partnerships have been established and influenced by the historical background of the region and the common trends and comparable approaches for tackling issues and challenging higher education systems to implement the Bologna Reform. Algerian students have benefited from mobility through Erasmus Mundus partnerships and their share in the Maghreb and SM region as a whole were respectively 32% and 14%. Mobility partnerships have annually increased in number and size, leading to a gradual increase in the number of students and staff involved in mobility schemes for Algerian HEIs. Staff and students visited countries, studied new courses, experienced new methods of teaching and learning, including e-learning platforms, learned from each other, and self-assessed themselves with their European peers. The objective of this chapter is to highlight the impact EU-South Mediterranean HEI partnerships have on higher education systems and institutions, through their contribution to EU funded Tempus and Erasmus Mundus programmes. A new dynamic involving academics from either side of the Mediterranean Sea encourages HEIs to share expertise while tackling common higher education issues related to modernization of curricula, quality assurance and adoption of graduates' competencies and qualifications in the labour market, based on needs and requirements.

1.6 Developing International Quality Assurance Standards in Africa: Reference to the Pan-African University as an Institutional Partnership in the Framework of the Bologna Process

In 1999, in what is known as the Bologna Process, 29 ministers of higher education (HE) signed the Bologna Declaration with the intention to create a European Higher Education Area, adopting a system of easily comparable degrees and establishing a credit point system to enhance student mobility and promote the employability of citizens. Since then, other regions of the world have adopted some of the process' basic underlying ideas, such as streamlining and harmoniously organizing a variety of degrees. This chapter investigates the potentials of upheaval on the African continent's higher education landscape – related to and partly inspired by the Bologna process, but by no means exclusively associated to it – through a case study from the Pan-African University initiative. It provides a spotlight on recent African higher education policy trends and presents the curriculum development process at the Pan-African University Institute of Water and Energy Sciences (including Climate Change – PAUWES) as an example of the application of new concepts. Furthermore, it introduces the question of the demand for qualification harmonization in the recruitment for excellent teaching programme, which occurred during the establishment of the PAUWES Institute and within the framework of a European Union (EU)/German cooperation. The chapter argues that new technologies, primarily illustrated by the Institute Learning Management System, play a major role in the crucial quality assurance and standardization processes. Lastly, it proposes an outlook on cross-border collaboration opportunities, with a focus on EU-African institutional partnerships, affirming that the EU's high interest for recognition in the context of Africa's higher education advancement has influenced its own reform.

1.7 Internationalizing Higher Education through Service Learning: The Case of the University for Development Studies, Ghana

The internationalization of university programmes is gradually gaining grounds in Ghana. Service Learning (SL) as a strategy for blending academic work with community life and industry practices has become an important window for the internationalization process of higher education. In efforts to promote SL for its students, the University for Development Studies (UDS) offers the Third Trimester Field Practical Programme (TTFPP) as a window for joint learning with communities and development agencies. While the programme has been largely localized, in the bid to internationalize, UDS has also hosted international students in search of community-based experiences. This paper examines the UDS TTFPP as SL for international studies. The key questions raised are: what factors/forces drive the internationalization of the UDS TTFPP as SL? How are the drivers shaping and defining the programme for its international actual and prospective audiences? To what extent can the programme be enhanced to service its current purposes while addressing the pressures to internationalize? What are the strengths, challenges, and options for the sustainable improvement of the programme? Through interviews, informal discussions and desk review a descriptive survey was employed, involving UDS students, staff, managers and administrators, as well as the community and NGO leaders. The survey found that, while the programme meets most of the criteria, the University has not been proactive in investing in the packaging and marketing of the programme. The chapter concludes with a discussion on how, despite the existing challenges, the TTFPP has strong potential for the University's internationalization process.

1.8 *Prospects and Challenges in North-South Curriculum Development Partnerships: The Case of a Finnish-Cameroonian University Project in Higher Education Studies*

The increasing phenomena of capacity building through European university-mentored curricula in the global south, from development cooperation funds, has not been appropriately captured in the literature on the internationalization of education. One of the consequences of this kind of curricula development related to capacity building has been the dearth of academic literature on the topic. Since projects are often lodged and evaluated by development agencies, there are evaluation reports in development agencies, but very little academic literature on the topic. This chapter sets out to examine the involvement of a Finnish university in a three-year curriculum project to develop a Master's programme in higher education management in Cameroon, within the framework of Finland's development cooperation work in Africa and the internationalization agenda of the Finnish University. The chapter is a result of a longitudinal observational study conducted by the author, and a desk review of the project documents. The methodology was strengthened by interviews with other participants in the project, who provided their views on the project as well. According to all the stakeholders of the project, the development of the Master's programme within the framework of cooperation development was key to its success and its final deliverables. The project's development also highlights several lessons that can be learned to strengthen these kinds of partnerships and the quality of similar projects. The chapter analyses the involvement of the Finnish University and the factors that favoured the implementation of the project and those that impacted its effectiveness in strengthening this type of curriculum development partnerships between the North and South regions of the world, and in the internationalization processes in general.

1.9 Prospects, Challenges, and Opportunities of International Exchange Programmes: The Case of a Double Degree Master's Programme

International exchange programmes (IEPs) contribute to the sharing and valuing of ideas among different nations and professional cultures, as well as the enrichment of host nations' academic and social programmes. While IEPs contribute tremendously to the progress of collaborating institutions, this also involves challenges. The shift from local to international adds value to the collaborators, and depending on the context and terms of the collaboration, these benefits can be shared. However, in designing different options, collaborating institutions can also face challenges. In 2012, the University for Development Studies (UDS) in Ghana and its partner, the University of Applied Sciences Dusseldorf (UASD) in Germany, embarked on a double degree Master's programme aimed at deepening an existing partnership programme that brought together faculty and students for a variety of intercultural learning experiences. In order to foster an effective collaboration in a new initiative between the two partners, efforts were placed on negotiations, research and consultations for the development of the partnership. After four years of implementation, it has been necessary to assess its successes and failures and to examine prospects, challenges, and options for promoting international exchange through the double degree Master's programme memes. This chapter seeks to generate insights for improving upon and institutionalizing the initiative as an avenue for internationalizing higher education in the two institutions. The evaluation revealed that the double degree Master's programme has prospects and opportunities, as well as challenges, for the students of UDS and UASD. The prospects for strengthening this partnership include extending the duration of the programme, introducing practical excursions, organizing orientations for students at the beginning of the programme, opening wider windows of interaction, putting more emphasis on academic writing, and increasing levels of participation and facilitation. Challenges include overloaded course contents, an inadequate academic writing component, lack of orientation for smooth take off, lack of support for proper socio-cultural adjustment, and effective time management for the completion of the curriculum. Opportunities include experiencing a new culture, making friends from around the world, becoming truly independent, studying in a global context, and travelling more widely. The chapter concludes by illustrating how, in efforts to institutionalize the initiative in either institution, there are high prospects for forging ahead, but that it is important to tackle challenges head-on.

1.10 Challenges and Prospects of Higher Education Partnership in Africa: Concluding Remarks

Higher education partnership between African and European institutions has passed through a number of historical trajectories that have involved both challenges and opportunities for all stakeholders involved. The forms, modalities, and structures of partnerships need to be understood through their processual character and, as the case studies in this book reveal, they have often evolved over time, with new developments in the higher education sector steered by global developments. How these developments are reflected in regional policies and in the specific programmes and projects launched with their respective frameworks, points to the importance of understanding the benefits of higher education collaboration on all levels, from the individual to the strategic. The final chapter summarizes and provides an analytical overview of higher education partnerships by highlighting the various processes involved and inciting future prospects and developments.

References

Bloom, D., Canning, D., & Chan, K. (2005). *Higher education and economic development in Africa*. Harvard University.

Gray, H. (1996). Theories of association: The social psychology of working together in educational consortia. In D. Bridges & C. Husbands (Eds.), *Consorting and collaboration in the education marketplace* (pp. 168–177). London: Falmer.

Kedia, B. L., & Lahiri, S. (2007). International outsourcing of services: A partnership model. *Journal of International Management, 13*(1), 22–37.

Mohiddin, A. (1998). Partnership: A new buzz-word or realistic relationship? *Development, 41*(4), 5–12.

Prichard, C. (1996). Managing universities: Is it men's work? *Men as Managers, Men as Managers* (pp. 227–238). London: Sage.

Tuten, T. L., & Urban, D. J. (2001). An expanded model of business-to-business partnership formation and success. *Industrial Marketing Management, 30*(2), 149–164.

van Ginkel, H. (1998). Networking alliances and consortia of universities: Focusing and strengthening international cooperation. In *International workshop on academic consortia proceedings* (pp. 35–46). Hong Kong: David C. Lam Institute for East-West Studies, Hong Kong Baptist University.

Wood, G. (2002). A partnership model of corporate ethics. *Journal of Business Ethics, 40*(1), 61–73.

CHAPTER 1

Higher Education Partnership in Africa: The Case of the Pan-African University Network and the Mwalimu Nyerere Mobility Programme

Emnet Tadesse Woldegiorgis

1   Introduction

African universities have been working in collaboration with other universities outside of the continent for many years, since the 1940s. Historically, modern higher educational institutions in Africa – in the form that we see them today – were introduced by European colonial administrations. This historical background facilitated conditions for African universities to not only inherit European higher education systems but to also continue to maintain higher education partnerships with Europe. However, these partnership trends and processes have not been linear or similar throughout the continent, but they have rather been segregated along the colonial and linguistic lines of Anglophone, Francophone, and Lusophone. In recent years, one can see a slight shift in trends, with diversifying partnerships among African universities and with countries that do not have colonial ties, such as the United States of America (USA), China, Canada, and Scandinavian countries, among others.

Partnership in higher education is a crucial means for sustainable collaboration among institutions, in order for them to share experiences, mobilize resources, and be connected to processes of international knowledge production and dissemination. The benefits of partnerships, however, can only be fully beneficiary for all sides if the partnership is based on the principles of mutuality, reciprocity, equality, accountability, and shared responsibility. Otherwise, it can lead to a donor-recipient kind of relationship, which eventually creates dependency of one institution towards the other.

This chapter discusses higher education partnership initiatives within Africa among African Universities and focuses on the Pan-African University (PAU) network and the Mwalimu Nyerere Student mobility programme. The PAU was established as a flagship institution to promote science, technology, and research in African higher education institutions. It was established in 2009 by the African Union Commission (AUC) as a network of five high-profile African universities to train students at Masters and Doctoral levels. Even though the

PAU is a network of African universities, different governments, and the European Union are also partners in the process. The Mwalimu Nyerere mobility scheme was initiated in 2007 by the AUC to facilitate student mobility of African students to undertake different degree programmes (at Bachelors', Masters' and Ph.D. levels) in Africa, in the areas of science and technology. The programme has been funded by the European Union since 2009, along with other partners as well.

These two cases are examples of both intra-African and inter-African higher education partnerships that facilitate cooperation, not only among African Universities but also with European agencies. This can be seen as a significant new paradigm in higher education cooperation that facilitates regionalization and harmonization of higher education systems within Africa. This chapter discusses the operationalization of these cases of higher education partnership systems, and critically examines the challenges encountered so far and the opportunities that can be tapped into for the future.

2   Partnership in Higher Education

Conceptualizing partnership in higher education has never been an easy venture. The concept itself has been mostly used and developed in the field of business and management rather than higher education. The way in which higher education institutions and business enterprises function is different, with the central motives, in the case of public higher education institutions, going beyond profit making. Partnership in the business world is an arrangement in which two or more enterprises share the profits and liabilities of a business venture, with the main goal being to maximize their profits.

In higher education institutions, partnerships reflect the social responsibility that is a part of the universal character of universities, to generate and disseminate knowledge for the advancement of the global community. In explaining the characteristics of higher education institutions, Burton Clark (1986) stated that knowledge is the epicenter of the higher education system around which activities are organized. Activities are organized around knowledge through disciplines, departments, faculties, and institutions. These institutions are not self-sustaining entities, they are rather embedded in common frameworks of societal expectations, regulatory frameworks, and co-operative or competitive linkages (Teichler, 2004). The terms of partnership in higher education are therefore more comprehensive and diversified than in the business world.

Partnership in higher education is manifested through joint programmes that promote student and staff mobility, academic exchanges, curriculum development, joint course delivery, research collaboration, joint bidding for research projects, and benchmarking (Bailey & Dolan, 2011). It also includes the creation and development of a wide range of strategic alliances that facilitate the exploitation of scarce resources among partner institutions. By initiating new paradigms that cross traditional administrative boundaries, partnership in higher education brings new perspectives that can bear competitive advantages for the partners and provides essential ways for introducing new voices to the operations of each university (Layton, 1997). It is within this framework that international partnerships and collaborations with other higher education institutions have become a growing phenomenon among African institutions and important venues for institutional development.

In explaining partnership patterns in higher education, different scholars have provided different frameworks and models of interaction. Wanni, Hinze, and Day (2010), have illustrated a 'model of reciprocity' that emphasizes the importance of negotiated roles and goals among the parties involved in the partnership. According to them, partners should share ownership of projects, and their relationship should be based on respect, trust, transparency, and reciprocity. Decisions should be taken jointly after negotiations have taken place between the partners. Each partner should be open and clear about what they are bringing to the partnership and what their expectations are. The model also argues that successful partnerships tend to change and evolve over time (Wanni, Hinz, & Day, 2010).

In studying education partnership in England, Husbands (1996) has introduced 'market-led' concepts in his model of partnership in higher education. According to his model, higher education partnership is a 'trade-off' activity that is driven by profit, and collaboration is a process that grows from a 'loose model of purchasing consortia' to a 'partnership model of collaboration' (Bridges & Husbands, 1996). This model argues that partnership is a process through which "[...] participating institutions develop a common identity [...] within which participating staffs have an opportunity to articulate shared values" (Bridges & Husbands, 1996, p. 4).

Hans de Wit (1998) has come up with a different model, explaining partnership in higher education in terms of 'academic association', 'academic consortia', and 'institutional networks', and putting more emphasis on the role of individuals. This model argues that it is individuals who work together and not institutions and that the success of any partnership also depends on individuals' performance, not just the institutions.

In all of these discourses on the nature of partnership reciprocity, mutuality, shared vision, sustainability, negotiated goals, and capacity of professionals come up as the main characteristics of a successful partnership. It is important to keep in mind that discourses on partnership in higher education vary depending on how the notion of partnership is conceptualized and understood, and on the context in which it is applied. Despite differences, the fundamentals of partnership schemes, of working together to achieve a common goal, persist throughout all partnership models in different contexts.

It is important to mention that the concept of 'partnership' has been used interchangeably with other concepts such as 'association', 'cooperation', 'collaboration', and 'joint decision making', implying that partners make joint efforts on certain issues and work together towards particular goals. Even though the concept of 'partnership' has been used interchangeably with other concepts, the high level of interaction and commitment among partners makes partnership stronger and different in comparison to the other concepts mentioned. Mohiddin (1998), for example, defines partnership as the "highest stage of working relationship between different [parties-individuals/institutions] brought together by a commitment to common objectives, bonded by long experience of working together, and sustained by subscription to common visions" (Mohiddin, 1998, p. 5).

Partnership can also be understood and conceptually differentiated from other forms of interaction through its characteristics. Bailey and Dolan (2011) have illustrated the specific characteristics of partnership, such as a long-term relationship (sustainability), based on shared responsibility, reciprocal obligation, equality, accountability, trust, and the principle of mutuality and joint decision-making processes (Bailey & Dolan, 2011). These characteristics are also comprehensively summed up in Wanni, Hinze, and Day's (2010) definition of partnership;

> …a dynamic collaborative process between educational institutions that brings mutual though not necessarily symmetrical benefits to the parties engaged in the partnership. Partners share ownership of the projects. Their relationship is based on respect, trust, transparency, and reciprocity. They understand each other's cultural and working environment. Decisions are taken jointly after real negotiations take place between the partners. Each partner is open and clear about what they are bringing to the partnership and what their expectations are from it. Successful partnerships tend to change and evolve over time. (p. 18)

Higher education partnerships are thus cooperative agreements among higher education institutions, and/or other distinct organizations, to coordinate activities, share resources, and divide responsibilities, in relation to specific projects or goals. Through this process, higher education partnerships are expected to entertain the characteristics and values mentioned above.

Due to the fact that partnership in higher education demands different higher education institutions, which operate in different settings, to come together and find common objectives worthy of the cooperation, partnership in higher education is generally believed to also facilitate harmonization of higher education policies. This harmonization process is also developed through various forms of internationalization processes in higher education. The concepts of internationalization and partnership are not the same and it is internationalization processes that reinforce partnerships. As Jane Knight (2008) defines it, internationalization is "the process of integrating an international, intercultural or global dimension into the purpose, functions or delivery of higher education" (Knight, 2008, p. 2). Integrating international and global dimensions in higher education can only be best achieved through partnership, hence partnership and internationalization are both essential for higher education institutions to remain relevant and competitive in knowledge production and dissemination processes.

The aim of partnership in higher education, however, goes beyond simply being an instrument for knowledge generation and dissemination. Partnership also contributes to institutional and human capacity building (Brinkerhoff & Morgan, 2010). International partnership and development cooperation in higher education sectors, associated with skill development through degree and exchange programmes, are important avenues for institutional capacity building and development pertaining to research infrastructure, organizational reforms, curriculum and pedagogical development, leadership and management, and human capacity building.

2.1   *Partnership in African Higher Education*

Due to their financial and technical power, higher education partners from the global North usually have more bargaining power in negotiations and have comparative advantages to impose their interests on the partnership. On the other hand, poor infrastructure, lack of funding, and weak institutional settings in Africa tend to situate African institutions in more vulnerable positions, in the process of negotiations with their partners. Within the hierarchy of the global North as provider and the global South as receiver of development assistance, it is difficult to establish equal partnership and cooperation. In the context of Africa, it is challenging to introduce the North-South partnership trend concept in the models of partnership outlined above, as most partnership schemes are not established on the principles of mutuality or reciprocity.

The history of higher education partnership trends in Africa highlights colonial legacies as well, since the early stages of independence, which relate to the fact that the higher education sector in Africa is mostly an outcome of European intervention. The higher education structure, curriculums, and mediums of instruction in Africa have thus been shaped by European higher education models, which also makes cooperation and partnership with European higher education institutions more straightforward. Higher education partnerships, involving the processes of scholarships, accreditation, research, curriculum development, examinations, and policy reforms have in fact primarily linked Europe to its former colonies in Africa.

Developments since the 1980s indicate that there has also been increasing diversification in partnership trends in higher education in Africa. The diversification relates to institutions that African higher education institutions collaborate with, and also to the donors that finance such initiatives. The new trends indicate that higher education partnership patterns have now moved from the classical historical basis of colonial lines to new partners from the USA, Canada, China, and European countries that do not have colonial ties.

There are various factors that have contributed to the shift in partnership trends in higher education in Africa, and the major factors include the African economic crisis of the 1980s and the misleading policies of the World Bank regarding higher education in Africa at the time. The economic crisis of the 1980s pushed African governments to look for more development partners, not only in higher education but also in other sectors. This resulted in various bilateral relations forming between African universities and countries to which they never had colonial ties. For instance, partnerships were forged with Canada, through the Canadian International Development Agency; with the Netherlands, through the Netherlands Universities Foundation for International Cooperation, the International Training Center, the Royal Tropical Institute, the International Agricultural Center, and the Institute of Social Studies; with Norway through the Norwegian Agency for International Development; with Sweden through the Swedish International Development Authority; and with the USA, through the Agency for International Development.

These new partnerships were formed in part as a result of misleading World Bank policies on African higher education that put higher education as the last priority for the continent, which led to the decline of public funding for higher education institutions in Africa, in the face of a growing student population. Starting from the 1990s, African institutions were thus pushed to search for more diversified partners in higher education. Following this period, the World Bank policy was also changed and higher education began to assume a priority position in the discourse on African renaissance and economic development (Bloom, David, & Chan, 2005).

Along with this change in orientation regarding the role of higher education in Africa, different donor institutions also began supporting higher education partnership initiatives with African higher education institutions. The AUC is one institution that took on partnership as a route for the revitalization of Africa's universities and played a critical role in its development. This is an excerpt from the document of the New Partnership for Africa's Development (NEPAD)

> ...higher education development requires partnerships not only with local and regional actors and stakeholders but also with the universities, businesses and governments of the developed world. (2005, p. 21)

African higher education institutions have engaged in a number of partnerships with development organizations from the global West to improve the higher education system in the continent. Some of the major partnership initiatives that facilitate cooperation with African higher education institutions are: the Higher Education Institutions Institutional Cooperation Instrument (HEI-ICI) in Finland; the Austrian Partnership Programme in Higher Education and Research for Development (APPEAR); the Norwegian Programme for Capacity Building in Higher Education and Research for Development (NORHED); the Netherlands Organization for International Cooperation in Higher Education (Nuffic) and its sub-programme, the Netherlands Initiative for Capacity Development in Higher Education (NICHE); the Swedish International Development Agency (SIDA); the Partnerships with Higher Education Institutions in Developing Countries (DIES) and the German Academic Exchange Service (DAAD) in Germany; the Agence Française de Développement (French Agency for Development (AFD) in France; the Japan International Cooperation Agency (JICA); the Spanish Agency for International Cooperation (AECID); the United Kingdom Department for International Development (DFID); and the U.S. Agency for International Development (USAID).

Partnership schemes are not limited to the bilateral relationships mentioned above, and in order to keep up with the global changes in higher education, Africa as a continent has also engaged in multilateral partnerships with other regions. The Africa-EU partnership, the Africa-U.S. partnership, the Africa-China partnership, and the Africa-Canada partnership are leading examples so far in this regard. Regional representatives or university associations, like the Association of African Universities (AAU) and the already mentioned AUC, play a facilitating role in the process of negotiating partnerships along regional lines, but partnerships also happen in isolation, based on open calls from donor institutions. The Africa-EU partnership, for instance, has been negotiated through the AUC and in the case of the Africa-Canada partnership, the AAU played a facilitating role. The Africa-U.S. partnership, on the other hand, was based on open calls that directly dealt with higher education institutions. The Africa-China partnership reflects a combination of the two, involving regional, national and institutional actors in the process of negotiating partnerships.

Sub-regional organizations have also engaged in regional partnerships in higher education. In this regard, a good example is the Southern Africa–Nordic partnership, which is a higher education cooperation between institutions in Southern African countries, such as Malawi, South Africa, and Zambia, and 25 research-led higher education institutions from Denmark, Finland, Iceland, Norway, and Sweden. Even though all the higher education partnership schemes Africa has with the USA, Canada, and China are worthy of academic discussion, this particular chapter focuses only on the Pan-African University network and the Mwalimu Nyerere mobility schemes, which are cases that fall in the framework of Africa-Europe partnerships.

3 The Pan-African University Network

As higher education researchers have documented (Damtew & Greijn, 2000; Ilon, 2003; Assie-Lumumba, 2006), African universities have more collaboration with European universities in student exchange and degree programmes than with universities within Africa. This trend has proved to produce the unintended consequence of perpetuating Africa's state of dependency and making the retention of skilled manpower difficult to maintain within Africa. In the 1980s and 1990s, most African scholars who benefitted from higher education partnerships did not return to their home countries after their exchange programs to European universities and this gradually weakened the capacities of higher educational institutions in Africa. These weakened capacities have been repeatedly highlighted by the Conference of Ministers of Education of the African Union (COMEDAF), which states that African higher education institutions have a marginal role in the production of knowledge, especially in the field of science and technology. The African Development Bank (AfDB) has highlighted how, "on average, Africa has 35 scientists and engineers per million inhabitants, compared to 168 in the case of Brazil, 2,457 in the case of Europe, and 4,103 in the case of the United States" (AfDB, 2013, p. 12).

Alongside inter-Africa partnerships between Africa and the rest of the world, the promotion of intra-Africa partnership, with partnerships between

African universities, is of paramount importance for capacity building and expert retention in African universities. Since the adoption of the Second Decade of Education for Africa, the AUC has taken the promotion of science and technology and the establishment of centres of excellence as the main way forward to address these challenges in the continent. The establishment of the PAU is an example of this and it was set up to facilitate collaboration among African scientists and researchers throughout the continent.

The PAU was established in 2009/10 by the AUC as a leading post-graduate training and research institution, for the promotion of science and technology in Africa. It focuses on Master's and Doctoral level programmes and has created an intra-regional partnership of high-level academic institutions and researchers in the area of science and technology. This initiative is believed to enhance the attractiveness and global competitiveness of African higher education and improve the retention of skilled African academics and professionals.

The PAU is structured as a network of high-profile African universities across all five regions of North, South, East, West and Central Africa. Each geographic region is expected to host one thematic subject area that is coordinated by one university, which is selected from one sub-region, on a competitive basis. Each coordinating university is also linked to ten "satellite campuses", located in various African countries. The PAU includes 55 African institutions, with 5 coordinating universities and 10 satellite universities for each coordinating university. The five thematic areas identified by the AUC for each region are: (i) Science, technology and innovation, hosted in East Africa; (ii) Water and energy sciences, hosted in North Africa; (iii) Life and earth sciences hosted in West Africa; (iv) Space Sciences, hosted in Southern Africa; and (v) Governance, Humanities and Social Sciences, hosted in Central Africa (See Table 1.1). Even though the AUC took the initiative to establish and lead the PAU, other actors, including the AAU, sub-regional economic communities, and donors (leading partners), are actively involved in the process as well.

The PAU is therefore not a single university setting located in one particular place, but it is rather a network of already operating high-ranking African universities, which are coordinated by the AUC, with the objective of creating a flagship university that "shall be globally competitive and locally relevant" (African Union, 2013, p. 2). As stated in the statute, "the main campus [is] linked to a network of satellite campuses scattered across a particular region of Africa" (African Union, 2013, p. 3), hence the PAU does not aim at constructing a new higher education infrastructure, but uses existing university facilities in satellite campuses across the continent. In this way, the university is set up to facilitate partnerships among top African universities, mainly in the field of Science and Technology.

TABLE 1.1   Thematic areas of the Pan-African University

Sub-regions	Thematic areas	Host countries	Host institutions	Major donors
East	Basic science, technology, and innovation	Kenya	Jomo Kenyatta University of Agriculture and Technology	Japan, African Development Bank, the EU
West	Life and earth sciences	Nigeria	The University of Ibadan	India, Development Bank, the EU
Central	Governance and human and social sciences	Cameron	The University of Yaounde	Sweden, African Development Bank, the EU
North	Water and energy sciences	Algeria	University of Tlemcen	Germany (through GIZ), African Development Bank, the EU
Southern	Space sciences	South Africa	–	EU, USA, African Development Bank, the EU

In the first enrolment of students in 2013/2014, the PAU admitted students from 11 African countries in three thematic institutes, the Institute for Governance, Humanities and Social Sciences at the University of Yaounde II in Cameroon, the Institute for Life and Earth Sciences (including Health and Agriculture) at the University of Ibadan in Nigeria, and the Institute for Basic Sciences, Technology and Innovation, at the Jomo Kenyatta University of Agriculture and Technology in Kenya. A total of 135 students were registered to pursue their studies in different areas of specialization. Out of the total intake, 18.5 percent of the first batch of students were female.

In the second PAU student enrolment in 2014/2015, a total of 236 students from 37 African countries were enrolled and the percentage of female students was 35.7. The second programme comprised of master's students at the Institute for Governance, Humanities and Social Sciences at the University of Yaounde II in Cameroon and the Institute for Water and Energy Sciences (including Climate Change) at the University of Tlemcen in Algeria, and both

Master's and Ph.D. students at the Institute for Life and Earth Sciences, at the University of Ibadan in Nigeria, and the Institute for Basic Sciences, Technology and Innovation, at the Jomo Kenyatta University of Agriculture and Technology in Kenya. The call for students for the academic year 2016 attracted 5629 applicants, representing an overall increment of 361 percent from the previous year, and the 2016 student population stands at 573 (174 females and 399 males), with a breakdown of 435 Masters students (133 females and 302 males) and 138 Ph.D. students (41 females and 97 males).

There are some limitations to the PAU initiative. One limitation is that it has been donor dependent and was designed to ensure that each thematic area is supported by different donors, which the AUC refers to as "thematic partners". However, apart from Germany and the European Union Commission, the promised funding from other donors has not been fully provided yet. The AUC and host countries have also not fully committed to providing a sustainable means of funding for the partnership, making the sustainability of the programme questionable as it continues to depend on foreign sources of funding, without mobilizing needed funding from African governments.

Since the PAU is utilizing already established universities in the five thematic areas instead of establishing new ones, it may also not add any value of excellence to African higher education systems. In the selection process for host universities, being a top-ranking university was the criteria used by the AUC for admitting universities into the PAU network. Thus, instead of taking average universities and investing in them to build their capacity and make them centres of excellence, the PAU initiative has taken already existing universities as qualified centres of excellence.

Additionally, even though the PAU recommended that a wide cluster of professors, from both Africa and the African Diaspora, be a part of the project, most of the professors involved thus far have been local professors from host countries and the Diaspora involvement has not been reached yet. The recruitment process for professors has been difficult in general, taking more than one year in some cases, and with continued difficulties in getting the desired expertise.

One of the most important pillars of higher education is the existence of autonomy and academic freedom in daily activities and in the pursuit of knowledge. The PAU, however, is a product of the AUC and abides by the bureaucracy and regulations of this political organization. As a result, it is sometimes difficult to make simple decisions without the approval of the Commissioner, and activities can be delayed for months or sometimes years because of this. For instance, until recently, the AUC was working on the appointment of the rector and on setting up the board members of the PAU, according to the statute of initiatives. Despite some efforts, it took almost two years to set up the basis for this process to be completed and, due to this delay, many other bureaucratic delays in relation to financial regulations, recruitment of staff and students, curriculum development, approvals, and setting up administrative teams also followed. Because of the tight bureaucracy at the AUC and complications at host institutions, in some cases, students and staff have also had to wait months before getting paid. Despite these challenges, the PAU has been operational and its first students graduated in 2015/2016.

4 Mwalimu Nyerere Student Mobility Programme

The Mwalimu Nyerere programme was established with the objective of promoting student and staff mobility across various higher education institutions in Africa, in both undergraduate and post-graduate programmes. Higher Education partnerships for the promotion of mobility of students have been among the core objectives of most higher education collaboration processes, not only in Africa but in other regions as well. For instance, the Bologna process has the same programme to promote the mobility of students, which is called the Erasmus programme. The Mwalimu Nyerere programme is a student mobility scheme and partnership framework among African institutions, which is funded by the European Union Commission, and partly administered by the AUC. The programme is designed so that students can be provided a scholarship to participate in the programme, with a binding agreement that they will work in Africa from two to five years after graduation. This agreement is put in place in order to retain African graduates to serve the continent, at least for the time proportional to the scholarship they receive.

The programme is named after an icon of Pan-Africanism and the first leader of Tanzania, Julius Nyerere. Nyerere was known by the Kiswahili honorific as Mualimu or Mwalimu, which means 'teacher', and this was his profession prior to politics. Re-affirming the Pan-African legacy of Julius Nyerere, the Mwalimu Nyerere mobility scheme was initiated in 2007 "to develop and retain high-quality human resources for Africa's development while enhancing intra-Africa institutional networking, academic mobility, and quality" (European Commission, 2013, p. 2).

The Mwalimu Nyerere mobility programme is the first continental initiative launched by the AUC to foster partnership among African institutions and to promote student mobility in the region. In the beginning, the programme had the ambitious objective of providing scholarships and promoting academic and staff mobility across all parts of Africa. However, due to the fact that the programme was poorly financed by its stakeholders, this ambitious objective was not achieved as planned. After a year of its establishment in 2008, the Nyerere mobility programme provided scholarships to only 19 African students from the whole of the continent. This number did not show much improvement afterward and, by 2013, only a total of 150 students had been through the program, which is an insignificant number in comparison to a large number of African students and the objectives set by the AUC to promote intra-regional student mobility.

The programme also only provides scholarships to students in Science and Technology and disregards other disciplines, such as Social Sciences and Humanities. Even though the reason for this is to address the shortage of African scholars in Science and Technology, the Institute's limited targeting disregards the objective of promoting student mobility on a general scale. In order to establish and promote a culture of intra-regional student mobility in Africa, the Nyerere programme should, in fact, include more students from all disciplines and institutions. When compared to the European student mobility scheme through the Erasmus programme, for example, one can see how the Erasmus programme is open to all disciplines, across all intuitions, and how it has managed to accommodate 3 million students in the programme.

In order to address the financial challenges of the programme, the process of mobilizing funding and minimizing costs was taken on by the AUC. One of the decisions made to minimize the costs of mobility was to wave tuition fees for the participants of the programme at their host university. On the Fourth Ordinary Session, at the Conference of Ministers of Education (COMEDAF IV), held in Mombasa, Kenya from November 23rd to 26th, 2009, the AUC pushed to finalize the preparations needed to ensure the timely scaling up of the programme and passed the decision demanding member states to consider the Nyerere Scholarship award holders in the mobility programme as resident students in their host universities (AU/MIN/EDUC/RPT(IV), 2009).

Under the Africa-EU partnership scheme, the AUC also decided to call upon the European Commission to provide support for the Nyerere programme. The issue of including the Nyerere programme in the Africa-EU partnership scheme was discussed at the 3rd Africa-EU Summit held in Cape Town, South Africa, on November 23rd and 24th, 2010. At the conference, the EU pledged to support and fund the Mwalimu Nyerere African Scholarship Scheme and help boost the mobility of students and staff in higher education in Africa. Since then, the Nyerere scholarship programme has been funded by the European Development Fund (EDF) and technically supported by the European Commission. The EDF provided Euro 41.5 million in 2010, and an additional Euro 30 million between 2011 and 2013 (European Commission, 2013).

The involvement of the EU in the Mwalimu Nyerere programme and its place within the framework of the Africa-EU partnership has further expanded the objectives of the programme and now includes mobility of African students beyond Africa as well. The Africa-EU partnership has different thematic areas and within the thematic area of "migration, mobility and employment", the EU has developed a partnership scheme called the World University Mobility Programme, which is a student mobility initiative that promotes collaboration between higher education institutions and supports student exchange programmes between Africa, the Caribbean and the Pacific (ACP) regions. As stated by the European Commission Education Audio-visual and Culture Executive Agency (EACEA):

> This programme builds on the African Union's Mwalimu Nyerere programme for Africa, granting additional funding, and setting up a similar scheme for the Caribbean and Pacific regions. It is funded through the European Development Fund (EDF). (EACEA, 2014)

Despite its place within Africa-EU and world partnerships, the main challenge remains the context in which the Nyerere mobility programme is implemented. The current higher education systems and the infrastructure in Africa restrict this partnership from living up to its expectations because the programme has been launched with the absence of necessary and enabling factors for mobility. For example, the existence of a working Credit Accumulation and Transfer System (CATS) is an important factor for student mobility, which facilitates mobility and enhances comparability of study programmes and qualifications of studies (Tempus Study, 2010). So far, there is no functioning CATS in Africa. The adoption of a full-fledged credit transfer system would allow students to move between universities in different countries without losing the credits they have accumulated.

Generally speaking, student mobility is also a mirror of various other elements, including political stability, availability of quality higher education infrastructure, availability of instruments of recognition of studies, flexible entry mechanisms, smooth visa procedures, and harmonized/comparable higher education systems. The enabling factors mentioned above are rarely available in most countries in Africa, and this is a challenge to the development of intra-regional partnerships for student mobility within the continent. In order to facilitate the smooth movement of the whole partnership process and to address the challenges mentioned, a collaboration between the AUC and sub-regional economic organizations is crucial.

When compared to the European Erasmus programme, the objectives there go beyond the provision of scholarships to students, but rather encourage all European students to spend at least 6 months in other European universities, outside of their home country, with or without a scholarship. The programme is an important opportunity for European students to have an enriched study experience and exposure to different cultures. The Nyerere mobility programme, on the other hand, mainly focuses on scholarship opportunities for a few African students, and it has not yet been institutionalized as a continental instrument for student mobility with the same procedures as the Erasmus programme in Europe. When compared to the Erasmus programme, which is financially sustainable and receives an annual budget of 489 million Euros from member countries, the AUC has a significant amount of work to do financially, in order to achieve the objective of making the Nyerere mobility programme an instituted and stable intra-regional student mobility programme in Africa.

5 Conclusion

Historically, higher education partnership in Africa has been mostly characterized by donor-recipient dynamics, within the framework of North-South partnerships, which are not established and based on the principles of mutuality and reciprocity. Nowadays, most partnerships are donor dependent and the terms of partnership and interests are defined along the demands of donors. Partnerships among African institutions can create an alternative ground or opportunity to establish partnership schemes that are actually based on the principles of mutuality and reciprocity. The PAU network and the Mwalimu Nyerere mobility programmes are pioneer attempts at creating higher education partnership among African institutions and need more tools and opportunities to scale up.

References

AfDB. (2013). *AfDB approves US$45 Million grant for creation of Pan-African University for science, technology, and innovation*. Retrieved October 9, 2014, from http://www.afdb.org/en/news-and-events/article/afdb-approves-us-45-million-grant-for-creation-of-pan-african-university-for-science-technology-and-innovation-12155/

African Union. (2013). *Establishment of the Pan-African University – Department of human resources, science and technology*. Addis Ababa: AUC.

African Union. (2010). *Decision on the establishment of the Pan-African University Doc.EX.CL/579(XVII)*: Adopted by the fifteenth ordinary session of the assembly of the Union. Kampala: AU.

Assie-Lumumba, N. T. (2006). *Higher education in Africa. Crises, reforms, and transformation.* Dakar: CODESRIA.

AU/MIN/EDUC/RPT(IV). (2009). *Report of the fourth ordinary session of the conference of ministers (COMEDAF IV).* Mombasa: African Union Department of Human Resources, Science, and Technology.

Bailey, F., & Dolan, A. (2011). The meaning of partnership in development: Lessons for development education. *Policy and Practice: A Development Education Review, 14,* 30–48.

Bloom, D., Canning, D., & Chan, K. (2005, March). *Higher education and economic development in Africa.* Boston, MA: Harvard University Press.

Bridges, D., & Husbands, C. (1996). The education market place and the collaborative response: An introduction. In D. Bridges & C. Husbands (Eds.), *Consorting and collaboration in the education market place* (pp. 1–6). London: Falmer.

Brinkerhoff, D. W., & Morgan, P. J. (2010). *Capacity and capacity development: Coping with complexity.* Retrieved from http://www.gsdrc.org/go/display&type=Document&id=3788

Clark, B. (1986). *The higher education system: Academic organization in cross-national perspective.* Berkeley, CA, Los Angeles, CA, & London: University of California Press.

Damtew, T., & Greijn, H. (Eds.). (2000). *Higher education and globalization: Challenges, threats and opportunities for Africa.* Maastricht: Maastricht University Centre for International Cooperation in Academic Development (MUNDO).

de Wit, H. (1998). International networks in higher education. In *Proceedings of the International Workshop on Academic Consortia* (pp. 119–128). Hong Kong: David C. Lam Institute for East-West Studies, Hong Kong Baptist University.

EACEA. (2014, August 28). *Navigation path European Commission EACEA.* Retrieved from http://gai-edu.eu/academic-mobility-scheme/

European Commission. (2013). *Thematic partnership on migration, mobility and employment action plan 2011–2013 fiches on priority initiatives.* Addis Ababa: AUC and EUC.

Husbands, C. (1996). Schools, markets and collaboration: New models for educational polity? In D. Bridges & C. Husbands (Eds.), *Consorting and collaboration in the education market place* (pp. 9–20). London: Falmer.

Ilon, L. (2003). Foreign aid financing of higher education in Africa. In D. T. Altbach & D. T.

Knight, J., & de Wit, H. (1995). Strategies for internationalization of higher education: Historical and conceptual perspectives. In H. de Wit (Ed.), *Strategies for internationalization of higher education* (pp. 5–32). Amsterdam: European Association for International Education Publications.

Layton, R. A. (1997, August 20–22). *The strategic significance of inter-university linkages.* International Conference on Inter-university Cooperation and Exchange, Beijing University, Beijing, China.

Mohiddin, A. (1998). Partnership: A new buzz-word or realistic relationship? *Development, 41*(4), 5–12.

NEPAD. (2005). *Renewal of higher education in Africa.* Report of AU/NEPAD workshop 27–28 October. Johannesburg: AU.

Teichler, U. (2004). Changing structures of the higher education systems: The increasing complexity of underlining forces. In *Diversification of Higher Education and the Changing Role of Knowledge Research* (pp. 3–17). Paris: UNESCO Forum Regional Scientific Committee for Europe and North America.

Tempus Study. (2010). *State of play of the Bologna process in the Tempus countries of the Southern Mediterranean (2009–2010).* Armenia: European Commission Education Audiovisual and Culture Executive Agency.

Wanni, N., Hinz, A., & Day, R. (2010). *Good practices in educational partnerships guide: UK-Africa higher and further education partnerships, the Africa Unit, UK/Africa Partnerships in HE/FE.* Retrieved from http://www.hea.ie/files/Good_Practice_Guide 1.pdf

CHAPTER 2

A Critical Assessment of the Internationalization of Higher Education: The Case of Sub-Saharan Africa

Sintayehu Kassaye Alemu

1   Introduction

Internationalization processes are among some of the most important instruments in higher education partnerships. The notion of higher education partnership can be understood as a broad umbrella concept within which internationalization processes exist as instruments. The internationalization of higher education is understood as an increasingly transformative process and strategy that enables institutions to adjust and improve their standards, increase their national, regional, international and global competitiveness and collaborative visibility in the creation of knowledge and innovation, and improve their teaching and services. However, the transformative power of internationalization processes in higher education is not equally evident everywhere.

Internationalization of higher education affects different higher education institutions differently. According to the separation of centre and periphery in our global world, central higher education institutions are considered to be institutions with better academic capacity and research infrastructure while peripheral higher education institutions are institutions with less academic capacity, research infrastructure, governance experience, and tend to reproduce and benchmark central institutions. From this perspective, central higher education institutions are in a leading position, not only in terms of knowledge production, but also in terms of initiating internationalization processes, and tend to benefit more from internationalization processes than peripheral higher education institutions do. In this regard, the context of higher education institutions in sub-Saharan Africa has a peripheral landscape and the process of the internationalization of higher education institutions in Africa ties back to the period of colonialism. Africa, the second largest and second most populous[1] continent, has been connected to the Western system of higher education through the colonial bonds established since the 18th century, and colonial systems and models have replaced traditional and indigenous higher learning institutions in Africa. For administrative purposes, during the colonial period, colonial powers established regional administrations where different nations established mutual collaboration among themselves. The 'post-independence' period witnessed the shattering of the colonial regional collaborations and encouraged more narrow national focus, limited to links or partnerships with the ex-colonial powers and international aid agencies. From this perspective, in their model, scope, dimension, participation, and benefits, higher education systems in Africa have been the most internationalized and, at the same time, the most peripheral and marginalized (Damtew, 2014).

Unequal global market competition as an imbalanced form of internationalization has replaced the old cooperative and supportive forms of internationalization and widened the gap between higher education institutions in Africa and the rest of the world. African higher education institutions/universities have been weakened by several factors, including the colonial legacy, receiving external 'policy advice', unequal link formations, deep internal socio-economic and political crises, brain drain, and sheer states of negligence. The challenges are further exacerbated by the massification of higher education in the region. African research has been negatively affected by considerable financial, infrastructural, and quality difficulties and scholarships in student mobility programmes have caused a brain drain that has affected research, knowledge production, learning and socio-economic development in the continent. Higher education institutions in the continent have engaged in the process of internationalization with all the internal and external difficulties and challenges mentioned above and these situations have incapacitated higher education institutions in Africa from playing their regional and national in development. Internalization in the form of unequal partnership formation has also resulted in a dependency syndrome.

Despite the prevalence of many and complex factors that affect sub-Saharan African higher education, this chapter tries to focus on and analyse the challenges caused by unequal global processes of internationalization of higher education institutions. Through a qualitative review of related literature, this chapter critically analyses the challenges caused by internationalization on research, publication, and academic mobility in Africa. The chapter is organized in an introduction and an overview of the concepts of internationalization, research, and academic mobility. These issues are a part of the main framework of analysis and debate regarding the challenges of internationalization, particularly on higher education institutions in sub-Saharan Africa.

2 An Overview of Internationalization and Higher Education in Sub-Saharan Africa

2.1 *Conceptual Review*

Internationalization is deep-rooted in history. Centuries of movement of scholars and knowledge around the world and the concept of 'universe' in naming 'universities' as the first formal institutions of higher learning bear witness to the historical dimension of internationalization (Rüegg, 1992; Sehoole & Knight, 2013). Even though internationalization is not a new phenomenon, in recent years, its complexity has grown, particularly due to diversified actors, interpretations, impacts, rationales, activities, and consequences. Internationalization has emerged, since the 1990s, as one of the defining global processes in higher education and it has gained increasing attention from higher education institutions and researchers worldwide (IAU, 2010).

Ancient universities of Africa, Asia, and Europe were designed and served as regional communities of learning and scholarship (Scott, 2000). Internationalization of higher education is a collaborative process and strategy by which higher education institutions around the world establish a partnership to improve their academic experiences and achievements. It is often closely related to the physical mobility of scholars and students, academic cooperation and knowledge transfer, and international education (Knight, 2004).

However, due to globalization, the neoliberal philosophy, the knowledge society and the modern concept of academic mobility of people, programmes and providers, the process of internationalization has entered into a more competitive and market-oriented scenario in which new and diverse actors and rationales play crucial roles (Rivza & Teichler, 2007). Both the activities and the concept have become more complex and different and internationalization has increasingly become a key factor in shaping higher education management, funding, teaching, research, and academic mobility strategies. Since the 1990s, internationalization of higher education has incorporated a wider range of competitive academic mobility and integration of people programmes and providers (Meek et al., 2009), and is now often associated with competition and market-steering, transnational education, and commercial knowledge transfer (Teichler, 2004).

Internationalization has exposed higher education institutions not only to cooperation and competition but to dominance and dependency as well. Higher education institutions in developing countries and regions (commonly referred to as "peripheries") have become increasingly influenced and dominated by higher education institutions in advanced countries (commonly categorized as "centres"), and increasingly dependent on the achievements of these countries and their institutions. Peripheral higher education institutions have become victims of the impacts of the hegemonic dominance of the centres by directly adopting their standards, policies, and curriculums.

In addition to accelerating cooperation and competition, the development of global and international education and research has challenged national values and cultures. The expansion of the English language at the expense of national languages is a common phenomenon of the process as well. Internationalization has also paved the way for the development and framing of more commercial fields of studies, inducting the academic cultures of different programmes and institutions. The process requires institutions in the peripheries to develop new instruments and arrangements in order to challenge the dominance and influence of globalization. Moreover, it pushes peripheral higher education institutions to invest from their meager resources towards standardization, which may be unattainable (Dale, 2005).

Internationalization of higher education is driven by a diversity of rationales, expressed in a variety of activities, and results in multiple benefits, risks, and unintended outcomes and it means something different to different people, countries, and institutions. For some, internationalization of higher education refers to a series of international activities such as, "academic mobility of students and teachers; international linkages, partnerships, and projects; new international academic programmes; and research initiatives" (Sehoole & Knight, 2013, p. 4). Others focus on higher education internationalization as a process of cooperation with universities in other countries, to reform and modernize curricula and pedagogy. Others yet may focus on the delivery of education programmes in other countries, using a variety of face-to-face and long-distance techniques and different types of arrangements, such as branch campuses or franchises. Still, others consider international development projects or the increasing emphasis on commercial cross-border education as the crux of internationalization (Sehoole & Knight, 2013).

The most cited definition reads that internationalization is "the process of integrating an international, intercultural or global dimension into the purpose, functions or delivery of post-secondary education" (Knight, 2008, p. 11). Because internationalization is also a strategy and process of integration and expedites mobility, a new definition has been developed by the "Universities in the Knowledge Economy" (UNIKE) Ph.D. project. It reads as follows: "Internationalization of higher education is an approach-oriented strategic process of cross-border (departmental, sector, local, national, institutional, regional, international) mobility, integrity, and interaction of academic people, programmes, and/or institutions of tertiary education to achieve academic, cultural, economic, social and/or political benefits" (Sintayehu, 2016, p. 312).

2.2 Higher Education in Sub-Saharan Africa

African higher education institutions engage in the complex process of internationalization without adequate preparation and capable background. According to MacGregory (2015), by 2015, Africa possessed nearly 2,000 public and private higher education institutions, with growing diversification and differentiation. In varying degrees, African higher education institutions share common challenges. Some of the most common challenges of higher education institutions in Africa include: shortage of faculty and poor faculty development; poor and unstable governance, leadership, and management; problems of quality and relevance; weak research and innovation capacities and infrastructures; brain drain; financial austerity and lack of capacity to diversify funding resources; poor physical facilities and infrastructures; and low access and equity (Sy Habib, 2003; Damtew & Altbach, 2004a; Sichone, 2006; Teichler, 2004; Knight, 2013). The difficulties of African higher education institutions are deeply rooted in the legacy of colonialism and they are also further exacerbated by the unequal and imbalanced phenomena of globalization and internationalization (Sy Habib, 2003; Dale, 2005).

Since colonialism, African higher education institutions' internal developments have been exposed directly to influences from Europe and donor policies (Altbach, 2004b; Mohamedbhai, 2008; Brock-Utne, 2003). Thus, modern higher education institutions in Africa have followed the models of the Western world. Mohamedbhai (2008) has traced the historical background of Africa higher education to Western and American influences.

> The history of the modern African University, as it is now known, can be traced back to the period between 1930 and 1960, when the few African Western-educated elites, who saw European education as a strong tool to fight against colonialism, demanded the creation of European systems of education in Africa firmly believing that anything that was good for the Europeans was also good for the Africans. Most of the countries in sub-Saharan Africa eventually had universities created but, in the majority of cases, it was after they had attained independence from their colonial masters. Most of these African universities were, however, modelled on specific institutions of the colonial powers and during the period spanning the beginning of the 20th century and the 1950s, all higher education programmes in Africa reflected the major trends in philosophical discourse and policy debate among the major western powers i.e. the colonial powers and the USA. (Mohamedbhai, 2008, p. 2)

In the immediate post-independence period, African higher education institutions played an important role in the socio-economic and cultural developments of the continent and were considered "development universities" (Meek et al., 2009; Vessuri, 2007; Muche, 2006; Ogachi, 2011). This was triggered by the return of the first generation of African scholars from abroad, the new African leaders' emphasis on higher education, and the financial support channelled by the ex-colonial countries, which became the major sources of financial support and funding of African universities (Mohamedbhai, 2008; Assie-Lumumba, 2005; Mkandawire, 1995). For instance, Cote d'Ivoire, supported by France (its former colonial power), and allocated 7.4% of the GNP (Gross National Product) to education in 1965, which grew to 31.7% in 1973, and 45.0 % in 1981. Other countries were also assisted by their ex-colonial powers and spent between 25% and 30% of their GDPs on education. The share of higher education was higher and significant during the 1960s and 1970s when foreign support was available (Assie-Lumumba, 2005).

In the 1980s and 1990s, because of 'policy advice' from the World Bank, African governments began to give due attention to basic and secondary education. Higher education in sub-Saharan Africa suffered from a serious lack of attention and financial support, not only from the ex-colonial powers but also from other international donors (Woodhall, 2003). The World Bank, for instance, dropped its general financial aid to Africa from 17% in 1985–1989 to 7% in the years between 1995 and 1999 (Bloom et al., 2006). As a result, higher education funding in sub-Saharan Africa dropped from 19% between 1980 and 1984 to 15% between 2000 and 2005 (Ezeh, 2008). The situation became even drier in the poorest countries of the continent, where no more than 0.63% of the GDP was allocated to the higher education sector (World Bank, 2010).

Due to its weakened local capacity, African academia continues to be largely shaped by Euro-American intellectual paradigms, and theoretical, epistemic, and methodological orientations that tend to reproduce and reinforce Western knowledge. This lopsided global knowledge and innovation system, with its centre in the industrialized world, is not desirable and favourable for Africa's future (Zeleza, 2012). Africa has also engaged in the arena of contemporary internationalization in higher education with multiple internal and external socio-economic and political problems that have strengthened its peripheral position, and African higher education institutions face considerable challenges in generating, accessing and disseminating knowledge, and in providing meaningful responses to both the challenges of their situations and the broader issues posed by internationalization.

According to the IAU (2010, p. 21), the most pertinent rationale for sub-Saharan African higher education institutions' engagement in global internationalization is to "strengthen research and knowledge capacity production". However, as home to the largest number of developing countries, Africa faces a multiplicity of drawbacks in its engagement with and attempts to respond to the challenges of internationalization (Jowi, 2009). Brain drain is ranked the highest challenge and risk for Africa (IAU, 2010). The key challenge to African universities has also been to explore how academic programmes can be aligned to support local and regional economic development, the eradication of poverty, and the promotion and sustainable use of natural resources. There has been an increasing intention to create a situation in which knowledge creation in higher education institutions is connected to Africa's research needs and priorities (Ogachi, 2011; Barrett et al., 2014), and internationalization of higher education in Africa has been intended more and more "to increase the visibility of African universities in areas such as Research and Development, and increase the contribution that the institutions are making to the development of Africa, and open channels for Africa to benefit from the global stock of scientific knowledge" (Ogachi, 2011, p. 14). These goals also touch upon increasing research networking, capacity building and the establishment of partnerships (Sawyerr, 2004; Ogachi, 2011; Barrett et al., 2014).

Internationalization has also been imagined as a potential tool for increasing mutual socio-cultural understanding between people and nations. It intends to broaden the scholarship attitude of students and scholars and enhance the production of diversified, high-quality research. It widens learning opportunities for students in developing countries, challenges traditional education systems and influences institutions towards a form of standardization that involves innovative programmes, delivery methods, and competitive environments (Meek et al., 2009). Internationalization also diversifies funding and allows institutions to benefit from links with prestigious institutions, mainly in developed countries (Meek et al., 2009). With some drawbacks related to context, the internationalization of research and research training is also often hailed as an important tool for raising the quality of research in developing countries (Vessuri, 2007; Muche, 2006).

Internationalization has, however, posed more challenges than rewards for peripheries or developing countries and regions like Africa. The student mobility piece of internationalization has resulted in a devastating brain drain process in the continent, which has had far-reaching negative repercussions on research. Internationalization of higher education has seduced or deceived higher education institutions in sub-Saharan African countries to incorporate inappropriate and expensive standards for unequal competition and returns.

In relation to research, the scenario under which it has been carried out in developing countries, particularly in sub-Saharan Africa, has raised some essential questions: how much of the researches carried out in universities are directly relevant to the needs, suitability and priorities of the socio-economic, political, and cultural contexts of the region? How much do local researchers manage, possess, and utilize collaborative/joint venture researches? Whose policies, methods, and priorities are being respected and implemented? What are the standards and parameters for researchers' competency and the quality of research?

These kinds of inquiries can illustrate the biases and dilemmas regarding international research paradigms in developing countries. Researchers in developing countries tend to measure researchers' competence and research quality on Western parameters and eventually lose their own foundation for their own independent research endeavors. Subsequently, African researchers have become highly dependent on Western research approaches, methods, training, and teaching systems, remaining disconnected from their own context. Papoutsaki (2008) has explained this dilemma as follows:

> With the increasing internationalization of higher education, developing countries are ill-prepared to absorb and appropriate yet more foreign influences and demands of international organizations...The needs of institutions to develop within a global academic and research community and thereby adopt the predominant Western models of higher education and the development needs of these countries are often clashing, posing a dilemma between satisfying market forces and the need to nurture education within socio-cultural specificities of the country. The challenge of how to be locally relevant and at the same time with international standing is a big challenge for these higher education institutions. The internationalization of higher education is making it more difficult for local knowledge to prevail. (p. 246)

As a result of these complex internal and external challenges, and the imbalances inherent to internationalization, African higher education institutions have become strongly marked by influences from the global North that can become more alienating than liberating and empowering, and remain disconnected from African theoretical orientations and development strategies that can serve the interests of African peoples (CODESRIA, 2011).

In the next sections, the challenges and risks are discussed in terms of the academic mobility and research partnership major features and aspects of internationalization.

3   Academic Mobility and Brain Drain

The pattern of scholarship and partnership in the international networks of African higher education institutions has a paradoxical and challenging impact on brain drain. Adams et al. (2010) have presented brain drain and lack of investment as the main causes for developing countries' dependency on donors or developed centres:

> A problem for Africa as a whole, as it has been for China and India, is the hemorrhage of talent. Many of its best students take their higher degrees at universities in Europe, Asia, and North America. Too few Africans return. The African Diaspora provides powerful intellectual input to the research achievements of other countries but returns less benefit to the countries of birth. That is at least in part because of a chronic lack of investment in facilities for research and teaching, a deficit that must be remedied. (p. 1)

Higher education in developing countries has genuine risks and challenges. Scholars such as Wilson (2013) have acknowledged these risks and challenges as follows:

> As the global pressure to develop knowledge societies accelerate, there is a risk that the gap between the developed and the developing countries will continue to widen. Brain drain, the large-scale emigration of highly skilled human capital, is a major concern to society at large, and for the higher education and research community. In spite of attempts to promote "brain circulation", it will surely remain a major concern in the decades to come. (p. 33)

Wealthier nations constitute 16% of the workers of the world and 60% of their workforce is composed of global migrants (Spring, 2008). At the beginning of the new millennium, of the 150 million migrants in the world, more than 50 million were estimated to be from Africa. By 2005, there were 191 million people living outside their home country and the share of Africa was 9% (UNESCO, 2008). This process has been reinforced by globalization and internationalization, and internationalization is what is particularly attractive to academics. One of the features of the internationalization of higher education is academic mobility of students, teachers, and researchers. Academic mobility of students, scholars, and graduates has increased because of increased global opportunities, declining national control, the promotion of global socio-economic interconnectedness, and favourable and attractive policies framed by the developed countries of the world to recruit the brightest and best talents from the developing world.

UNESCO (2008) has shown that over 20 million Africans with tertiary education, aged 25 or over, were living in the Organization for Economic

Co-operation and Development (OECD) countries in 2000. This number was 12 million in 1990. According to UNESCO (2008), Africa loses 30% of its scientists due to brain drain annually, and this does not include the loss of other professionals. In fifteen years, from 1960 to 1975, Africa has lost 27,000 people from its skilled human capital population, the number increased to 40,000 between 1975 and 1984, and it has been calculated that, since 1990, at least 20,000 qualified Africans to leave the continent every year (UNESCO, 2008).

The World Bank (2002) has estimated that some 70,000 highly qualified African professionals, experts, scholars, and managers, with internationally marketable skills, leave Africa every year, and that more than 40,000 African Ph.D. holders were working abroad in the early 2000s (Teklu, 2008). In 2003, the United Kingdom (UK) alone approved work permits for 5880 health and medical personnel from South Africa, 2825 from Zimbabwe, 1510 from Nigeria, and 850 from Ghana. It has been estimated that about 60% of doctors trained in Ghana during the 1980s have left the country, and, according to the estimates of the Commission for Africa, this percentage increased to around 70% in the 1990s.

It has been estimated that there are more African scientists and engineers working in the USA than in the whole of the continent of Africa. The National Association of Social Workers in Zimbabwe has estimated that half of (1,500) their well-trained (3000) social workers have immigrated to the UK over a period of 10 years. In addition, studies on the 1995, 1996 and 1997 graduate cohorts from the College of Medicine of the University of Nigeria (which were around 468) show that 40% of graduated students left the country. From the Department of Physics, in Addis Ababa University (Ethiopia), 20 faculty members have been sent abroad to study for their Ph.D.s (the majority destined for the US) and none have returned. With institutional variation, the extent of brain drain from Ethiopian universities might be more than 50% (Habtamu, 2003) and Ethiopia has lost about 74.6% of its human intellectual capital from various institutions, between 1980 and 1991. From the 2009 Erasmus Mundus higher education programme Ethiopian team (of which the author of this article was a part of), only 33.3% of the students returned home. In order to cover vacant positions, the country has spent over $5.3 million every year on hiring expatriates (Amazan, 2014). Table 2.1 shows compilation data on brain drain.

The academic mobility between the centre and periphery – has been further increased by the initiation of internationalization and brain gain policies in the global North, from countries such as Australia, Canada, the United Kingdom, and the United States. While there has always been mobility across borders, an increasing number of national governments around the world are developing and publicizing policies and strategies with regards to the internationalization

TABLE 2.1   A compiled data on brain drain: Sub-Saharan Africa (SSA)

Year	Number	Source	Destination	Remark
1960–1975	27,000	Africa	Unspecified	Skilled working force
1975–1984	40,000	Africa	Unspecified	
Since 1990	20,000/year	Africa	Unspecified	
Since 2000	70,000/year	Africa	Unspecified	
1990	12 million	Africa	OECD	
2000	20 million	Africa	OECD	
2000s	40,000	Africa	World	Ph.D. holders
2003	5,880	South Africa	UK	Medical personnel
	2,825	Zimbabwe	UK	Medical
	1,510	Nigeria	UK	Medical
	850	Ghana	UK	Medical
1980s	60%	Ghana	Unspecified	Physicians
1990s	70%	Ghana	Unspecified	Physicians
2002	200	Ghana	Unspecified	Physicians
2006	20	Ethiopia	USA and others	Physicist, AAU
1980–1991	74.6%	Ethiopia	Unspecified	Scholars from HEIS
2003/2004	26,780	Africa	Outside EU	students

SOURCE: UNESCO (2008; WORLD BANK (2002); TEKLU (2008); UNIVERSITIES UK (2005); SPRING (2008); AMAZAN (2014) AND HABTAMU (2003)

of their higher education sector. For example, Canada's International Education Strategy document has focused on attracting talent from developing and emerging economies (Canada, 2014).

Some scholars have advocated the advantages of studying abroad, highlighting better resources and exposure to better experiences. Brain gain or brain circulation is an important aspect of internationalization but it requires innovative approaches to academic and professional credentials. Examples of brain circulation and brain gain may include the Silicon Valley Information Technology expertise returning to India, mobilization of the African Diaspora, and burgeoning cooperative arrangements such as joint professorship, and joint venture in research (Meek et al., 2009).

These important aspects related to and able to promote brain gain are not feasible in Africa for various reasons, including lack of financial, organizational and system capacity. Hence, more than in other continents, brain drain continues to be a striking challenge of the internationalization processes of higher education in Africa and it significantly affects the research paradigm and socio-economic development in general.

The impact of brain drain can increase unexpected and additional financial expenses,[2] develop worries and hesitations to subsidize the education of students who may ultimately go abroad, and distract academic environments from focusing on teaching, learning, and research (Meek & Teichler, 2009; Damtew, 2008). The financial expense has further diminished research funds and increased higher education institutions' dependency on foreign aid. According to the World Bank (2002), most research activities, between 70% to 90%, in Africa are in fact largely funded by external agencies.

4 Internationalization and Research in Sub-Saharan Africa

Knowledge has become the primary and most commonly dependable resource for national and international economic and social prosperity, and both a private and public good that facilitates individual and national economic growth and social inclusion. The erstwhile boundaries that previously contained knowledge within higher education institutions and research centres no longer create the barriers and limitations they used to, and technology facilities movements of people, programmes, and providers that has blurred boundaries and made them more easily permeable.

Governance of knowledge and knowledge-based institutions are shared and often contested between the state, economic markets, and academic institutions. Current knowledge production has begun to emphasize problem-solving or applied knowledge (also referred to as Mode II knowledge), establishing strong links between society and industry. Mode II knowledge often involves multidisciplinary approaches and collaboration with a wide range of non-university and university institutions through internationalization processes and programs (Salazar-Clemena & Meek, 2007).

However, these new features of knowledge have been shaped by the global North or the centre, and this has created knowledge of totalitarianism or unitary knowledge. According to the International Association of Universities (IAU) (2014) survey, the "dominance of a Western epistemological approach" is the top risk of internationalization in Africa. Internationalization, coupled with technological advancement and the hegemonic power and pressure of the global North, has also changed the context of knowledge (Salazar-Clemena & Meek, 2007). The global South or "periphery" appears to be the consumer and its knowledge production is considered cultural and not scientific.

Foucault (1980) analyzed the ways in which the developed world considered knowledge production in developing countries and regions like Africa as "subjugated knowledge", as "disqualified or unqualified", "insufficiently elaborated" and "located low down on the hierarchy, beneath the required level of recognition or scientificity" (Foucault, 1980, p. 82). Africa's role in knowledge production seems to fall in line with this consideration that Foucault made.

Through research partnerships, collaborations, and other capacity-building initiatives, internationalization can help address the low research capacity of many African universities. However, according to a researcher from Mekelle University (Ethiopia), even though it is believed that international research ventures have the capacity to integrate African researchers within the international research community and provide needed funding and infrastructure, the language used, the areas of research dealt with, the methods applied, and the coordinating positions within the international research community are determined by funding agents and not by African members of the community. Furthermore, most international collaborative research themes related to Africa deal with agriculture and health studies only and they tend to treat "nations of the Global South simply as sites of empirical research" while "the application of theories [is] developed elsewhere" (Rizvi & Lingard, 2010 p. 48). Examples of this kind of unequal collaboration in research are the UK's Medical Research Council in which Gambia and Uganda are the sites for long-term research on tropical diseases, and the British Welcome Foundation's similar research investments in Kenya and Malawi (Adams et al., 2010). These examples are a part of the processes through which research carried out in Africa has significant intellectual benefits that are secured outside of Africa.

In spite of the fact that research is an important aspect of higher education and of the internationalization of higher education, research that is a product of internationalization and its dissemination is challenging to African universities. The legacy of dependency, lack of qualified and skilled researchers, unequal collaboration and the subsequent loss of self-esteem among local scholars, brain drain, unsustainable foreign financial support and research projects, financial austerity, and poor research infrastructures are some of the most challenging hurdles for most African universities. The issues within the academic research scenario in sub-Saharan Africa can be analysed in terms of the lack of value placed on African researchers, external pressures, unequal partnership formations, language, and publication, which are challenging aspects of global internationalization in general.

4.1 *African Researchers*

Mkandawire (1995) has categorized African post-independence researchers into three generations. He argues that the USA trained the first generation through programmes such as the African Students Programme in American Universities (ASPAU) and that Europe was the other destination of this first generation of post-independence African students, who mostly travelled in their post-graduate studies. He argues that the most recent generation of post-independence African scholars has travelled as undergraduate students to the USA and Europe and that the most significant distinction of the first generation was that most scholars returned after completing their post-graduate studies to their respective home countries. He argues the first generation was the first set of indigenous scholars in the 'indigenization' of the African 'development' universities, and that their return was motivated by both material and moral incentives. Relatively good living conditions, the euphoria, and prospects of independence, and the "intoxicating mystique of emergent Africa" attracted the first generation to return home (Coleman & Court, 1994, p. 90). However, these scholars returned with a Western education and academic culture, and with the perception that what was good for the West would be equally useful to Africa. The political environment looked favourable, "most intellectuals shared the state's 'developmentalism' ideology, and some even rationalized the authoritarian cast with which the 'developmentalism' ideology was to be molded by pointing to supposedly universal exigencies of development" (Mkandawire, 1995, p. 76). During this time, foreign financial support was still attractive and the vibrancy of the work of this generation enabled them to publish articles in major journals and books by international publishers. As a result, this first generation enjoyed the recognition and collaboration of the international academic community (Mkandawire, 1995).

A significant number of the second generation of African researchers have also trained abroad, usually after their undergraduate studies in their home universities. The major characteristic of this group, unlike the first generation, was that many of them did not return, and those who did return did not stay for long in their home countries. They constituted the first wave of the African 'brain drain' (Mkandawire, 1995). The failure of the members of the second generation to return home after the completion of their studies abroad created a generational succession gap, and the gap was further exacerbated by the retirement of many scholars from the first generation (Mkandawire, 1995).

The third generation of African scholars is mostly locally based. The setting up of local graduate school programmes undercut much of the rationale for sending students abroad, obviated the need to do so and paved the way for doubting the wisdom of sending students abroad since it had mostly encouraged professionals to seek 'greener pastures' (Mkandawire, 1995). With slight national differences, the third generation is also characterized by a training attained in extremely difficult academic and political environments, in lacking material conditions. The third generation of African scholars has also been working in a situation in which universities are facing identity crises. Having supposedly achieved their mission of 'meeting the high-level manpower needs of the nation', in the eyes of the state, the public and international aid agencies such as the World Bank, African universities seem to have lost their original raison d'être (Mkandawire, 1995; Woodhall, 2003). This situation has intensified the dependency syndrome, which is manifested in the form of partnerships or link formations with other non-African universities.

4.2 Link Formation

Higher education institutions around the world are increasingly becoming the most significant places and centres for knowledge creation, dissemination and accumulation, and training of skilled labour force. Moreover, through the process of internationalization, higher education institutions collaborate with other higher education institutions to learn from and contribute to each other's work and to enable them to gain inputs and understand the status and competence of their institution on an international level (Salazar-Clemena et al., 2007).

The role of international institutions and agencies in shaping and steering scientific knowledge in particular, on the African continent, cannot be underestimated. International institutions and agencies have, to a large extent, managed to sustain minimal scientific production in many countries where Science and Technology structures have failed to develop or have seriously declined. For example, the continuing support of SIDA to Addis Ababa University in Ethiopia, since 1976, has sustained a minimal scientific output in the natural and health sciences field of the country.

On the other hand, it can be argued that some international organizations and agencies have been more interested in pursuing their own research agendas and have not done enough to ensure the long-term sustainability of a local science base in Africa (UNESCO, 2008). "Few areas have been funded in a more fragmented way than research. Project support is still the most common, and in many cases, grants go to researchers in the funding country with researchers from low-and-middle-income countries as invited collaborators" (Meek et al., 2009, p. 33). Moreover, until recently, both national governments of developing countries and external funding agencies have had the conviction that "relevant research may be better done internationally, and that low-income countries should rely on research findings produced elsewhere rather than invest in local research" (Meek et al., 2009, p. 29).

International aid agencies and organizations such as the International Monetary Fund (IMF) and the World Bank have made strong impacts on national policies in Africa. The impact of the 1980s Structural Adjustment Programme on the education sector is an example worth mentioning. During that time, due to the striking poverty that prevailed in sub-Saharan countries in Africa, there was a tendency to de-legitimize African universities' endeavours for the establishment of higher education research infrastructures. In the eyes of the World Bank, higher education was a luxury for Africa (Brock-Utne, 2003). Consequently, the World Bank enforced the idea that "most African countries were [...] better off closing universities at home and training graduates overseas. Recognizing that its call for a closure of universities was politically untenable, the Bank subsequently modified its agenda, calling for universities in Africa to be trimmed and restructured to produce only those skills that the 'market' demands" (Brock-Utne, 2003, p. 30; Cloete et al., 2015).

The World Bank also argued to shift resources towards basic education, including secondary and tertiary education and suggested that higher education, though important for development, failed to support the development endeavours needed in the poorest parts of the developing world. It labelled universities and other higher education institutions in developing economies, as institutions that did not produce original and new knowledge. The World Bank thus proposed to increase the proportion of basic education from 11% to 27% and to reduce the share of higher education from 40% to 30% (Brock-Utne, 2003, p. 29). In 33 sub-Saharan African countries the annual foreign financial aid per student thus dropped from $ 6,800 in 1980 to $ 1,200 in 2002 and later dropped further to $ 981. This policy officially delinked African universities from the development mission (Cloete et al., 2011). Furthermore, it advised African leaders to privatize institutions and demand that students pay for the cost of their education, increasing the student fees and creating loan schemes through the introduction of a cost-sharing system (Brock-Utne, 2003). Following the funding cuts for higher education, the dependence of Africa on studies overseas increased. African institutions of higher learning have become once more staffed with expatriates or people who have been trained overseas, on mostly Western or, at least, non-African concepts, ideas, outlooks, and research methodologies. The academic and financial starvation of higher learning institutions has thus exacerbated and sustained the process of brain drain. Sub-Saharan Africa has lost 30% of its highly skilled workforce between 1960 and 1990, largely to countries of the European Union. The United Nations Economic Commission for Africa estimates that, since the 1960s, more than 50% of Africans who pursued tertiary studies in chemistry and physics in the United States, never returned to Africa. This situation has increased the need for external link formations, through foreign aid, expatriate staff and foreign partners. More than 100,000 expatriates from industrialized countries are employed in different countries in Africa (Brock-Utne, 2003). This dynamic, coupled with internal socio-economic and political challenges, has contributed to an environment of academic underdevelopment and foreign dependency. The tendency to uncritically and unconditionally adopt foreign policy paradigms, methods, and approaches has also drastically destroyed the national research potential, capacity, and endeavours.

In reconsidering the potentials of higher education for African development, link formation has been suggested as a solution for African higher education to "keep up" with the rest of the world. Academics and higher education institutions in Africa feel compelled to seek expertise and donor support for their departments, faculty, and research institutes, through links with more affluent universities in the industrialized world. They thus depend on these external links for support in funding, research, publications, sustaining journals, and training staff (Brock-Utne, 2003). This link has assumed a donor-recipient kind of relationship, which has eroded equality and mutual support and disempowered the role and potential of African research. Brock-Utne (2003) has commented on the dynamics inherent to link formations in higher education as follows:

> The reinvigoration of the research and teaching qualities of the African universities are assumed to be found in the search for the 'missing link' where African institutions of higher learning have to go into link arrangements with more affluent universities in the North or seek direct support from Western donors. 'Experts' from the North coming to teach and distribute the Western curricula are normally part of the link phenomenon. So are books are written in the West, computers from the West, and scholarship for master's and Ph.D. students to go to the West to study the curricula offered there [...] for professors in the south to be visiting professors teaching in the north. No wonder, then, that many academics in the South develop a Westernized outlook. (p. 36)

The February 1990 issue of the Newsletter of the Academic Staff Assembly at the University of Dar es Salaam also commented explicitly on the link pretense as follows:

> Here, in the midst of filthy toilets and classrooms with broken windows and furniture, thrives the LINK phenomenon. Virtually every department, under the threat of material and intellectual starvation, has been forced to establish links with one or more institutions, mostly from the West. We depend on the links for the training of our junior staff, for teaching material and equipment, and a host of other things. The link agreements are, almost without exception, as unequal as would be expected. This is

> despite some efforts to include clauses suggesting reciprocity [...]. What is primarily at stake is that as we lose confidence in our own ability to sustain our education system, we shall also have to abandon the pretense of determining our educational future. (UDASA, 1990, p. 1)

Hirji (1990), who is staff of the University of Dar es Salaam, has made an analogy of the link phenomena with the 19th century colonial partition; "As one goes around the Faculty of Medicine, one wonders whether, after a hundred years, after Karl Peters landed here, the second partition of Africa is in progress or not. The Dental School seems to be run by the Finnish, the AIDS research programme by the Swedes, community health programmes by the Germans, with the British, Italian, Danish all having their own corners" (Hirji, 1990, p. 23).

Since North-South cooperation in higher education can generally enhance capacities reciprocally on both sides, the issue is how the partnership, cooperation or link is established, governed and managed. Most of the time, external support to African higher education institutions comes with conditions and follows the Programme-Based Approach (PBA), also sometimes referred to as 'basket funding' (Meek et al., 2009, p. 32), which considers research capacity building as something secondary, even if research capacity building is of primary importance for Africa's engagement in internationalization. In fact, strategies for developing higher education research initiatives in Africa should be contextualized to the prevailing local conditions of institutions and should be developed by local researchers and policy-makers rather than be planned and organized by external donors or agents and foreign researchers who cannot have a clear picture of local scenarios and priorities.

Papoutsaki (2008) explains the lop-sidedness of the link phenomena established between the global South and global North in research partnerships as follows:

> Research into donor-based programmes of cooperation between institutions from the North and South has indicated an inequality in the relationship. Because the Northern donors provide the funding, [...] knowledge, [...] [they] often decide on the model and activities to be chosen, despite the fact that the Southern institution is obviously being better placed to determine the needs and priorities [...]. The Northern institutions benefit from these programmes in terms of the internationalization of courses, attracting researchers, establishing collaborations with partner institutions in the South, and getting access to research grounds in developing countries. (p. 247)

4.3   Language

Another problematic aspect of internationalization in developing countries is also the use of a foreign language at the expense of local languages. According to Brock-Utne (2003), in the North-South dynamic, "culture, including language, was offered in exchange for material goods. The West exports its ideas and languages and imports Africa's riches" (Brock-Utne, 2003, p. 45). Research and publication in sub-Saharan Africa have in fact been constrained partly due to the use of foreign languages in research projects and publications (Brock-Utne, 2003), and language is what determines the success rates for getting international funding, with more opportunities to obtain international grants for researchers who master the English language versus any African vernacular (Mamela, 2014).

Due to colonial history and its influences, there is no university in sub-Saharan Africa that uses indigenous African languages as a medium of instruction, and the languages of research and instruction at universities remain colonial languages such as English, French, Portuguese, Dutch (in South Africa), and Italian (in Somalia) (Brock-Utne, 2003; Damtew, 2008). Ethiopia, an African nation that was not colonized, also uses English as a medium of instruction in its universities.

Some efforts are in progress to lessen the colonial language dominance. For example, Sudan has been trying to use Arabic as the main medium of higher learning instruction, and South Africa is strengthening Afrikaans and Zulu languages in its institutions of higher education. Following the entrance of English-speaking leaders and intelligentsia in political positions of power in Rwanda, English has been increasingly used at the expense of French in Rwandan universities. The African Union has also recognized Kiswahili as a language (Damtew, 2008).

Colonial language diversity within Africa has limited internal regional communication and collaboration as well. For example, Anglophone Gambian and Ghanaian researchers prefer to collaborate with the British instead of their next-door neighbours, the francophone Senegalese researchers. Figure 2.1 shows the internal collaborative network trend that has been shaped by colonial and modern global internationalization language and cultural influences.

As can be seen from the chart, there are significant research partnerships among countries of North Africa, who share a similar language and culture. With the exception of Egypt, which has extended its collaboration to South Africa, the Maghreb region does little research with the rest of Africa. This internal language diversity that has influenced collaboration with countries of similar language outside of Africa has hindered the development of strong regional collaboration and the establishment of an African Research

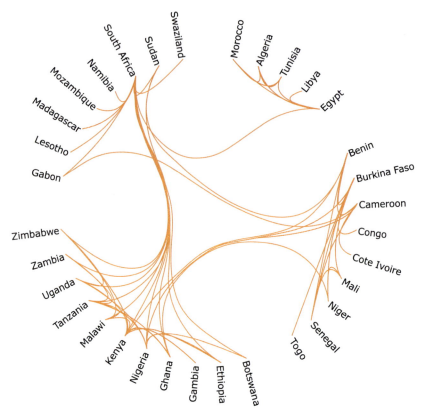

FIGURE 2.1   Network of internal research collaboration (from Adams et al., 2010)

Area (ARA). Moreover, research conducted in colonial foreign languages has also alienated higher education institutions from their societies and the local people, and from the role they can play in local development. In this respect, Gorostiaga (1993) questions the merits of the African University as follows:

> What, then does it mean to train 'successful' professionals in this sea of poverty? Does an institution that does not confront the injustice surrounding it that does not question the crisis of a civilization that is ever less universalizable to the great majorities of the world, merit the name "university"? Would not such an institution be simply one more element that reproduces this unequal system? (p. 29)

4.4   Publication

Academic publication has been another feature of internationalization. Countries in Africa have initiated a relatively good deal of publications and journals at different times. These have been funded and supported by international and regional organizations, and higher education institutions in the USA, UK, France, Germany, Italy, and Australia, among others. However, with few exceptions, due to lack of sustainable support and low considerations for African research outputs, most African academic journals have disappeared and publications have dropped. In discussing the decrease in African research, which is linked to its publications, UNESCO (2008) observation reports that:

> These diminishing shares of African science overall do not reflect a decrease in an absolute sense, but rather an increase in publication output less than the worldwide growth rate. Africa has lost 11% of its share in global science since its peak in 1987; sub-Saharan science has lost almost a third (31%). The countries in Northern Africa; Egypt and the Maghreb countries (Algeria, Mauritania, Libya, Morocco, and Tunisia) accounted for the modest growth of the African share of the worldwide output during the years 1998–2002. Part of this decline of sub-Saharan science can be attributed to discarding African journals from the Citation Indexes. Notably, the number of South African journals dropped from 35 to 19 during the years 1993–2004. (p. 34)

Even though, through international collaborations and increased production of internationally co-authored publications, it is generally observed that sub-Saharan Africa has improved both the quantity and quality of its research output in a decade, from 2003 to 2012, its global rank is still at the bottom of the hierarchy and its global share has been limited to 0.44% (2003) and 0.72% (2012) (World Bank, 2014). Moreover, one might expect that international partners have been part of local research capacity-building, creating effective organizational and managerial structures, which can enable the production of co-publications. Many research publications remain co-productions between African-based researchers and their foreign research partners, which are more often colleagues in Europe, Asia or the United States (Tijssen, 2015). Table 2.2 shows the declining trend of publication in Africa in general, and particularly in sub-Saharan Africa, with Africa lagging behind in publications compared to the rest of the world. For instance, in 2007, the scientific research published in sub-Saharan Africa was the least, only to be followed by the Middle East and North Africa taken together (see Table 2.2).

Between 1999 and 2008, research production in Africa was mainly dominated by three countries, namely, Egypt (30,000), Nigeria (10,000), and South Africa (47,000). In the same period, in central Africa, 37 countries, produced 7,100 research papers per year. In northern Africa, in Egypt, Tunisia, Morocco,

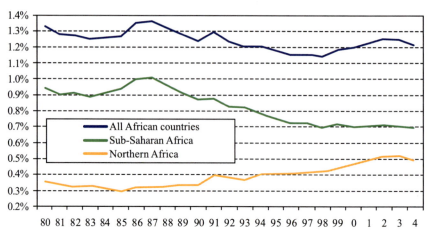
FIGURE 2.2   Trends in African research article output in the international journal literature, 1980–2004 (from Tijssen, 2007, p. 308)

Algeria, and Sudan, more than 10,500 research papers were generated in 2008 alone. In southern Africa, the Republic of South Africa and the other ten countries produced more than 10,000 papers. On average, the continent of Africa has been producing about 27,000 research papers per year (Adams et al., 2010).

Figure 2.3 depicts the regional research output share in the years between 1999 and 2008.

Damtew and Altbach (2004) have described brain drain, lack of infrastructure and commitment, low funding and massification as the major hurdles to the development of research capacity and publication in Africa.

> By all measures, research and publishing activities in Africa are in critical condition. The general state of research in Africa is extremely poor, and its research infrastructure is inadequate. Scarcity of laboratory equipment, chemicals, and other scientific paraphernalia; a small number of high-level experts; poor and dilapidated libraries; alarmingly low and declining salaries of academic and research staff; a massive brain drain out of the academic institutions; the "expansion" of undergraduate education; poor oversight of research applicability; and declining, non-existent, and unreliable sources of research funds all remain major hurdles to the development of research capacity across the continent. The paucity of local publications is complicated by many other factors, including the small number of researchers with the energy, time, funds, and support needed to sustain journals; the lack of qualified editors and editorial staff; a shortage of publishable materials; a restrictive environment that

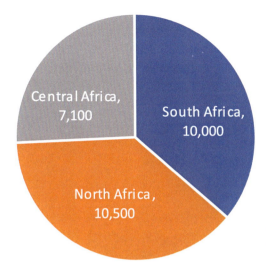

FIGURE 2.3
Regional research production, 1999–2008 (adapted from Adams et al., 2010)

inhibits freedom of speech; and a lack of commitment to and appreciation of journal production by university administrators. (pp. 38–39)

Table 2.2 illustrates how sub-Saharan Africa occupies the lowest number of scientific research and patent applications in 2007. Europe and Central Asia have taken the lead in publication, while East Asia and the Pacific regions are frontrunners in patent applications.

According to Dell (2014), most scientific papers produced in Africa are collaborative, and this has affected the continent's research evolution and priorities. Collaborative research endeavours in Africa have reached 66% of the continent's research in a five-year period (2004–2008), while single author articles, by contrast, appear to be "on the verge of extinction" (Dell, 2014). Most African research papers are produced in collaboration with foreign countries such as the USA, UK, France, Germany, Italy, Spain, Australia, Belgium, the Netherlands, China, Japan, and Saudi Arabia. The research collaboration has internal dimensions as well. The threshold of this dimension of collaboration produces a minimum of five research papers per year (Adams et al., 2010). In spite of this, due to the factors described by Damtew and Altbach (2004) and reported above, the scientificity, applicability, and sustainability of publications remain limited. In most cases, publications in African universities are done for academic promotion purposes and left on the shelf, with limited local utility due to its low quality, relevance, and poor funding, which ties to the idea that research in Africa should be considered a regional priority, to avoid lessening its socio-economic relevance and utility. The consequence is

TABLE 2.2 Regional comparison of scientific publications and patent applications in 2007

Regions	Scientific publications	Patent applications
East Asia and the Pacific	14,817	65,506
Europe and central Asia	34,905	32,728
Latin America and the Caribbean	10,093	40,003
South Asia	8,896	2,143
The Middle East and North Africa	3,123	926
Sub-Saharan Africa	3,499	101

SOURCE: DAMTEW AND GRELJN (2010)

a vicious cycle; underdevelopment of research competence, productivity, and knowledge feeding into dependency and gross academic and socio-economic underdevelopment of the region. Table 2.3 illustrates the collaborative publications in sub-Saharan Africa. The table shows how the UK and USA are frequent global research partners of six key African countries, namely Algeria, Tunisia, Egypt, Kenya, Nigeria, and South Africa.

Research and publications are also hampered by poor remuneration, heavy teaching loads resulting from increasing numbers of students, inability to monitor young faculty, inadequate infrastructure, and the inadequacy of research systems, which are both cause and effect of the region's knowledge poverty and serious material deprivation. All of these problems are the ones that have fallen on the 'third generation' of the African scholars (Sawyerr, 2004).

Poor academic environments, with poor knowledge productivity and low quality of academic scholars, in peripheral higher education institutions, are also further burdened by cross-border education programs, which is one of the features of internationalization that has further negatively affected higher education and research in developing countries. In their lack of consideration of the host country, cross-border programmes and providers can appear to be commercial and phony, awarding degrees that are not relevant to the context in which they are awarded, and facilitating frauds such as the diploma mills. Through internalization and cross-border programs, the export of fake and unqualified programmes and institutions have been found to occur (Knight, 2007). Internationalization of higher education also means the opening of branch foreign campuses with already overloaded staff members and meager resources from the local public universities, which also affects the potentials for improving research and human resources (OECD, 2007; Knight, 2012).

TABLE 2.3   Percentage of collaborative scientific paper production

Top African research countries	Foreign collaborators and % of collaboration				
Algeria	USA, 2.6%	UK, 2.3%	France, 42.0%	Italy, 2.6%	Spain, 2.6%
Egypt	USA, 9.6%	UK, 4.0%	Germany, 5.2%	Saudi Arabia, 6.0%	Japan, 3.7%
Kenya	USA, 32.0%	UK, 23,6%	Germany, 6.8%	Holland 5.8%	Belgium, 4.8%
Nigeria	USA, 7.4%	UK, 5.9%	Germany, 2.9%	Italy, 1.8%	China, 1.5%
South Africa	USA, 15.1%	UK, 11.7%	Germany, 5.7%	Australia, 4.5%	France, 3.9%
	USA, 2.8%	UK, 2.1%	France, 32.6%	Italy, 2.7%	Spain, 2.5%

SOURCE: BASED ON ADAMS ET AL. (2010)

These factors can result in brain drain and the emergence of poorly formed graduates, who are incapable of undertaking quality research. Ultimately, *brain drain* and *minds in drain* produce poor research and sustain academic under development. Developing countries also fear that cross-border providers will lead to increased social costs for higher education, a return to elitist systems, and the gradual disappearance of national systems that fail to compete with foreign providers (Bubtana, 2007).

5   Concluding Remarks

Internationalization of higher education has many positive benefits for students, academic scholars, higher education institutions, countries, and regional academic hubs. However, it is not without challenges. The challenges are more severe in developing countries than in the developed parts of the world. This chapter stresses the interconnected challenges imposed by global internationalization on research, publication and academic mobility of sub-Saharan African higher education institutions, which tend to be duplicates of colonial higher education institutions in terms of curriculum, research method, governance, funding system, and reforms.

Higher education in Africa has also suffered from the broader issues of poor economic resources, political instability, and lack of indigenization that have characterized post-colonial Africa in general. These difficulties have incapacitated African higher education institutions from playing their key role in development have kept this field dependent and stifled in its own knowledge production.

Reforms and policies influenced by international financial institutions such as the World Bank, the International Monetary Fund and other aid agencies, have led sub-Saharan African higher education to become dependent on foreign support for its research, publication and academic capacity building, and have challenged its knowledge production, publication, and academic capacity building. Most HEIs in sub-Saharan Africa are operating under the financial aid of foreign organizations and countries and internationalization has become a necessity for research capacity building of higher education institutions in sub-Saharan Africa. International partnerships have further triggered policy shifts to the interests of foreign partners.

The academic scholarship piece of internationalization has been initiated and eased by developed nations' recruitment policies and overall global academic migration, which has brought Africa to lose many of its academic scholars. Brain drain has further negatively affected the regional research paradigm and debilitated regional academic development and quality, which is key to knowledge production. Consequently, African research has also found itself at the bottom of the global research output ladder, which further affects the competitive power of Africa, while sustaining its socio-economic problems. This overall situation has resulted in dependency and unequal partnerships, which have resulted in the deterioration of self-esteem and worth on individual, national, and regional levels in African academia. Coupled with the legacy of colonialism and the 'post-independence' internal socio-economic and political difficulties, the challenges of internationalization in sub-Saharan Africa higher education are thus considerable and conspicuously debilitating.

Africa has to reconsider its engagement in global internationalization. One way of minimizing challenges is to guide and support engagement through consciously prepared policy paradigms. Another option is to strengthen regional or continental forms of internationalization. De Wit (2013), for instance, states that "until recently 'internationalization' of 'international education' was predominantly a Western phenomenon, in which the developing countries played only a reactive role" (de Wit, 2013, p. 6). He recommends the need to "de-internationalize" or indigenize higher education in Africa, to move away from the dominance of Western structures, concepts, and learning models, and to develop its own style of internationalization. The 2012 action plan of the International Association of Universities (IAU) also calls for new visions and strategies to challenge traditional views on the internationalization of higher education. Moreover, Mohamedbhai (2013) has proposed that African higher education institutions that share common challenges need to contextualize and prioritize their internationalization activities in a regional context.

The sensitivity of the issue of brain drain has compelled the Network of African Science Academies (NASAC) (2009) to submit a joint statement to the heads of state attending the G8 +5 Summit in Italy, in July 2009where the following issue was addressed: "One-third of all African scientists lives and works in developed countries. This outflow represents a significant loss of economic potential for the continent, especially in today's global society where scientific and technological knowledge drive development" (NASAC, 2009, n.p.). Consequentially, Africa remains the world's least scientifically proficient region and the world's poorest continent. Even though, the future of Africa rests on Africa's own internal resources, the NASAC (2009), statement also called upon the G8+5 countries to adequately invest on African higher education and research, extend financial support to young African scientists, launch regional and international centres of excellence in areas of study that are important to African development, and encourage the African Diaspora to participate in African development initiatives and endeavours.

Assie-Lumumba (2005) has also proposed to reinvigorate sub-Saharan universities on the ground of an African education philosophy. He sustains that Africans should possess, transform, and indigenize higher education through the fusion of international experiences with local socio-historical, economic, and cultural contexts. She suggests that "education in its various disciplinary forms, including its philosophy, science, technology, and knowledge base, must be reconnected to the African culture". In line with Assie-Lumumba's (2005) ideas on the importance of the African philosophy concepts of *botho* or *Ubuntu,* which refer to communal relationships and emphasize how an individual is always connected to and understood in relation to others, this paper also supports the idea that this humanistic philosophy can and should provide the foundation for African education in general, and higher education in particular, and re-centre African education around the collective well-being of the African people.

Notes

1 The size of Africa is 11,677,239 square miles (30,244,049 square km) and ranks second next to Asia, which occupies 17,139,445 square miles (44,391,162 square km)

(http://geography.about.com/od/lists/a/largecontinent.htm). The African population was estimated at 1.033 billion people in 2013. The population is projected to be 1.2 billion and 2 billion by 2025 and 2050, respectively (AFIDEP, 2012).

2 For example, sub-Saharan Africa spent $4 billion annually on the salaries of approximately 100,000 western professional expatriates; the cost of training, for a non-specialized doctor in a developing country is about $60,000 and for a para medical specialist it is about $12,000; brain drain has cost South Africa 8.4 billion Rand of lost income tax and 285 billion Rand in potential contributions to the GDP between 1994 and 1997. It is generally estimated that Africa loses over $US 13 billion in brain drain (Damtew, 2008).

References

Adams, J., King, C., & Hook, D. (2010). *Global research report, Africa*. Leeds: Thomson Reuters.

African Institute for Development Policy (AFIDEP). (2012). *Population, climate change, and sustainable development in Africa*.

Altbach, P. G. (2004a). The past and future of Asian universities: Twenty-first century challenges. In P. G. Altbach & T. Umakoshi (Eds.), *Asian Universities – Historical perspectives and contemporary challenges* (pp. 13–32). Baltimore, MD: Johns Hopkins University Press.

Altbach, P. G. (2004b). Globalization and the University: Myths and realities in an equal world. *Tertiary Education and Management, 10*, 3–25.

Amazan, R. C. (2014). When the Diaspora returns: Analysis of Ethiopian returnees and the need for highly skilled labour in Ethiopia. In B. Streitwieser (Ed.), *Internationalization of higher education and global mobility* (pp. 169–185). Symposium Books Ltd.

Assié-Lumumba, N. T. (2005). *Higher education in Africa: Crises, reforms, and transformation*. Senegal: Council for the Development of Social Science Research in Africa (CODSERIA).

Barrett, A. M., Crossley, M., & Fon, T. P. (2014). North-South research partnerships in higher education: Perspectives from South & North. In B. Streitwieser (Ed.), *Internationalization of higher education and global mobility* (pp. 59–71). Symposium Books Ltd.

Bloom, D., Canning, D., & Chan, K. (2006). *Higher education and economic development in Africa*. Washington, DC: World Bank.

Brock-Utne, B. (2003). Formulating higher education policies in Africa: The pressure from external forces and the neoliberal agenda. *Journal of Higher Education in Africa, 1*(1), 24–56.

Bubtana, A. R. (2007). WTO/GATS: Possible implications for higher education and research in the Arab States. In V. L. Meek, U. Teichler & M.-L. Kearney (Eds.), *The impact of globalization on higher education and research in the Arab States* (pp. 95–112). Rabat, Morocco: Regional Research Seminar.

Canada. (2014). *Canada's International Education Strategy: Harnessing our knowledge advantage to drive innovation and prosperity*. Canada.

Cloete, N., Bailey, T., & Maassen, P. (2011). *Universities and economic development in Africa: Pact, academic core and coordination*. Cape Town: Centre for Higher Education Transformation (CHET).

Cloete, N., Maassen, P., & Bailey, T. (Eds.). (2015). *Knowledge production and contradictory functions in African higher education*. Cape Town: African Minds. Retrieved from https://chet.org.za/books/knowledge-production-and-contradictory-functions-african-higher-education

CODESRIA. (2011). *Africa and the challenges of the twenty-first century* (13th CODESRIA General Assembly, 5–9 December 2011). Morocco: Rabat.

Dale, R. (2005). Globalization, knowledge economy, and comparative education. *Comparative Education, 41*, 117–149.

Damtew, T. (2008). The international dimensions of higher education in Africa: Status, challenges, and prospects. In T. Damtew & J. Knight (Eds.), *Higher education in Africa: The international dimension* (pp. 44–79). Boston, MA: CIHE.

Damtew, T. (2014, February 21). The "soft power" proof the pudding-not in the branding. *University World News*, Issue No. 308.

Damtew, T., & Altbach, P. G. (2004). African higher education: Challenges for the 21st century. *Higher Education, 47*, 21–50, 2004. Dordrecht: Kluwer Academic Publishers.

Damtew, T., & Greijn, H. (2010). Introduction: Globalization and African higher education. In T. Damtew & H. Green (Eds.), *Higher education and globalization: Challenges, threats and opportunities for Africa* (pp. 1–7). Dordrecht: Maastricht University Centre for International Cooperation in Academic Development.

Dell, S. (2014, February 7). International collaboration in African research – Who wins? *University World News, 306*.

de Wit, H. (2013). Reconsidering the concept of internationalization. *International Higher Education, 70*, 5–7.

Ezeh, A. C. (2008). *Consortium for Advanced Research Training in Africa (CARTA): A model for training and retaining the next generation of African academics*. Powerpoint presentation for the University Leaders' Forum: Next Generation of Academics hosted by Kenya, The University of Ghana.

Foucault, M. (1980). *Power/Knowledge: Selected interviews and other writings 1972–1977* (C. Gordon, L. Marshall, J. Mepham, & K. Soper, Trans.). New York, NY: Pantheon Books.

Gorostiaga, X. (1993). New times, a new role for universities of the South. *Envio: The Monthly Magazine of Analysis on Central America, 12*(144), 29–40.

Habtamu, W. (2003). 'Ethiopia'. In T. Damtew & P. G. Altbach (Eds.), *African higher education: An international reference handbook* (pp. 316–325). Bloomington, IN: Indiana University Press.

Hirji, K. (1990). Academic pursuit under the link. *UDASA Newsletter/Forum, 10*, 11–26.

International Association of Universities (IAU). (2010). *Internationalization of higher education: Global trends, regional perspectives*. Paris: IAU.

International Association of Universities (IAU). (2012, April). *Affirming academic values in internationalization of higher education: A call for action*. Retrieved December 25, 2014, from http://www.iau-aiu.net/sites/all/files/Affirming_Academic_Values_ in_Internationalization _of_Higher_Education.pdf

Jowi, J. O. (2009). Internationalization of higher education in Africa: Developments, emerging trends and policy implications. *Higher Education Policy, 22*(3), 259–261.

Knight, J. (2004). Internationalization remodeled definition, approaches, and rationales. *Journal of Studies in International Education, 8*(1), 5–31.

Knight, J. (2007). *Implications of cross border education and GATS for the knowledge enterprise*. Submitted to UNESCO Forum on Higher Education, Research and Knowledge.

Knight, J. (2012). Concepts, rationales, and interpretive frameworks in the internationalization of higher education. In D. Deardorff, H. de Wit, J. Heyl, & T. Adams (Eds.), *The Sage handbook of international higher education* (pp. 27–42). Washington, DC: Sage Publications.

Knight, J. (2013). The changing landscape of higher education internationalization-for better or worse. *Perspectives: Policy and Practice in Higher Education Journal of the Association of University Administrators, 17*(2), 1–11.

MacGregor, K. (2015, March 13). 50% Higher education participation in 50 years – Summit. *University World News*, issue No. 358.

Mamela, A. (2014, March). Lost in translation. *Research Africa Roundup, 4*. Retrieved May 27, 2014, from https://www.researchprofessional.com/media/pdf/Research_ Africa_News_Roundup-March_2014.pdf

Meek, V. L., Teichler, U., & Kearney, M. (Eds.). (2009). *Higher education and innovation: Changing dynamics*. Kassel: International Centre for Higher Education Research Kassel (INCHER-Kassel).

Mkandawire, T. (1995). Three generations of African academics: A note. *Transformation, 28*, 75–83.

Mohamedbhai, G. (2008). *The effect of massification on higher education in Africa*. Retrieved April 28, 2010, from http://www.boomerangbooks.com.au

Mohamedbhai, G. (2013). Internationalization of African higher education: A different approach? In H. de Wit, F. Hunter, L. Johnson, & H.-G. van Liempd (Eds.), *Possible futures: The next 25 years of the internationalization of higher education* (pp. 138–141). Amsterdam: European Association for International Education.

Muchie, M. (2006, November 29–December 1). *The challenges and opportunities of re-inventing higher education as centers of research capacity-building.* A paper presented in the Colloquium on "Research and Higher Education Policy, Universities as Centers of Research and Knowledge Creation: An Endangered Species, Paris.

Network of African Science Academies (NASAC). (2009). *Brain drain.* Kenya: Network of African Science Academies.

OECD. (2007). The internationalization of higher education: Towards an explicit policy. In *Education policy analysis 2008: Focus on higher education.* Paris: OECD Publishing.

Ogachi, O. I. (2011, December 5–9). *21st Century 'academic imperialism', internationalization of higher education and threats to indigenization of research and innovation for development in African Universities.* A paper presented on the 13th CODESRIA General Assembly, Rabat, Morocco.

Papoutsaki, E. (2008). The need for local research approaches: De-Westernizing research methodologies for higher education curricula in developing countries. In U. Teichler & H. Vessuri (Eds.), *Universities as centre of research and knowledge creation: An endangered species?* (pp. 241–254). Rotterdam, The Netherlands: Sense Publishers.

Rivza, B., & Teichler, U. (2007). The changing role of student mobility. *Higher Education Policy, 20*(4), 457–476.

Rizvi, F., & Lingard, B. (2010). *Globalizing education policy.* New York, NY: Routledge.

Rüegg, W. (1992). Themes. In W. Rüegg (Ed.), *A history of the university in Europe, Vol. I, Universities in the nineteenth and twentieth centuries (1800–1945)* (pp. 3–34). Cambridge: Cambridge University Press.

Salazar-Clemena, R. M., & Meek, V. L. (Eds.). (2007). *Competition, collaboration, and change in the academic profession: Shaping higher education's contribution to knowledge and research.* UNESCO: UNESCO Forum on Higher Education, Research and Knowledge.

Sawyerr, A. (2004). African universities and the challenges of research capacity development. *Journal of Higher Education Area, 2*(1), 211–240.

Scott, P. (2000). Globalization and higher education: Challenges for the 21st century. *Journal of Studies in International Education, 4*(3), 3–10.

Sehoole, C., & de Wit, H. (2014). The regionalization, internationalization, and globalization of African higher education. *International Journal of African Higher Education, 1*(1), 217–241.

Sehoole, C., & Knight, J. (Eds.). (2013). *Internationalization of African higher education: Towards achieving the MDGs.* Rotterdam, The Netherlands: Sense Publishers.

Sichone, O. (2006). Globalization and internationalization of higher education in South Africa: The challenge of rising xenophobia. *JHEA/RESA, 4*(3), 33–53.

Sintayehu, K. (2016). *Conceptualizing the internationalization of higher education and the academic profession with a comparative analysis of Europe, Asia-Pacific, and Africa* (Ph.D. dissertation). University of Ljubljana, Slovenia.

Spring, J. (2008). Research on globalization and education. *Review of Educational Research, 78*(2), 330–363.

Sy Habib, J. (2003). Partnership in higher education in Africa: Communications implications beyond the 2000s. *Africa and Asian Studies, 2*(4), 577–610.

Teichler, U. (2004). The changing debate on internationalization of higher education. *Higher Education, 48*(1), 5–26.

Teklu, A. (2008, October 13–14). *Education system in sub-Saharan Africa: Trends and developments.* A paper presented to the Norwegian Agency for Quality Assurance in Education (NOKUT) Annual Seminar.

Tijssen, R. (2015). Research output and international research cooperation in African flagship universities. In N. Cloete, P. Maassen, & T. Bailey (Eds.), *Knowledge production and contradictory functions in African Higher Education* (pp. 61–74). Cape Town: African Minds.

Tijssen, R. (2007). Africa's contribution to the worldwide research literature: New analytical perspectives, trends, and performance indicators. *Sceintometric, 71*(2), 303–327.

UDASA. (l990). The squeeze of education. *UDASA Newsletter/Forum, 10.*

United Nations Educational, Scientific and Cultural Organization (UNESCO). (2008, January 16–18). *Regional report on Sub-Saharan Africa: Symposium on comparative analysis of national research systems.* Paris: UNESCO.

Universities UK. (2005). *Patterns of higher education institutions in the UK: Fifth report.* London: Universities UK.

Vessuri, H. (2007). Training of researchers in Latin America and the Caribbean. In M. Mollis & M. N. Voehl (Eds.), *Research and higher education policies for transforming societies: Perspectives from Latin America and the Caribbean* (pp. 141–152). Paris: UNESCO.

Wilson, L. (2013). The internationalization of higher education and research: European policies and institutional strategies. In H. de Wit, F. Hunter, L. Johnson, & H.-G. van Liempd (Eds.), *Possible futures: The next 25 years of the internationalization of higher education* (pp. 28–33). Amsterdam: European Association for International Education.

Woodhall, M. (2003). Financing higher education: Old challenges and new messages. *Journal of Higher Education in Africa/Revue de l'enseignement supérieur en Afrique, 1*(1), 78–100.

World Bank. (2002). *Constructing knowledge societies: New challenges for tertiary education.* Washington, DC: World Bank.

World Bank. (2010). *Financing higher education in Africa. Cost sharing and accountability – Current European developments*. Washington, DC: World Bank.

World Bank. (2014). *A decade of development in Sub-Saharan African Science, Technology, Engineering, and Mathematics Research*. Kigali, Rwanda.

Zeleza, P. T. (2012, March 21–22). *Internationalization in higher education: Opportunities and challenges for the knowledge project in the global south.* Keynote address, presented at Conference organized by the Southern African Regional Universities Association, the International Association of Universities, and Universidade Eduardo Mondlane, Maputo, Mozambique.

CHAPTER 3

Reflections on the Role of Africa in Research for Development: A Plea for Collaboration

Brook Lemma

1   Introduction

One impetus for higher education partnership is creating a favourable research environment that mobilizes a diverse set of funding and a pool of expertise. Partnership in higher education enables institutions and researchers to put resources together and achieve common goals, generating and disseminating knowledge to the wider community.

Over the past few years, among higher education institutions and researchers, there has been increasing interest in the different modalities of research collaboration. With regards to research collaboration between the developed and developing countries, the discourse is quite diverse, ranging from a neo-colonial conception of partnership, which presupposes structural dependency of African institutions on European institutions, to a more mutual collaboration that aims to achieve win-win outcomes for all parties involved.

Despite a range of debates on research partnership, collaborative research among different institutions, across different geographical and institutional jurisdictions, has become a necessary condition for higher education institutions to excel in their innovation and development. This chapter highlights the importance of collaborative research as a means for sharing possibilities and also responsibilities. It discusses the link between research and development as a process for the accumulation of knowledge and for refining basic questions for humankind, that are connected to research for development.

2   The Meaning and History of Research

Research is seen as a systematic and organized way of thinking and acting in order to find answers to problems. By its nature, research is also unpredictable, in some cases moving in unforeseen directions, with unexpected consequences, sometimes giving rise to significant but bizarre outcomes, which should still be applauded and not curbed (Taylor, 2006). Research outcomes that are gathered make up a mass of knowledge that humans use to guide their competitiveness in this world.

However, research is not the only way humans use to create knowledge with. If we look back to the forms of thinking and combining information, from which humans have formed and stored knowledge for future use, we can see that humans acquire knowledge through more or less four ways. These are:
- *Intuitive learning*, whereby humans naturally come up with ideas that guide them on some level of improved action. An example of this kind of knowledge could be cracking a shell with a stone instead of using bare hands or putting the shell in one's mouth to try and crack it open with the pressure of the jaw muscles and sharp edges of the teeth.
- *Authoritative learning*, where information is gathered from others through questioning, asking subordinates to come up with information, or learning from books or, in more modern times, from searching the Internet.
- *Logical reasoning*, where humans reason that if A is equal to B and B is equal to C, then A must be equal to C.
- *Empirical learning*, where humans apply their abstract thinking to critically observe and/or experiment in relation to a given problem, and come up with outcomes that can solve the problem that triggered the experiment. This is the formal way of learning in academic research.

Empirical knowledge can be basic or applied (Roll-Hansen, 2009). Basic research (BR) is experimental or theoretical and done primarily to acquire new knowledge, without any particular foreseeable application or use in sight (Calvert & Martin, 2001). Examples of basic research are space research or research on human origins, which may seem to have no significant value or use for most people on earth but may actually have applications in the future.

As knowledge accumulates it generates certain combinations that eventually make packages of technology with usable or applicable qualities. As Mahatma Gandhi of India once said, "What you do is not important, but the important thing is that you do it."[1] This points to the big picture that comes out of cumulative research, over a long period of time, conducted by generations of people, not only in one country but around the globe. The outcomes of basic research thus accumulate piece by piece, through the experiments conducted by different generations, in different parts of the world, and eventually become applied to and impact the lives of humans, in often substantive ways.

Most basic research undertakings are done in universities and institutes of research that are meant specifically for such purposes, in universities like Addis Ababa University in Ethiopia, Harvard University in the United States (USA), the Max Plank Society in Germany, or the Ethiopian Institute of Agricultural Research (EIAR) in Ethiopia.

Unlike basic research, applied research (AR) is mostly conducted or lead by industries, and it is conducted in the same way as basic research, with the use of standard experimental or theoretical frameworks. However, unlike basic research, applied research is guided by its usefulness to mankind, setting out to provide products or services through its experiments. It is also necessary to note that some applied research activities that are meant to be so, revert to basic research when they become short of new ideas.

According to Cattell (1906), research was previously referred to as "investigation" or "inquiry" and with the establishment of universities and the concentration of academics in the same place the word "research" came into being. Throughout the development of research, there was no mention of industrial research until the need for applied research surfaced as the logical step for boosting production of quality, marketable products. According to Cattell (1906), a turning point in the history of research occurred when, in 1920, Mees wrote that basic research, applied research and development appeared to be in a linear model, with the latter being an outcome of the research process, such as in the following diagram:

Basic research → Applied research → Development (Mees, 1920)

This understanding of research was adopted by President Hoover of the USA in 1927 when he stated that, "Research is the soil of civilization", implying that the civilization which the world is proud of was an outcome of its predecessors, and basic and applied research.

After 1945, development shifted from being a subcategory of research to being complementary to it, and the two started appearing with the familiar acronym R&D, standing for research and development. Furthermore, measurements were put in place to see if projects were designed in R&D models and, as Mees had originally suggested, they were examined to see if they delivered the desired outcomes.

In 1965, Novick (1965) wrote a famous article entitled "The ABC of R&D" in which he accepted the same sequence of events in research and development, but added a fourth component, giving an evaluation of each step (see also Godin, 2006). He suggested the following steps:

> *Step 1: Basic research* involves efforts to understand the universe and to organize knowledge about it in order to (a) permit major changes in ways of looking at phenomena and activities; (b) create new devices and methods of accomplishing objectives; and (c) identify phenomena and activities that permit revolutionary changes in existing products, methods and

approaches. The promise in Step 1 is great but not identified to a specific purpose, and the possibility of fulfillment (application) is highly uncertain.

Step 2: Applied research involves singling out or identifying specific potentials or applications with a view to developing the new general knowledge obtained in Step 1. In this type of active application of usefulness is identified, but the economy, efficiency, and acceptability of the proposals remain highly uncertain.

Step 3: Product development, product testing, product evaluation, and pilot production. Specific devices or methods appear as likely solutions but must be brought reasonably close to the final application to determine effectiveness, economy, and acceptability. Do-ability has been established and major advances are reasonably certain.

Step 4: Product application, application research, applied testing and application evaluation. New uses and applications, or modifications of existing uses and applications, are sought for existing methods, products or components, which may result in substantial benefits to users or producers. Success is reasonably assured because it is evolutionary rather than revolutionary.

In order to make research profitable and independent from commitments to financiers Novick (1965) also suggested some level of separation between research and development through apportioning one-third of available resources (financial, human, facilities, etc.) to research, and allocating two-thirds to development.

As shown in the model in Figure 3.1 known as the push-pull (supply-demand) model of research, from 1970 to 2011 extensive and complex changes took place in the organization, conduct, and applications of research outcomes.

The model (Figure 3.1) presupposes that our world is headed towards an insatiable hunger for growing quality of life (Stage I). This serves as the push or supply side, which is mostly driving universities and industries to go into basic research. With appropriate government policy setups that verify the need to convert some of the research outcomes from Stage I and to establish appropriate linkages between universities and the industry, sizable BR outcomes can be changed into innovative technologies through applied research (AR) (Stage II). The innovative technologies generated from AR in Stage II can generate new and improved sets of goods and services that serve as the pull or demand side of the research cycle (Stage III).

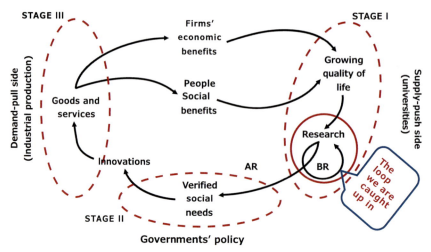

FIGURE 3.1 The push-pull (supply-demand) model of research (developed after Godin & Lane, 2005)

Eventually, firms that presuppose the demand of people are insatiable for improved quality of life reap their profits while the quality of life in society improves.

It is important to note that contemporary research conducted around the world, both in universities and industries, is of use to humanity and generates profits for those who sponsor it. This ties to the fact that there is more and more AR conducted today in universities, research centres, and industries. There are cases where industries or governments invest in BR that is predicted to have long-term profits (such as surveys for oil and gas consumption), comparative advantages, strategic importance (such as research in Antarctica, under kilometres of ice), or even political relevance that can give a certain position to nations in the context of global politics (such as competition to mark places on Mars by the USA, Russia, China, India, the European Union, etc.).

3   Research and Development in the Contemporary Global Neo-Liberal Scenario

The contemporary global neo-liberal scenario has introduced new dimensions to the exercise of research. The neo-liberal scenario presupposes a universe where every action of every being is a market transaction (commodity), and where transactions occur in an infinitely short time (globalization). The presupposition of the neo-liberal scenario regarding research is that it is an integral part of the global economy, where everything is for sale.

- it is considered a commodity.
- it should deliver more for less, unlike previous years
- it is accountable for its expenditures to the public that finances it
- it is expected to allow mobility of researchers for the purpose of exchanging new findings and collaborative work, and adding value to individual efforts (Figure 3.2 shows how the USA is the country that allows most mobility to its researchers, followed by the UK, Germany, and China).
- it is subject to globalization in a flat world
- it is expected to include full academic freedom and to operate poorly under control and management
- it is a personal activity that is dependent on individuals' ideas and imaginations
- it is competitive

Figure 3.3 illustrates how the above arguments translate into the research process, in contemporary times. The neo-liberal context has thus made the world economy a knowledge-based economy which, by default, amounts to continued calls for demand-driven research with verified assessments of added value to communities.

Figure 3.4 highlights the advantages of economically developed countries gain in the neo-liberal economy through their research investments. It is important to examine some of the details of operations of the current knowledge-based economy. The location where R&D is conducted matters for profitability. For instance, India and China are located in the heart of Asia, which has the largest world population, and Africa has intact natural resources

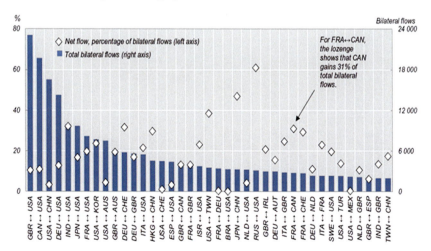

FIGURE 3.2   International flows of scientific authors (researcher mobility) from 1996 to 2011: Largest bilateral flows (Appelt et al., 2015; see also OECD, 2013; Hulten, 2013)

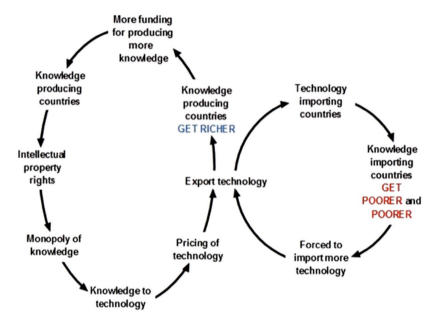

FIGURE 3.3   Model of the research process in neo-liberal times (Taylor, 2006; Knight, 2007; Meek & Davis, 2009; Jacob & Meek, 2012)

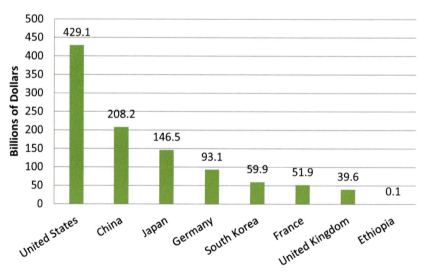

FIGURE 3.4   Investments in basic research for 2011 (from OECD, 2012, 2013a, 2013b; Hulten, 2013)

near them, which creates ample opportunities for these countries to conduct demand-driven research that encompasses the needs of people in two major continents. Firms with both domestic and foreign R&D activities also make significantly higher profits than those that carry out solely domestic R&D.

When countries produce products for local markets only, protectionism that bans or exorbitantly taxes the import of similar products from outside and discourages national consumers from using imported competitive items follows. Such exercises discourage the innovativeness of research and the production of competitive items that would be going into international trade, and this influences the degree to which R&D contribution is undermined in national development.

The profitability of R&D and its role in the advancement of national economies thus requires governments to put certain conditions in place. These are as follows:
- appropriate policies that create enabling contexts (collaboration, researcher mobility, etc.) should be in place for R&D to succeed nationally and internationally
- Free trade should be accepted
- Civil society should be engaged in knowledge creation
- Regional engagement should be the first priority and countries should assess comparative advantages that can put them in leadership positions within their regions and seize opportunities to enhance these positions. An example of this is Ethiopia's desire to generate clean energy from hydropower to supply energy to countries in the Horn of Africa and in East Africa.
- Countries should aim at being centre stage in global engagements and to do this by examining the world economic situation and what can put that particular country at the forefront. Examples of this are when Brazil decided to host the Rio Climate Summit in 1992, which placed it as the leading nation in the international arena, or when Ethiopia came up with the Climate Resilient Green Economy Strategy, which attracted worldwide support for its efforts in building structures for the production of clean energy (hydropower, wind and solar energy, electric powered-train and research in biotechnology) and the production of crops that are resilient to drought.

It is necessary to emphasize the significance of global politics on research and development, as there is no one nation today that is economically successful without interfacing its activities with other nations. von Hau et al. (2012) have highlighted the following four strategies that can be used by countries to assume a prime position in the global politics of research and development:
- *Issue leading:* Being a part of global issues and aligned policies (e.g., the Brazil Rio Conference and Ethiopia's Climate Resilient Green Economy Strategy mentioned above).

- *Opportunity seeking*: Establishing close bilateral relations, in the form of trade agreements, with strategic investment in selected countries (e.g., China offering Africa the African Union Building; Ethiopia hosting the African Union, which provides a platform for discussion of issues related to the Horn of Africa and important dialogues such as the current ones between Sudan and South Sudan).
- *Region organizing:* Leadership in geographical and culturally defined areas (e.g. Russia in ex-Soviet countries, China in the Far East countries, the USA in North and South America, and Ethiopia in Eastern Africa.
- *Region mobilization*: Economic integration within a particular region (e.g. China established a banking system for Far Eastern Countries, which is comparable to the World Bank and IMF in the West).

4   Research and Development for Africa – The Case of Ethiopia

In an African country such as Ethiopia, research institutes and universities tend to get caught up in Stage I the Push-Pull (Supply-Demand) Model of Research, and basic research continues to be done with taxpayer funds. Developing countries tend to lack the appropriate policy setups that can verify the need for research outcomes to convert to innovative technologies that can generate goods and services, which can be of use locally or internationally. Countries such as China and India have broken out of this cycle of basic research and today their products are generated out of both BR and AR and they are developed to address the needs of the international community, passing through Stages II and III of the cycle. As a consequence, investments in research that are based on demands of the global community have enabled them to reap their profits and satisfy the needs of the international community, with improved quality of life at cheaper prices.

Most applied research activities today are done in developed countries versus developing countries. An example of this split in applied and basic research, in developed and developing countries, is research in developed countries having produced technologies for developing high yielding varieties, harvesting and threshing facilities for the most common crops used by humans, such as wheat, barley, and maize. As a developing country, Ethiopia has imported improved crop varieties and facilities to speed up production processes for these common crops but, *Teff,* which is a cereal that is cultivated exclusively in Ethiopia, did not have well-developed varieties, or harvesting or threshing technologies. Ethiopian agriculture researchers have only been doing basic research that has left Ethiopian farmers toiling with old traditional farming systems, varieties and technologies. As the world came to estimate the importance and value of *Teff*, the Dutch developed an improved variety of the cereal and they now own the patent for that variety, even though the original seeds were taken from Ethiopia. Students from the American University developed *Teff* threshing machines for which they too own the patent. Hence, Ethiopia is now in the position of having to import these technologies as it cannot reinvent the wheel due to the high costs of research, or copy products that are protected by patents. This is a telling example of the benefits that can result from the implementation of basic findings into applied research, in developing countries. The example also points to the imbalances inherent to the use of basic research findings in one part of the world and their exploration in other parts of the world. Consequently, it also a sign of how global neoliberal research economy does not involve mutually benefitting collaborations and partnerships.

Partnership in research for development and academic mobility, in particular, can significantly enhance the quality of research. Ethiopia used this strategy by bringing international universities on board in collaborative research projects that would enhance academic mobility of faculty members and students among collaborating institutions. With this strategy, between 2008 and 2009, there was a great turning point for the emergence of Ethiopian higher education, with a rise in the number of universities from mere two universities to thirty-four in 2016. This was also a time when Ethiopia was prepared for an overhaul of its economic development, which was meant to be supported by high-level capacity building and acquisition of research outcomes relevant to its development plans, consisting mostly of the Growth and Transformation Plan I, with the opening of new universities and with the Addis Ababa University (AAU) taking on the main responsibilities for delivering the research and development mandates.

This was not a simple task for AAU since, as Harle (2013) has pointed out, institutional growth and expansion are less often accompanied by additional funding. In fact, the AAU had to look for alternative ways of delivering its mandate in the development plans of the nation, and of increasing and delivering training and research outcomes (Moges Yigezu, 2013).

International funding was what ultimately allowed the AAU to fulfill its role, and the internationalization of its programmes, with academic mobility, is what allowed the university to grow, take centre stage and win grants. Currently, among others, the AAU continues to work with Swedish universities, and with the support of Sida, and the World Bank it has established three major Academic Centres of Excellence for Eastern and Southern Africa. In these Centres, African students and students from other continents now come to Ethiopia for

Ph.D. level training, and faculty members from African and other international universities travel to Addis Ababa to take part in the university's programmes. The European Union has opened the International Business School at AAU and international students and faculty members are a part of this school as well. This kind of academic mobility and internationalization has enhanced the research outputs at AAU, contributed to national development, and improved the university's rank among African universities, going from thirty-two in ranking in 2008/09, to fifteenth in 2015.

5 Concluding Remarks

Scholars agree today that executing planned or strategic research to reach specific development aims and goals is embedded in human nature and an important aspect of research and development worldwide. Today, countries that wish to conduct research on their own terms and based on their own domestic capacities and markets, do not have a chance to do so in the global knowledge-based economy, and their economies cannot succeed in a highly competitive world. There is, therefore, a need for research to be collaborative and based on mutual engagement and accountability. While many efforts continue to make research have added value towards development, the endeavour of making research sustainable, with due consideration towards natural resources, must persistently forge forward.

The world economic order has clearly indicated how countries that have greatly invested in research, and particularly those that have linked their research to development, have benefited from this investment and now govern the world economy. Countries who are leading in research, development and the world economy have also had it easier in reaching the stage they have achieved. Countries such as China and India have had to spend less in terms of finance and time and, without re-inventing the wheel, they have been able to copy or adapt their technologies to the needs of contemporary society. Appropriate policies and good governance systems, and the use of technology and collaboration in a globalized world has allowed these countries to decrease their time and efforts.

Countries that intend to invest in research, with the understanding that research can someday support itself financially, need to take centre stage as movers of knowledge and bring out the comparative advantages of research. As challenging as it may be, changes in policy, joining the free trade market and opening financial systems to global competition in fields such as banking, telecom, and insurance, should be the inevitable courses of action to work towards this. Research and development efforts should not be left in the hands of government institutions (such as universities and ministries) alone. As long as they are committed to delivering the desired outcomes for social change and development in the economy, civil societies, private universities, and international organizations should also be invited to compete for grants in research.

Countries should have complete clarity with regards to their research and development priorities, outlining a roadmap of where the country wants to go in the coming twenty, fifty or more years. An example of clarity in terms of priorities for development in Ethiopia, where, in the past, there was an understanding that promoting agriculture would transform the country economically, which lead to the intention to develop the country's agriculture. Today, that understanding and roadmap has changed and the country's development plans have indicated that science and technology can promote the country's green, climate resilient industry and economy, which is the research and development strategy that has now gained the foreground and placed the country in a more competitive position, within the global context.

A country that needs to develop its R&D, in the contemporary global context, needs to create the necessary bases that can allow academic mobility and freedom, engage consumers and industries for quality improvement, build science parks and developer platforms, and work towards mixed method research synthesis (MMRS) and meta-analysis (Sandelowski et al., 2006: Voils et al., 2008 & Heyvaert et al., 2011). With these elements, research can prove itself to be a commodity that can finance itself. R&D that does not have the proper grasp on the bigger picture of economic development and the global economic system, and that does not operate in harmony with the ecosystem, cannot flourish and reach its necessary and attainable potentials for improving both higher education systems and the economy of a given country.

Note

1   Quote by Mahatma Gandhi retrieved from https://www.goodreads.com/quotes/

References

Antonio, A., Astin, H., & Cress, C. (2000). Community service in higher education: A look at the nation's faculty. *Review of Higher Education, 23*(4), 373–398.

Appelt, S., Beuzekom, B. V., Galindo-Rueda, F., & Pinho, R. (2015). *Which factors influence the international mobility of research scientists?* OECD Science, Technology and Industry Working Paper, 2015/02. Paris: OECD Publishing. http://dx.doi.org/10.1787/5js1tmrr2233-en

Calvert, J., & Martin, B. R. (2001, October 29–30). *Changing conceptions or basic research? SPRU – science and technology policy research*. A paper presented at the Workshop on Policy Relevance and Measurement of Basic Research, Oslo, University of Sussex, Falmer, Brighton.

Cattell, J. M. (1906). A statistical study of American men of science, the selection of a group of one thousand scientific men. *Science, 24*, 658–665, 699–707, 732–742.

Godin, B. (2006). Research and development: How the 'D' got into R&D. *Science and Public Policy, 33*(1), 59–76.

Godin, B., & Lane, J. (2005). *Research or development? A short history of research and development as categories* (Published in German in Gegenworte Special Issue on Basic or Applied Research). Retrieved from sphhp.buffalo.edu/content/dem/sphhp/cat/kt44t/pdf/research-ordevelpemnt.pdf

Harle, J. (2013). Strengthening research in African universities: Reflections on policy, partnerships and politics. *Policy & Practice: A Development Education Review, 16*(Spring), 80–100.

Heyvaert, M., Maes, B., & Onghena, P. (2011). Applying mixed methods research at the synthesis level: An overview. *Research in the Schools, 18*(1), 12–24.

Hulten, C. (2013). *Stimulating economic growth through knowledge-based investment*. OECD Science, Technology and Industry Working Papers, 2013/02. Paris: OECD Publishing. http://dx.doi.org/10.1787/5k46dbzqhj9v-en

Jacob, M., & Meek, V. L. (2012). Scientific mobility and international research network: Trends and policy tools for promoting research excellence and capacity building. *Studies in Higher Education, 38*(8), 331–344.

Knight, J. (2007). *Implications of cross-border education and GATS for the knowledge enterprise*. Commissioned paper for the UNESCO Forum on Higher Education, Research and Knowledge, Paris.

Meek, V. L., & Davis, D. (2009). Dynamics in higher education and research: Concepts and observations. In V. L. Meek, U. Teichler, & M. Kearney (Eds.), *Higher education research and innovation: Changing dynamics* (pp. 41–84). Kassel: UNESCO/INCHER.

Mees, C. E. K. (1920). *The organization of industrial scientific research*. New York, NY: McGraw Hill.

Moges Y. (2013). Ph.D. training programs in Ethiopia: Challenges and prospects. In T. Negash & A. Daniel (Eds.), *Ph.D. training in Eastern and Southern Africa: The Experience of OSSREA* (pp. 83–108). Addis Ababa: Organization for Social Science Research in Eastern and Southern Africa (OSSREA). Retrieved from http://www.ossrea.net

Novick, D. (1965). The ABC of R&D. *Challenge, 13*(5), 9–13. Retrieved from http://www.jstor.org/stable/40718919

OECD. (2012). Science and technology indicators report.

OECD. (2013a). Science and technology indicators report.

OECD. (2013b). Science and technology indicators report.

Roll-Hansen, N. (2009). *Why the distinction between basic (theoretical) and applied (practical) research is important in the politics of science* [Online]. London: The London School of Economics and Political Science.

Sandelowski, M., Voils, C. I., & Barroso, J. (2006). Defining and designing mixed research synthesis studies. *Research in the Schools, 13*(1), 1–15.

Suwanwela, C. (2006). *Relevance and utility issues for research in developing countries.* Paper presented at UNESCO Forum on Higher Education, Research and Knowledge, Paris.

Taylor, J. (2006). Managing the unmanageable: The management of research in research-intensive universities. *Higher Education Management and Policy, 18*(2).

Taylor, J. (2006). Managing the unmanageable: The management of research in research-intensive universities. *Higher Education Management Policy, 18*(2), 1–25.

Voils, C. I., Sandelowski, M., Barroso, J., & Hasselblad, V. (2008). *Field Methods, 20*(1), 3–25.

vom Hau, M., Scott, J., & Hulme, D. (2012). Beyond the BRICs: Alternative strategies of influence in the global politics of development. European association of development research and training institutes. *European Journal of Development Research, 24*(2), 187–204.

CHAPTER 4

Relational Policies in Higher Education Partnership and Collaboration: Europe's Approach to Africa and the Special Case of Germany

Christine Scherer

1   Introduction

The field of education in Africa in general and higher education, in particular, has long been shaped and impacted by forces from outside the continent (Barbosa, 2010). The consequences of colonialism on national higher education systems in Africa's sub-regions have been analysed thoroughly (Teferra & Altbach, 2003). Assié-Lumumba et al. (2013) have highlighted how Africa's policy-makers have been catering to European and Western education standards for quite some time, "embracing European/Western education and human capital theory with all its flaws" (Assié-Lumumba et al., 2013, p. 3). The consequences of colonialism and its legacies, the pragmatics of policy-makers in national higher education systems in Africa today, and the ambiguities that come along with it are visible on all levels of education (Seepe, 2004).

Experts today claim that the time has come for Africa to shape its education systems in the continent (Abrokwaa, 2017). What is requested are 'African' solutions for the diversity of private and public institutions in Africa, the 'Africanization' of university curricula and teaching, and Africa-driven research funding, while situating the new continental quest of African research and higher education in a global context of competition (Cloete et al., 2015).

The current global knowledge economy has created a competition for 'excellence', and Africa seeks to play as much a role as Europe or any other region in the world. At the African Higher Education Summit entitled "Revitalising higher education for Africa's Future", which was held in Senegal's capital Dakar, in March 2015, late United Nations Secretary-General Kofi Annan recommended that Africa should harness Africa-driven collaboration and partnerships that are based on an understanding of the differentiated contexts;

> [...] we cannot truly realize Africa's potential, nor overcome its serious challenges, without increasing access to education, improving the quality and diversity of skills taught, and deepening the research capacity of

Africa's higher education. I serve as the chancellor of the University of Ghana and therefore see at first hand the scope and complexity of this challenge. I know too, that what works in Accra may not work in Cape Town, Nairobi or indeed Dakar. (Annan, 2015)

The Africa-driven discourse demands continental political agency and regional and national policies that can enhance the respective systems and their layouts and highlights the importance of valid frameworks and practices for international collaboration and balanced partnership. Despite knowledgeable inputs and frequently articulated desiderata from African partners in collaboration contexts, in higher education partnerships, patronizing approaches are what seems to prevail and foster 'partnership fatigue'. The prevailing imbalances of donor-receiver structures critically hint at a 'tyranny of partnership', which dictates structural frameworks of collaboration and influences large-scale research via funding priorities for specific research themes (Landau, 2012). As Cross and Ndofirepi (2017) have shown in their edited volumes *Knowledge and Change in African Universities*, the impact of this is central to the current discussion around higher education partnership in Africa. In fact, higher education and science, as both knowledge economies and terrains for innovation and development, are not neutral spaces, but interrelated fields of power in which 'excellence' as an epistemological category is under scrutiny:

> It is based on some of the core ideas of the epistemologies of the South: an ecology of knowledges and intercultural translation. Its starting point is the recognition of mutual ignorance and its endpoint is the shared production of knowledge. (Santos, 2016, p. 27)

The purpose of this chapter is to contribute to the understanding of the ecology of higher education collaboration. After explaining relational policies on a regional level in Europe, which foster the 'recognition of mutual ignorance', the case of German higher education policy towards African countries will be discussed. What becomes clear is how regional policy interests, in joint top-down agendas, such as the European Framework Programs (FP) and the more recent Horizon 2020, shape internationalization and collaboration beyond their own regions. What becomes clear is how a serious effort to understand the contexts in which potential partners act can support new agendas and foster constructive developments.

In describing selected schemes and projects of EU-Africa partnerships, within the EU context, two major phases of collaboration for research and development can be found to characterize the history; the first phase, between ca. 1980 and 2000, is based on the overarching notion of the 'neediness' of the African continent, and the second phase, from 2000 to 2016, is based on an understanding of Africa's 'challenges'. Both approaches reveal a mindset that has kept policy-makers from clear-cut arrangements and designs that work towards sustainable partnerships. This chapter argues that a third phase, which has already begun, needs to be embedded in a discourse that recognizes the strengths and weaknesses of both Africa and Europe.

As described in the second chapter of this book (Woldegiorgis), collaboration and partnership are essential ingredients for internationalization and can be conceptualized in specific ways. Internationalization is quantifiable through institutional strategies, Letters of Intent (LoI), Memoranda of Understanding, and collaboration contracts or agreements between institutions. However, the quality of a collaboration and partnership and the perceived reality for those who are interactively involved in the partnership is harder to quantify. This chapter is a combination of long-term observations as a professional practitioner in the field, expert interviews in distinct higher education settings and publicly accessible data.

2   The General Frameworks of Continental European and African Collaboration

For a better understanding of the case of partnership in Germany, it is necessary to analyse the overall developments of the European-African collaboration from the broader perspective that examines programme and/or research cooperation between the two continents. The basis for any kind of international academic collaboration between the continents of Europe and Africa has been the European idea of what was first called 'development aid' and later became known as development cooperation. The approach of the early European Economic Community resulted in collaborations with what were seen as 'developing', or 'less developed' countries in sub-Saharan Africa, the Caribbean and the Pacific (the ACP-Group). Alonso and Glennie (2015) have established four criteria for classifying development cooperation, which can be used to contrast this kind of cooperation to international academic collaboration. They highlight how development cooperation should aim at national or international development priorities, which should not be driven by profit or discriminate in favour of developing countries and should be based on cooperative relationships that seek to enhance developing country ownership.

In contrast, international academic collaboration is strictly driven by rationales such as social/cultural, political, economic, and academic rationales for integrating international academic standards (Knight, 2004).

2.1 From the European Development Cooperation to the Joint Africa-European Strategy (JAES)

Development cooperation has been an integral part of the European integration process from the beginning. The European Union (EU) and its member states are today the largest donors of official development assistance (ODA). Together, in 2013, European states provided 52% of the world's official development assistance granted during the same year and totalling € 56.5 billion (European Union, 2014).

What is called development or international cooperation today was initially set up in 1957, with the signature of the Treaty of Rome. This treaty inaugurated the common market in Europe and established the European Development Funds (EDFs), which aimed at providing financial and technical aid to African countries, some of which were still under formal colonial rule. A few years later, the conventions Yaoundé I (1963) and Yaoundé II (1969) came into being and focused on commercial advantages for former colonies in Africa, in order to build change in developing countries. The African countries addressed in these conventions were Benin, Burkina Faso, Burundi, Cameroon, Central African Republic, Chad, Congo (Brazzaville), Congo (Kinshasa), Côte d'Ivoire, Gabon, Madagascar, Mali, Mauritania, Niger, Rwanda, Senegal, Somalia, Togo, Kenya, Tanzania, and Uganda. On February 28th, 1975, the Lomé Convention was adopted and repeated three times with the Lomé II (1979), Lomé III (1984) and Lomé IV (1989) conventions, which were finally substituted by the Cotonou Agreement of June 23rd, 2000. This agreement is also the successor to the Yaoundé Agreements and signalled intensified action in Europe towards development cooperation with Africa (European Union, 2005).

The Cotonou Agreement became the overarching political framework for the EU's relations with African, Caribbean and Pacific (ACP) regions, and will be valid until the year 2020. So far it is the most comprehensive agreement, covering the EU's relations with 79 countries, including 48 countries from sub-Saharan Africa. The Cotonou Agreement aims at reducing and eventually eradicating poverty and has contributed to the gradual integration of the ACP countries into the world economy. It is based on three pillars: development cooperation, economic and trade cooperation, and related political dimensions. While the document mentions primary and secondary education and highlights it as a basic service that should be provided in societies, higher education is not mentioned once in the agreement (European Union, 2005).

The first steps towards an intensified political dialogue between Africa and Europe as neighbouring continents can be seen from the beginning of the new millennium. An important moment that marks this change was the political summit meeting between 27 countries of the European Union and 52 African countries, held in Cairo in April 2000, and initiated by Portugal. The meeting was an important moment that marked changing policies and forms of dialogue between the two world regions, and the first inter-sectoral action plan for the future collaboration between the European Union and Africa was announced at that time. The implementation of an institutionalized dialogue took some years and entered into the overarching framework of the African-European partnership as an inter-regional cooperation strategy, which was called the *Joint Africa-Europe Strategy* (JAES):

> [...] it is now time for these two neighbours, with their rich and complex history, to forge a new and stronger relationship that builds on their new identities and renewed institutions, capitalised on lessons of the past and provides a solid framework for long-term, systematic and well integrated cooperation. (African Union, European Union, 2007)

With the Lisbon Treaty entering into force in 2007, relations with Africa have become an integral part of the EU's overall political, economic, social, and humanitarian agenda. The treaty is meant to ensure greater consistency and coherence in the EU-Africa policy, and the EU's overall interests and ambitions, with Africa are seen as consolidating institutional architectures, providing a chance for mutual engagement on strategic levels, and allowing both continents to coordinate and align their positions.

As a follow-up to the intra-European Lisbon Strategy, in 2010, Europe also adopted the strategy "Europe 2020" for smart, sustainable and inclusive growth, which was more of an intra-European strategy. One of the aims of this strategy was that a minimum of 40 % of young adults, aged 30 to 34, would complete higher education for the enhancement of knowledge societies, by 2020. The focus of this intra-European strategy was on the key areas of knowledge and innovation, as well as sustainability, employment and social inclusion. Another key element of the Europe 2020 strategy is an enhancement of conditions for research and the objective to increase public and private expenditure for research and innovation to a total of 3% of the GDP (Gemeinsame Wissenschaftskonferenz (GWK), 2013).

The term 'partnership' has always been a part of the rhetoric in international collaboration. In higher education collaboration between the European Union and Africa, it has gained momentum during recent years. Partnership as a concept, condition, process, and practice is a wide-spread term that is self-evidently used in all policy documents, valid to describe collaborations between continents.

In their approach to higher education institutions, Amey, Eddi, and Ozaki (2007, p. 7) distinguish between what is rhetoric and what is functional in discourses on partnership, as well as the long-term and short-term levels of partnership, and provide a definition of partnership that focuses on the institutional level. Their approach can be useful for examining the processes involved on continental and regional levels when it comes to partnership. The authors highlight how partnership "[…] is multi-institutional and multi-functional and has long-term member support. Initial incentives […] typically revolve around academic issues such as cross-registration, faculty exchange, or use of other academic resources. Leadership at the highest level is typically required to make the […] partnership operate, especially if institutional policies and resources are centrally controlled".

Africa and Europe understood as neighbours, herein share the vision to,

> take the Africa-EU relationship to a new, strategic level with a strengthened political partnership and enhanced cooperation at all levels. The partnership will be based on a Euro-African consensus on values, common interests, and common strategic objectives. This partnership should strive to bridge the development divide between Africa and Europe through the strengthening of economic cooperation and the promotion of sustainable development in both continents, living side by side in peace, security, prosperity, solidarity and human dignity. (European Union, 2011, p. 17)

2.2 The Five Africa-EU Summits and Their Action Plans

The first continental summit between Africa and Europe, held in April 2000, in Cairo, Egypt and entitled "The 1st EU-Africa Summit: Partnership between Europe and Africa", institutionalized the beginning of an intercontinental mutual political dialogue. Under the aegis of the Organization of the African Unity (OAU) and the EU, the main document of the summit was adopted as the Cairo Declaration and covered the years between 2000 and 2005. It articulated the will "to give a new strategic dimension to the global partnership between Africa and Europe for the Twenty-First Century, in a spirit of equality, respect, alliance and cooperation between […] regions, […] committed to the basic objective of strengthening the already existing links of political, economic and cultural understanding through the creation of an environment and an effective framework for promoting a constructive dialogue on economic, political, social and development issues" (Cairo Declaration, 2000, p. 2).

Despite the constructive intentions, concrete action started only seven years later, when the second summit took place in Lisbon, Portugal, in 2007. The slight change in the title of the summit, from EU-Africa Summit in Egypt to Africa-EU Summit in Portugal is important to note. The policy document of this summit explicitly articulated the intention to quit the donor-recipient relationship in favour of identified, mutual and complementary interests based on "shared principles of ownership, partnership, and solidarity". Its adoption officially marked a 'new phase' in Africa-EU relations[1], with the following eight Priority Actions identified: (1) Peace and Security, (2) Democratic Governance and Human Rights, (3) Trade and Regional Integration, (4) Millennium Developments Goals, (5) Energy, (6) Climate Change, (7) Migration, Mobility and Employment, (8) Science, Information Society, and Space.

The Julius Nyerere Programme was introduced and initiated by the African Union Commission in 2005. Its aim was to contribute to high level African human resource development and retention, while supporting intra-African academic mobility, thereby mitigating the effects of brain drain in Africa. This scholarship programme was finally launched in November 2010. From then up until now, under the program, African students, scholars and academic staff receive scholarships for Master's and Ph.D. level studies, and the programme allows for the exchange of academics and administrative staff to occur between African universities. Overall, it is expected that, over the five consecutive rounds of the program's selection process, more than 2000 participants will have benefited from the program.

The third Africa-EU summit took place in 2010, in Tripoli, Libya, and defined the *Action Plan 2*, which was to be valid for the years 2011 to 2013, with modified aims compared to the Action Plan 1.

> In view of the overarching Summit theme "Investment, economic growth and job creation" the meeting underlined the essential link between a reinvigorated economic cooperation and regional integration via different sectors, including the private sector, with a reinforced cooperation in the thematic partnerships under the Joint Strategy: peace and security, democratic and economic governance and respect for human rights are prerequisites of development. These assets are essential for the creation of an investment-friendly environment that makes the best use of domestic resources and attracts investments. The development of Africa's vast human capital requires a focus on skills-development, innovation, and entrepreneurship, which should be complemented by a comprehensive

approach to social and labour market policies. Without a food-secure, educated and healthy population, both economic growth and poverty reduction remain elusive. Regional Integration, trade, migration and mobility, adaptation and mitigation regarding climate change together with sustainable investment in key sectors such as ICT, energy, raw materials or Science and Technology, agricultural research can build on these foundations to foster sustainable, knowledge-generating and competitive economies."[2]

In the fourth summit that was held in Brussels in 2013/14, entitled "Investing in People, Prosperity and Peace", five priority areas for a joint strategy between the years 2014and 2017 were highlighted: (1) Peace and security; (2) Democracy, good governance, and human rights; (3) Human development; sustainable and inclusive development, (4) Growth and continental integration; and (5) Global and emerging issues. Topics included education and training, women and youth, legal and illegal migrant flows between both continents, strategies for stimulating growth and creating jobs, investments towards peace, and strategies for enhancing EU support of African capacities to manage security in the continent.

At the time of the summit, in the field of higher education, the following projects gained momentum. The Pan-African University was created as a project driven by the African Union that aimed at exemplifying excellence, relevance and global competitiveness of African higher education and research. The project is a network of African higher education and research institutions, with thematic hubs in each of the five geographic regions of Africa (Eastern, Western, Central, Southern and Northern Africa), and the first four thematic institutes were launched in 2011.

Another project that was guided by the EU is the African Higher Education Harmonization and Tuning process. This initiative aims at reviewing the state of implementation for the mutual recognition of higher education certificates and qualifications in Africa. It involves an assessment of the potential benefits of using the European approach of 'Tuning'. The initiative includes the implementation of the African Quality Rating Mechanism, the popularization of the revised Arusha convention (1981, revised in Cape Town 2002), and the development of a roadmap for the harmonization of higher education in Africa. A pilot phase on the potential of using this tuning approach began in 2011.

The fifth summit took place recently, in Abidjan, Côte d'Ivoire, in November 2017, and addressed the employability and applicability of knowledge based on the idea that "Africa aspires to catalyse education and [a] skills revolution

[that] actively promotes science, technology, research, and innovation, to build knowledge, human capital, capabilities and skills required to drive innovation".

Table 4.1 provides an overview of the summits that have taken place so far between Europe and Africa, and the respective action plans and declarations that came out of the summit.

2.3 Relational Policies and Early Africa-Driven Higher Education Policy Initiatives in Higher Education

The year 2000 is an important marker for the rise of new relationships in Africa, which also influenced new approaches to collaboration in the higher education sector. Under the New Partnership for Africa's Development (NEPAD), founded in 2001, the African Union (AU) took the initiative to push African states to cooperate economically and jointly achieve progress in the continent's development. In 2003, and under the umbrella of NEPAD, the African Council of Ministers of Science and Technology (AMCOST) was founded and opened to all AU countries. In 2005, NEPAD, AU and AMCOST presented a strategic document for science and technology policy in Africa, which was a unique strategic document entitled, "*Africa's Science and Technology Consolidated Plan of Action* (CPA)"[3] through which all African states agreed on common priorities in science policy. The action plan names three 'flagship projects' as priorities: building an African online campus, fostering science education, and developing a joint science and technology policy. However, this first Africa-driven strategy could not easily find support and funding at the EU-level. UNESCO was a key partner of NEPAD and AU and supported the preparation of the CPA.

In January 2007, during the eighth Summit of the AU in Addis Ababa, the Heads of State adopted a statement that explicitly called upon the support of all international organizations towards the CPA. Again, UNESCO played a

TABLE 4.1   Overview of the Africa-EU summits since the year 2000

Year	African-European policy framework	Declarations and action plans
2000	1st EU-Africa Summit, Cairo, Egypt	Cairo Declaration
2007	2nd Africa EU Summit, Lisbon, Portugal	First Action Plan 2008–2010
2010	3rd Africa-EU Summit, Tripoli, Libya	Second Action Plan 2011–2013
2013	4th Africa-EU Summit, Brussels, Belgium	Declaration and Roadmap 2014–2017
2017	5th African-European Summit in Abidjan	Declaration and Roadmap 2018–2021

key role in assisting NEPAD and the AU in the implementation of the CPA. For the 177th session of the UNESCO Executive Council, in autumn 2007, UNESCO presented a plan to support the implementation of the CPA from 2008 to 2013 and focused on the research areas of Water Resources Management, Biodiversity, Drought and Desertification, and Geosciences. In order to build an African online campus, UNESCO provided a model for the African Mediterranean countries, which was implemented in 2002 and funded by the European Union.

UNESCO also cooperated directly with national governments in developing a science policy for Africa. The UN agency advised the governments of Ethiopia, Kenya, Rwanda, Malawi, Congo, Namibia, Lesotho, and Mozambique. The state of the scientific landscape in each country was evaluated in order to come up with recommendations for reforms and restructurings, in collaboration and accordance with national institutions. Similar projects were launched in Mauritania, Côte d'Ivoire, Togo, Benin, Egypt, Swaziland, Seychelles, and Tanzania as well.

The initial positive outcomes of these processes can be seen in the announcement by Nigeria, in 2006, of implementing a new national research funding institution for the channelling of 5 billion US Dollar of funds, to boost national research initiatives. Another example is the new science policy in Rwanda, which has led to a significant increase in national funding for research in the country. South Africa has also been investing significantly in science research, since 2007. Uganda has received a $ 25 million loan from the World Bank to advance new efforts in the field of science policy, and Zambia has also accepted a similar loan from the African Development Bank.

2.4 Africa in the EU Research Framework Programs from Framework Programme 1 to Horizon 2020

Science, technology, and innovation (STI) policies at the European level have become a crucial instrument for fostering and directing research and technological development in the last decades of the 20th century (Caloghirou et al., 2001). In Europe, the policy led to the implementation of the European Framework Programmes (FPs) for science and technology, research and development, and fostered the European Research Area (ERA), which was initiated in the year 2000. Under these policy frameworks, the European Union is funding or co-funding transnational, collaborative research and development projects that aim at supporting regional European and transnational collaborations. Other projects are also supporting transnational mobility. Since the inception of the FP1, in 1984, eight other FPs have been launched, including Horizon 2020, which is the latest one, with a time range from 2014 to 2020.

TABLE 4.2　Overview of the FPs

FP1	FP 2	FP3	FP4	FP5	FP6	FP7	FP8/Horizon 2020
1984–1987	1988–1991	1992–1995	1996–1999	2000–2003	2004–2007	2008–2013	2014–2020

Currently, Horizon 2020 is under review and stakeholders have met to set out the research policy agenda for the next FP 9, which will start in the year 2021.

The main aim of the European framework programmes has been to first and foremost strengthen Europe's global position in research in science and technology and to promote European competitiveness through the coordination of national policies in the EU region. Whereas at the beginning of the European FPs, African research institutions did not play any role, the official interaction between selected organizations participating together on projects started to emerge with FP 2. During this programme, Ethiopia, for example, was listed in the programme, with two of its institutions, Kenya contributed with seven institutions, Egypt with two, and Morocco with two as well. Senegal shows the highest number, with ten participating institutions in 12 involvements.

The story of partnership and collaboration between EU and African institutions changed slightly over time and upon examining the different projects sheets, from FP1 (1984–1987) to Horizon 2020 (2014–2020), it appears that it is only since the year 2008, with the implementation of the Framework Programme Seven (FP7) (2008–2013), which was in in direct relation to the three Action Plans of the framework of the Joint African European Strategy (2008–2010, 2011–2013, 2014–2017), that a significant number of African institutions in higher education, research and development became listed as participants in EU-funded research projects. Though these figures provide a snapshot of the numerical developments of a short history of research collaboration between Africa and the EU, they are not telling regarding the *quality* of the partnerships that were set up between African and European research institutions, within these frameworks.

Figure 4.1 gives an overview of the quantity and number of participant organizations in African countries in the Framework Programme Seven.

Figure 4.2 shows in comparison the number of participant research and development organizations from Europe and from Latin America.

Even though African institutions make up a small number of participants in the European research FPs, since 1984, a significant number of African

RELATIONAL POLICIES IN HE PARTNERSHIP AND COLLABORATION 87

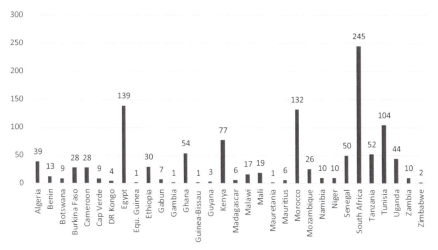

FIGURE 4.1   Participations of African R & D institutions in FP 7 (Source: Cordis FP 7 Organizations)

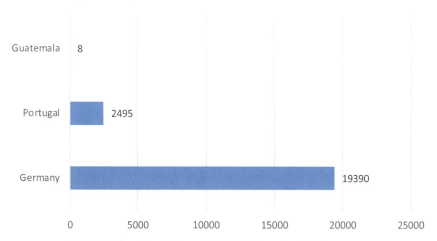

FIGURE 4.2   Participating nations (Source: Cordis FP 7 Organizations)

institutions has participated, especially since the FP 7 and the subsequent Horizon 2020, which opened its doors to third countries that are non-EU members or associated states. Even though the call outline does not state this explicitly, African countries are able to participate in Horizon 2020 projects.[4]

2.5   *African-European Platforms for Networking and Research Collaboration*

In the year 2008, with FP 7, the dialogue within the tertiary sector became accompanied and supported by the High Level Policy Dialogue (HLPD), which is a virtual forum that comprises commissions from both the African and the European Union, and is chaired by Egypt, Algeria, Nigeria, South Africa,

South-Sudan, Germany, France, Spain, and Portugal. HLPD has received and continues to receive practical project support, for example through the project *CAAST-Net* and *CAASTNet Plus* (2008–2017), or the projects *RINEA5* and PRO-IntensAfrica, which are all funded by the European Commission.

The Network for the Coordination and Advancement of Sub-Saharan Africa-EU Science and Technology Cooperation Network (CAAST-Net) was funded by the European Commission for the period 2008–2012. It is the predecessor project to CAAST-Net Plus, which ran from 2013–2017. The CAAST-Net project was initially a crucial platform for African and European stakeholders collaborating in research and development and aimed at increasing the quality and fostering the quantity of bi-regional cooperation in science and technology. Activities included FP7 information brokerage on the African continent, African sessions in European scientific conferences and fairs, networking events that addressed possibilities for cooperation in the FP7 calls, training sessions, activities around awareness of mobility instruments for brain circulation, and gathering information on obstacles to a fruitful cooperation.[6]

In order to bring together complementary related projects, such as CAAST-Net Plus, RINEA proposes three specific, measurable and complementary objectives, each addressing a core component of the bi-regional STI partnership that, when achieved, contributes to the overall goal of reinforcing and enriching the Africa-EU partnership in STI. The consortium encompasses 13 partners from six European and seven African countries, which also actively participate in the HLPD-office, thus allowing for a direct translation of political discussions on the HLPD level into measures to be developed and implemented by the RINEA consortium, upon request of the HLPD. Another important project is *ERAfrica,* which was initiated through FP 7, that had as its primary objective the creation of a "European Research Area Network" for the African continent: "[...]similar to other 'ERA-Nets' operating in relation to areas as diverse as Russia (ERA.Net RUS), India (New INDIGO) and the Far East (KorA-Net), funded by the European Commission, ERAfrica unites seven EU countries (France, Germany, Belgium, Spain, Portugal, Finland and Austria), as well as Switzerland and Turkey, with only three African partner countries (South Africa, Kenya and Egypt). As the project's website states: "ERAfrica aims to serve as a template for interactions between Europe and Africa in the field of science and technology research, and as a model for future cooperative ventures between the two continents".[7]

The network implemented five work packages in 2013:
- Information review and analysis of science & technology cooperation programmes in Europe and Africa;

- Communication and dissemination activities, including mobilization of other funders, and exchange of information and consultation with stakeholders and experts, to support ERAfrica implementation;
- Definition of a coordinated strategy for joint activities;
- Implementation and evaluation of joint activities;
- Joint management.

Each package is led by a different consortium member and aims at moving collaborative efforts from their theoretical inception through to the stages of conceptualization, policy formulation, and practical implementation, via funding of actual research projects or related initiatives. ERAfrica attracts participation from additional European and African governments.

It is important to note that, while ERAfrica is directed towards an entire continent, with more than fifty distinct nations or countries, other ERA.Nets (e.g. ERA.Net RUS) dedicate their actions towards single nations only. This highlights an unbalanced view regarding nations and regions, and hints to the perception, which is immensely difficult to overcome (not only) in Europe, since the beginning of collaborative relations with Africa, that views Africa as a continent that is somehow uniform to the rest of the world. Only slowly is Africa starting to become understood as an immensely diverse continent, with different countries that act as nations on their own behalf, within different sub-regions.

ERAfrica has been able to provide opportunities for new approaches involving shared ownership of research and innovation, in cooperation efforts between Europe and Africa. On January 15th 2013, funding parties from 15 African and European countries launched a joint call for projects in three thematic fields: Renewable Energies (addressing renewable energy projects); Interfacing Challenges (addressing projects conducted at the interface of key societal challenges); New Ideas (addressing idea-driven projects, generated in a bottom-up approach, with an emphasis on originality and novelty). Three lines of collaborative funding were made available at this time: collaborative research, collaborative innovation, and capacity building, with a total of 10.7 million Euros made available for funding projects. The call generated 124 proposals from which ERAfrica selected 17 projects to fund. The selected projects involved a total amount of 8.29 million Euros and 65 institutions (31 African and 34 European) from 18 countries (8 African and 10 European), working collaboratively on the projects.

Two projects that came out of the JAES Action Plan and Roadmap are PROIntensAfrica and AfriAlliance. Both projects are coordinated by Horizon 2020. ProIntensAfrica aims at developing a proposal for a long-term research and innovation partnership between Europe and Africa. The focus of this partnership relates to the improvement of food and nutrition security and the livelihoods of African farmers and scrutinizes the rich diversity of pathways that can lead to sustainable intensification of agro-food systems in Africa, with the support of the relevant environment policies.[8]

The website of the project states that "Africa-EU cooperation will be taken to a practical level by sharing (non-)technological solutions for local challenges, thus also identifying and boosting the sustainable market and investment opportunities. Demand-driven, problem-focused action groups will share knowledge between the identified stakeholders and networks at all levels to identify and address vulnerabilities effectively.[9]

Water and climate change research and social innovation (R&I) cooperation between Africa and Europe is the focus of AfriAlliance, a project that also receives its funding from the European Union's Horizon 2020. The overall action of the project refers to social innovation in the field of water and climate and it is headed by UNESCO (2016–2021).[10] The project serves to "identify demands, opportunities, and constraints at different levels and to develop strategic advice as short-term demand-driven R&I outlook and long-term R&I agenda for improving Africa-EU collaboration". From the perspective of the involved policy experts in such fora, particularly in the time span from 2005 to 2010, European stakeholders in science policy played a crucial role in learning to understand African contexts and vice versa. This was also a time when Germany's understanding of what is at stake in African countries deepened in relation to the field of higher education, research, and development, where exchanges were taking place.

3 Collaboration in Science, Technology and Innovation with Africa: Its Short History in German Science Policy

During the 1980s, the most important partner nations for Germany on the African continent were South Africa and Egypt for West Germany, while East Germany maintained close links to Angola and Mozambique. The first collaborative actions were driven from the German sides in their quests towards economic collaboration. Two major conditions characterize the collaborations, and these were stability and reliability, and, in the context of South Africa, the abolition of Apartheid.

The tradition of German collaboration with African countries in the specific field of higher education and research is more recent. Starting from the 1990s, in a newly united Germany, the impetus for the country's engagement with different countries became more intensive. In order to understand the dynamics of collaboration in a context of (economic) globalization, it became imperative to gain knowledge and understanding of distinct world regions. In order to position Germany as a reliable partner in research programmes, national frameworks of higher education systems in different regions became increasingly important to understand. The benefits and gains for German research in general, and for individual German researchers, were certainly the main drivers for an institutionalization of international collaboration with African countries in the tertiary sector. The early stage of these collaborations in the field of higher education, research and development is in fact characterized by the increasing necessity for the internationalization of research in Germany.

3.1 *Africa as a Field for German Research and a Terrain for Development Cooperation*

With the new millennium, when Europe as a region entered into a policy dialogue with Africa, through the previously mentioned JAES, higher education also became a field of interaction between the two regions, in accordance with their different respective action plans. Two strategic agendas were knit together in Germany; firstly, the agenda to learn to understand the continent as a neighbour, within a global context, and secondly, to combine the mission of development aid and collaboration with the mission of implementing science and higher education policy as a driver for sustainable development. However, until the year 2007, Germany held 43 agreements and memoranda of understanding for collaboration in science and technology on the national level world-wide and only two of these agreements were related to the African countries South Africa and Egypt. In addition, two memoranda of understanding existed with Morocco and Tunisia (Bundesministerium für Bildung und Forschung, 2008).

The beginnings of Germany's short history of research and development collaboration with Africa can be understood from the fact that, for many years, South Africa was an important location for German collaboration efforts in research and development. This is due to South Africa's natural environment, its flora and fauna, which makes it a prime location for European observation and technology. From a research policy perspective, Africa was seen as a great location for German scientists to research social and/or natural contexts, and for the placement of specific technologies related to space observation.

In 1999, under the German presidency of the European Union, the country initiated a focus on development cooperation as a central topic for the EU. A year later, in June 2000, the ministers of the Federal Republic of Germany decided to concentrate bilateral development cooperation regionally and sectorally and developed the concepts of *priority partner countries* and *partner countries*. In the priority partner countries of the bilateral development cooperation, a full range of development policy instruments were implemented. For partner countries, the focus was placed on selected aspects only. In addition, a list of other potential cooperation countries was created to include those countries in which development cooperation was seen as something that was impossible due to a political crisis or armed conflict, but that could be resumed if conditions changed. The concept was implemented and coordinated with other donor states of the European Union and multilateral development institutions.

At the time, the priority partner countries in the context of development collaboration for Germany were Benin, Burkina Faso, Ghana, Cameroon, Kenya, Malawi, Mali, Mozambique, Namibia, Rwanda, Zambia, South Africa, Tanzania, and Uganda. Côte d'Ivoire, Guinea, Lesotho, Madagascar, Burundi, Nigeria, Niger, Senegal, Chad were classified as partner countries. Ethiopia, Eritrea, Angola, Congo (DR), Sierra Leone, Zimbabwe, Sudan, Togo were classified as potential cooperation countries. The focus of the collaboration projects was placed on democracy and civil society, education (especially basic education), health, food security, environmental policy, economic reform, energy, transport, and communication. Collaboration in higher education, research, and innovation on the tertiary level, or partnerships connecting bilateral agendas was not a theme with neither for science policy nor for international collaboration policies.

In January 2008, the German government, represented by the state secretaries of two main national players, the Federal Ministry for Education and Research (BMBF) and the Federal Ministry for Economic Cooperation and Development (BMZ), agreed that science and technological cooperation and development cooperation should also be included in partnership projects with Africa, and respective measures should be coordinated. A reason for the accelerating interest in higher education collaboration is the notion that universities in Africa are drivers for economic growth, development and innovation. In order to implement this kind of cooperation, the desideratum was articulated to improve the collaboration between the ministries of the collaborating countries.

While internally trying to coordinate and relate activities, Germany became a member of the African-European High-Level Policy Dialogue (HLPD) in the European Union and took over the responsibility of ensuring a continuous interaction between the tertiary sectors on regional levels. The German Federal Ministry for Education and Research (BMBF) pushed towards a balanced approach for the support of its project agency, and, in order to introduce greater diversity in Germany, promoted collaboration with African countries.

The respective ministries' responsibility for a content-driven national research policy was guided by two complementary approaches; benefitting the national research agenda and campaigning for internationally connected programmes. The mandate and approach of the BMBF towards higher education complemented the approach of the German Federal Ministry for Economic Cooperation and Development (BMZ). The latter traditionally develops and directs national strategies for development cooperation and, within this framework, focuses on education (primary and secondary) and vocational training. However, by the end of the first decade, this traditional focus shifted.

The desideratum for coordination obviously underestimates institutional demarcation. Despite the official declaration to follow a joint and complementary mission in Africa, the Pan-African University (PAU) is an example of overlapping agendas that highlight unilateralist leanings and competition on the practical level. The Ministry for International Cooperation (BMZ) supports a close collaboration with the African Union Commission (AUC) and the Pan African University Institute of Water and Energy Sciences (including Climate Change) (PAUWES), which is one of the five hubs of the Pan African University (PAU) that is hosted at the University of Tlemcen, Algeria. This engagement fits in well with BMBF, however, in these partnerships, the German ministry mostly involved traditional agents for development and international cooperation. The German Academic Exchange Service (DAAD) and the Society for International Collaboration (GIZ), are commissioned with the implementation and consultancy of the doctoral training and rectorate of this partnership. BMBF initiatives saw their role in establishing research collaboration through the creation and funding of international networks of researchers in universities in Germany and researchers in universities in distinct African countries. Such initiatives resulted, for example, in the BIOTA AFRICA network, which operated between 1999 and 2006, and did research on the sustainable use and conservation of biodiversity. In this network, participating institutions jointly governed the network by electing representatives for a national BIOTA steering committee, which controlled the daily operations of the network and enabled national strategic discussions and decisions. The network was logistically subdivided into four regional networks, BIOTA East Africa, BIOTA Southern Africa, and BIOTA Morocco, and research activities were coordinated through a large number of subprojects.[11]

Other examples with this approach are the projects GLOWA-Volta, and GLOWA-IMPETUS, which operated between 2000 and 2012, both fostering research on sustainable water management and food security.[12] or SASSCAL (Southern African Science Service Centre for Climate Change and Adaptive Land Use) in Windhoek, Namibia,[13] and WASCAL (West African Science Service Centre on Climate Change and Adapted Land Use) in Ouagadougou, Burkina Faso.[14] Both SASSCAL and WASCAL initiatives became centres of competence with their respective databases, graduate programmes, and structures for research, training, and service, and operated until 2016.

According to an expert of the project agency at the time, these programmes are conceptualized in a way so that Germany "only serves as a catalyst and does not play a formal role". However, the GIZ is a partner that funds and administers the funding, the partnership, and the expert admits in the interview, hence the idea that Germany only serves as a catalyst and the sustainability of the projects by means of the partners in Africa is not entirely consequential and self-evident.

Figure 4.3 traces the amount of funding towards the distinct research and research funding institutions dedicated to collaboration and partnership in preparation of the 'Africa-Strategy' that was launched in Germany in 2014. The figures point to the respective developments of the German Academic Exchange Service (DAAD), the German Research Association (DFG), the Wilhelm Gottfried Leibniz Gemeinschaft (WGL), the Fraunhofer Gesellschaft (FhG), the Helmholtz Association (HGF), and the Alexander von Humboldt Foundation (AvH). It illustrates the steady growth, especially of the DAAD, which is the national agency for individual and programme support that is dedicated to academic mobility and international collaboration. The annual budget is provided by the Federal Ministry for Foreign Affairs, the Federal Ministry for Education and Research, the Federal Ministry for Economic Cooperation and

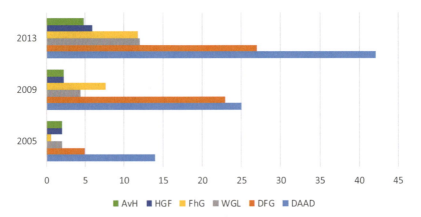

FIGURE 4.3   Funding development of German research and research funding institutions (2005–2013) (Source: Internationales Büro (DLR), May 2014)

Development, and the European Union. The German Research Association is the main national research funding agency for bottom-up-research proposed by individual researchers or collaborative research groups and grew remarkably between 2005 and 2009, only slightly increasing the means for the purpose afterward.

A look at Figure 4.4 shows a general increase of all funding for collaborative research programmes and projects between 2005 and 2013, by the respective institutions mentioned above, which were dedicated to the regions of Northern Africa, sub-Saharan Africa, and the Republic of South Africa. With the agreement on collaboration in science and technology of 1996, South Africa played and continues to play a crucial role as an addressee of programme and project initiatives. The funding increase of individual, programme and project funding for all regions in Africa accompanies a decrease in funding that is visible for South Africa.

These developments point to the start of a new phase of understanding, dialogue, collaboration and partnership in and with Africa, which reached 2014. An analysis of programmes and projects initiated by Germany reveals that collaboration became both a basis and a matter of negotiation. Programmes initially clarified the situation of various partners involved and subsequently placed desiderata and necessities of African interest into the programmes and research projects. One example of this is the German Research Foundation (DFG), the national research funding agency in Germany, which supports

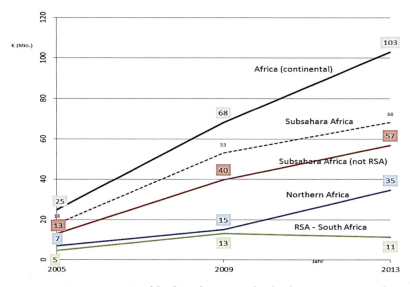

FIGURE 4.4   Germany's regional funding of science and technology programmes and projects (Source: International Office, May 2014)

bottom-up ideas. With the launch of the first 'Africa-Initiative' in 2010, 25 teams of researchers from German universities and from universities in different African countries received a budget of 20 million Euros to jointly conduct research on neglected diseases and built intra-African research capacities.

3.2   The Africa Strategy(ies) in Germany since 2014

In the aftermath of the April 2014 Fourth EU-Africa Summit in Brussels, the Roadmap 2014–2017 formulated the new direction of national German science and research policies in connection to the topics articulated in the interregional European-African policy agenda:

> Investments in science, technology and innovation (STI) are vital to promote growth and employment, improve competitiveness and identify and address pressing global societal challenges such as climate change, affordable renewable energy and energy efficiency, infectious diseases or food and nutrition security. EU-Africa cooperation on STI is cross-cutting in nature, contributing to the attainment of all other socioeconomic development objectives. We will work towards reinforcing cooperation between research communities and the creation of joint academic research programmes, with a special focus on innovation and the productive sector including research infrastructures. In addition, we will develop a long-term, jointly funded and managed research and innovation partnership, in particular in the areas of food and nutrition security and sustainable agriculture. We will take an integrated approach recognizing the important cross-cutting nature of innovation/entrepreneurship, research infrastructures, and technical skills development in Africa and Europe. To this end, the EU-Africa High-Level Policy Dialogue (HLPD) on science, technology, and innovation will be the key platform in the JAES for priority-setting and implementation design. A HLPD expert working group will be set up that will be tasked with developing a detailed roadmap defining the scope and outlining the different steps to be taken towards this new partnership. Financing will come from the European Research and Innovation Program, Horizon 2020, and other contributions from EU and African stakeholders. (European Council, 2014)

The passage of the AU-EU Roadmap also illustrates the change of paradigm in Germany's approach to partnership and collaboration with Africa. In the policy document entitled 'Afrikapolitische Leitlinien der Bundesregierung'[15] and launched in 2014, the potentials of the continent became explicitly acknowledged and the aim to partner with Africa at 'eye level', in order to jointly foster research projects to find answers to global, regional and national challenges, became articulated. Education in Africa, in terms of structure and content, and vocational training especially became a priority. For the higher education sector, the identification and support of talented young individuals became key, and an example of this was the support provided to the African Union to build the Pan-African University and to contribute to the fields of research on water, energy and climate change, which are crucial cornerstones to the European Framework programme as well.

What became explicitly mentioned was a change of paradigm in the approach towards collaboration in research, with the aim to facilitate the establishment of top-level research capacities and centres of excellence for joint research and to foster the sustainability of such endeavours by explicitly requesting contribution to funding schemes. The potentials in Africa for the innovation of research are seen as collaborative research programmes and projects that serve as models to strengthen tertiary systems in Africa.

The challenges listed in the AU-EU Roadmap hint at the prevailing mindset that sees Africa as a continent in crisis, and despite the 'visible growth' of national economies, 'destabilizing potentials' are listed. Another challenge that is articulated in the 'Leitlinien', is the 'fragility of African states', with the need for collaboration to be intensified. The document furthermore states that fragility fosters migration, human trafficking and social instability. It hints at gaps between regions and countries, and speaks about the immediate effects for Europe. Apart from the necessity to gain knowledge and learn to understand what other world regions plan in Africa, in the document, Germany states its strategic interest to foster credibility and influence of Europe in Africa.

To implement credibility and influence, the idea has developed to support regional integration in Africa through the African Peace and Security Architecture (APSA), and to support measures for the prevention of conflict and violence, the fight against poverty, sustainable urbanization, good governance, and the actualization of social security and sustainable employment policies. A clear priority is the reduction of the causes of migration through contributions towards the improvement of employability and income-generating activities. Education, including cultural education at all levels, is another aspect that is identified as an important field for collaboration and partnership in science, research, and development. Creative industries, for example, are taken as an option and opportunity for youth everywhere in Africa, and support measures in this area are intensified in programmes. All these aspects highlight the focus and impact of the regional European-African strategy and shed light on Germany's policy agenda.

When the German federal government launched its Africa strategy, the main entity that is traditionally responsible for research, the BMBF, and the entity that takes care of development cooperation in Africa, the BMZ, were both rapid in claiming their respective policy positions and each articulated their own 'Africa strategy' to gain territory within the national policy context. There have, however, been claims regarding Germany's lack of strategy in Africa, and comments that a complimentary German approach towards collaboration in and with Africa seems to be missing. The agency of programmes is obviously influenced by frictions between ministries, each representing their own interests and overlapping their tasks, and a complementary approach and collaborative agenda within Germany's policy is key.[16] It remains an interesting aspect of the current Africa policy in the making that the distinct and relevant resorts each do follow an overall 'Africa strategy'.

4   Conclusion

The history of Germany's partnership with African countries and institutions in the field of higher education is a relatively recent one. Despite the broad number of interrelated policies and agencies between Europe and Germany on one hand, and Germany and African countries on the other, two main phases of collaboration can be highlighted, and in both phases underlies a specific mind-set that continues to influence in part the interaction and strategies we find today.

The first phase includes the last two decades of the 20th century when engagement in Africa was driven by the overarching notion that Africa is a continent in need and in crisis. Higher education was not a field in which collaboration and partnership were seen as meaningful options for a mutually benefitting collaboration. The policy approach and instrument that was developed was development cooperation, and the main German agency that carried this forward was the BMZ.

Research collaborations were rare in this phase. If they were present, highly motivated individual researchers pushed for them on both sides and connected researchers in institutions for a certain time span, in a few selected countries, and when funding was available. This development cooperation approach led the participants involved to note the imbalances that came with it, with an imbalance in monetary funding and partnership rhetoric often prevailing. The frustration that surfaced had to do with the dynamic of funding agencies in the Northern hemisphere having the final say in developing, conducting and gaining acknowledgment for research on, in and with Africa.

During this phase, one of the African countries with which Germany started to collaborate on the tertiary level, since the 1980s, was South Africa. In South Africa, German researchers were able to conduct research that they could not conduct somewhere else. However, on a policy level, it was difficult for politicians to legitimize this collaboration since apartheid was the major force that prevented balanced collaboration:

> Regrettably, we encounter a political crisis in Southern Africa and negative economic developments that engross the entire continent capture the vigour of governments and politicians. This results in the impression that Africa-policy consists of political and economic crisis management. [...] We need lively academic exchange in both directions. By this, bridges are built between people without whom bilateral relations between governments will freeze.[17]

With the start of the new millennium and the implementation of high-level policy dialogue with more countries in Africa, a more differentiated view of the continent began to inform both Europe and Germany and influence ideas regarding the potentials and explicit demands for a more balanced exchange and approach for improving collaboration. A switch in perception that occurred in the context of Europe's and Germany's Africa-policy agendas, was the understanding that Africa is not just South Africa or the sum of the continent's countries, but that each country is diverse and distinct. Despite some positive changes, mostly in single actors' minds, there is no doubt that imbalances still guide the ideas and approaches of an overall 'Africa-strategy' (BMBF) or, more recently, a presumptuous 'Marshall Plan for Africa' (BMZ).

Nevertheless, the Joint African-European Strategy (JAES) brought a more interrelated and balanced approach for a second phase of what Sousa de Santos calls the "mutual acknowledgment of ignorance". It fostered an intercontinental high-level dialogue and supported the oscillation of input and exchange between top-down and bottom-up policy levels. With reference to European science policy, the mutual acknowledgment of ignorance influenced the development of positions and the articulation of desiderata in the field of higher education, which made African countries become eligible participants in the European Research Framework Programs, for example in the Horizon 2020 program. In this programme, joint research projects with a clear top-down approach meet bottom-up ideas anchored to African contexts.

The history thus far highlights the ways in which intercontinental policies and dialogue have influenced the current collaborative relationships between Europe and Africa in general, and between Germany and different African countries. What becomes clear is that the third phase of collaboration and partnership needs to be initiated and based on differentiated acknowledgments of mutual ignorance, in combination with a quest for mutual understanding and mutually learning from one another. This is the prerequisite for a revised view of the potentials of any collaboration between Africa and Europe, and between Germany and distinct nations and regions in Africa. This acknowledgment and mindset can eventually substitute the one that is still prevailing, with a one-dimensional mindset towards Africa. Eventually, policy could create differentiated collaborative measures that are based on a new perspective of partnership and on multidimensional policy dialogues that could fix the hidden imbalances in the field of higher education partnership between Europe and Africa, and between Germany and single countries, institutions, and individual researchers.

Notes

1. https://ec.europa.eu/europeaid/regions/africa/continental-cooperation/joint-africa-eu-strategy_en
2. http://www.africa-eu-partnership.org/sites/default/files/documents/03-jeas_action_plan_en.pdf
3. http://www.unesco.org/fileadmin/MULTIMEDIA/HQ/SC/pdf/sc_plan_action_en.pdf
4. http://ec.europa.eu/research/participants/data/ref/h2020/other/wp/2018-2020/annexes/h2020-wp1820-annex-a-countries-rules_en.pdf
5. http://www.rinea.org/en/558.php
6. https://caast-net-plus.org
7. http://www.erafrica.eu/en/159.php
8. http://www.intensafrica.org/background/
9. https://afrialliance.org/project-description/
10. https://afrialliance.org/project-description/
11. http://www.biota-africa.org/aboutus_struc_ba.php?Page_ID=L900
12. https://www.pik-potsdam.de/glowa/pdf/glowa-broschuere_dt-eng.pdf
13. http://www.sasscal.org/?page_id=172
14. http://www.wascal.org/fileadmin/user_upload/Documents/WASCAL_Cooperation_Agreement.pdf
15. https://www.auswaertiges-amt.de/de/aussenpolitik/regionaleschwerpunkte/afrika/afrika-leitlinien-node; author's translation from German.
16. http://www.faz.net/aktuell/politik/ausland/afrika/deutsche-aussenpolitik-strategielos-in-afrika-12996094.html

17 Speech of Helmut Schäfer, Minister of State in the Ministry of Foreign Affairs, 19 February 1988; Grundpositionen der Afrikapolitik der Bundesregierung. 2 March 1988, Bulletin 30-88.

References

Abrokwaa C. (2017). Colonialism and the development of higher education. In E. Shizha & N. Makuvaza (Eds.), *Re-thinking postcolonial education in sub-Saharan Africa in the 21st century*. Rotterdam, The Netherlands: Sense Publishers. https://doi.org/10.1007/978-94-6300-962-1_12

African Union & European Union. (2007). *International cooperation and development* [Online]. Retrieved from http://www.africa-eu-partnership.org/sites/default/files/documents/eas2007_joint_strategy_en.pdf

Alonso, J. A., & Glennie J. (2015). *Global Policy Online Journal* [Online]. Retrieved from http://www.globalpolicyjournal.com/blog/01/06/2015/what-development-cooperation-four-criteria-help-define-it

Amey, M. J., Eddy, P. L., & Ozaki, C. C. (2007). Demands for partnership and collaboration in higher education: A model. *New Directions for Community Colleges*, 5–14. doi:10.1002/cc.288

Annan, K. (2015, March 21). Higher education and Africa's social and political progress. *University World News* (Issue Africa Edition). Retrieved from http://www.universityworldnews.com/article.php?story=20150321104235 40

Assié-Lumumba, N. T., Mazrui, A. A., & Dembélé, M. (2013). Critical perspectives on half a century of post-colonial education for development in Africa. *African and Asian Studies*, 12(1–2), 1–12.

Bailey, F., & Dolan, A. (2011). The meaning of partnership in development: Lessons for development education. *Policy and Practice: A Development Education Review*, 14, 30–48.

Barbosa, A. (2010). Modern colonialism in African education: The wave of foreign investment in sub-Saharan Africa. *The Vermont Connection*, 31(1), 4.

Caloghirou, Y., Tsakanikas, A., & Vonortas, N. S. (2001). University-industry cooperation in the context of the European framework programme. *The Journal of Technology Transfer*, 26, 153. https://doi.org/10.1023/A:1013025615518

Cloete, N., Maassen, P., & Bailey, T. (Eds.). (2015). *Knowledge production and contradictory functions in African higher education*. Cape Town: Centre for Higher Education Transformation (CHET). Retrieved from https://chet.org.za/books/knowledge-production-and-contradictory-functions-african-higher-education

Cross, M., & Ndofirepi, A. (2017). *Knowledge and change in African Universities: Volume 1 – Current debates*. Rotterdam, The Netherlands: Sense Publishers.

European Union. *The Africa-EU partnership.* [Online]. Retrieved from http://www.africa-eu-partnership.org/en/about-us/what-partnership

European Union. (2005). *Development and relations with African, Carribean and Pacific States* [Online]. Retrieved from http://ec.europa.eu/development/body/cotonou/lome_history_en.htm#

European Union. (2011). *The Africa-European Union strategic partnership: Meeting current and future challenges together.* Brussels: European Union.

European Union. (2014). *Entwicklung und Zusammenarbeit* [Online]. Retrieved from https://europa.eu/european-union/topics/development-cooperation_de

Gemeinsame Wissenschaftskonferenz (GWK). (2013). *Steigerung des Anteils der FuE-Ausgaben am nationalen Bruttoinlandsprodukt (BIP) als Teilziel der Lissabon-Strategie und der Strategie Europa 2020* [Online]. Retrieved from http://www.gwk-bonn.de/fileadmin/Papers/GWK-Heft-31-Lissabon-Strategie-2013.pdf

Knight, J. (2004). Internationalization remodeled: Definition, approaches, and rationales. *Journal of Studies in International Education, 8,* 5–31.

Landau, L. B. (2012). Communities of knowledge or Tyrannies of partnership: Reflections on North-South research networks and the dual imperative. *Journal of Refugee Studies, 25*(4), 555–570.

Santos, B. d. S. (2016). Epistemologies of the South and the future. *From the European South: A Transdisciplinary Journal of Postcolonial Humanities, 1,* 17–29.

Teferra, D., & Altbach, P. G. (2003). *African higher education: An international reference handbook.* Bloomington, IN: Indiana University Press.

CHAPTER 5

Higher Education Partnership between Maghreb and European Higher Education Institutions during the 2002–2013 Decade

Baghdad Benstaali

1   Introduction

At the beginning of the third millennium, three North African countries, Algeria, Morocco, and Tunisia joined the Tempus programme and engaged their higher education institutions (HEIs) as actors in project partnerships. Within the consortia of European Union–South Mediterranean (EU-SM) partners, since 2002, Algerian HEIs have participated in various joint projects and structural measures that have created a real momentum for change and improvement in the curricular areas, support structures and services related to the functioning of Algerian HEIs. Algerian membership to EU-SM partnerships in 2002 preceded the 2004 implementation of the Reform of the three-cycle system (Bachelor-Master-Doctorate), whose key priorities were similar to the Tempus program's three pillars: Curricular Reform, Governance Reform, and Higher Education and Society.

Constructive collaboration in projects through the Tempus programme has led to innovation in the design of new higher education curricula, to the development of new models of governance, and to beneficial partnerships between higher education and society, that meet the needs of both academic institutions and socio-economic partners. The involvement of stakeholders in Tempus has helped HEIs open up their environments and listen carefully to the demands and requests of socio-economic partners. The mobility of academic and administrative staff and students has led to the transfer of knowledge, skills, and expertise, and the exchange of enriching practices and experiences.

A review of the implementation of the Tempus programme in Algeria has been necessary and a regular process of assessment has become essential to evaluate the achievements of the members of the programme. An analysis of the outcomes can help identify strengths, weaknesses, and deficiencies in higher education in general, and in potential stakeholders' implementation of the Tempus project in particular.

This chapter presents the characteristics of partnership that were created following Tempus and Erasmus Mundus annual calls for proposals, their follow up, and the progress made in the field of cooperation between HEIS. It reviews partnership accomplishments through the contribution of Algerian HEIS in projects covering ten years of implementation of the Tempus and Erasmus Mundus programmes. At the time of implementation, the Education, Audio-visual and Culture Executive Agency (EACEA) in Brussels financed the projects, and National Tempus Offices were in charge of monitoring and evaluating each partner country.

2   Overview of the North African Higher Education Setting

2.1   *Challenges and Needs*

Higher education systems in North African countries face similar challenges and trends and have led policymakers to adopt appropriate strategies and convenient methods to lessen the pressure on their higher education systems. Algeria, Morocco, and Tunisia all face increasing rates of new student registration and need to create new seats every year to absorb incoming students. Algerian universities aim to reconcile the needs of democratic access to higher education with those of higher quality training in a changing world, characterized by the advent of a knowledge and information society, and economic globalization. They also face an increasing rate of unemployment of graduates and need to match their programme outcomes with graduate skills that are required by the labour market. These challenges require a gradual transition out of a strict administrative model of management system to one that is based on the principles of "governance", where student services play a leading role in implementing the principles of democratic access to higher education. The old model of management no longer seems to be able to meet the initially assigned objectives of Algerian HEIS and should, therefore, involve greater participation of the larger community in the management of institutions.

Furthermore, one of the strategic challenges is to train large numbers of instructors needed yearly for the increasing student body. Algeria, Morocco, and Tunisia all also intend to establish a culture of internal quality assurance and external evaluation and to implement international quality standards in order to improve the internal output of their HEIS and achieve international recognition. The latter can be achieved by reforming course programmes and diversifying the range of efficient and high-quality courses in academic and applied disciplines.

Due to the challenges facing Maghreb countries, engineering and technological development are common strategic goals. Moreover, there is also a need to rethink and develop a regional system for the evaluation of HEI activities in the field of academic and scientific research. In this regard, the obligation to achieve these results and improve the general efficiency of the higher education system are common actions and activities that should be required at the regional level. The accomplishment of these goals will have an impact on the development of all components of national economies and improve overall regional standards.

2.2 Different Approaches

The main objective of policymakers in the field of higher education and scientific research is to establish an efficient, high-quality system of training and research. All countries aim to build international relationships and promote national and international student mobility. Universities focus on the development of research activities by enhancing local academics' and newly recruited researchers' participation in teaching and research activities, by providing them with new regulations, sophisticated materials, and well-equipped laboratories, and by creating mobility incentives.

Throughout the years, the Algerian government has made considerable efforts that have resulted in the expansion of the university network and the training of thousands of staff. These efforts continue to achieve the desired objectives, both quantitatively and qualitatively. As mentioned in the Higher Education in Algeria report (EACEA, 2012b) matters related to the development of human resources require particular attention, especially in regards to upgrading the status of teachers and researchers.

Higher education objectives in Morocco have focused on increasing the autonomy of universities and involving learners in the management of the progress of their studies (EACEA, 2012g). They aim at diversifying funding sources, ensuring links with the world of employment, encouraging talent, innovating scientific and technological research, and motivating human resources through the establishment of a culture of monitoring and assessing progress. The Tunisian Higher Education approach is to establish a training system characterized by flexibility and international recognition of diplomas. By reinforcing certification in ICT and communication languages, its objective has been to create a new generation of versatile graduates, who are able to adapt to a changing global context (EACEA, 2012a).

Following Tempus III, stakeholders from the Maghreb region have stated that the Tempus programme has succeeded in introducing a culture of quality to the region's higher education systems, and have provided recommendations that focused on the consolidation of accomplishments rather than on the introduction of changes. Maghreb countries decided to maintain the Tempus programme management scheme based on transparency, clarity, and simplicity, and to give priority to the available structural and complementary measures for solving specific problems related to the university reforms, which can have direct impacts and introduce any necessary structural changes.

Stakeholders of the programme have encouraged academic staff from the Maghreb region to become grant holders for Tempus projects and to enhance e-learning and virtual teaching, either to deliver specialized courses in universities or to provide an option for low-cost continuing education for professionals. New science domains, such as new technologies or biotechnology, have been included in national priorities of all three countries involved in the program.

On the other hand, Mashriq countries have chosen to introduce career guidance centres in their universities, to work on improving central university management systems and internal quality control practices, to support the development of joint degree programmes between the EU and partner universities, to ensure sustainable projects, and to lessen the influence of country priorities in the selection process.

In order to encourage professionalization of curricula and facilitate graduates' mobility and employment, both Maghreb and Mashriq sub-regions intend to reinforce HEI links to the economic sector. They also aim to enhance international cooperation, with academics working with their European peers in joint and structural projects financed by the European Commission, and to tackle common regional issues together.

3 European Union-South Mediterranean HEI Partnerships

3.1 *Maghreb Countries' Higher Education Network*

There are various types of institutions in the field of higher education. Academic, professional, cultural and vocational institutions are under the supervision of the Ministry of Higher Education and Scientific Research; universities and university campuses, teacher training schools, national tertiary schools devoted to particular scientific or vocational disciplines, and public institutions are under the authority of other ministries and the educational supervision of the Ministry of Higher Education and Scientific Research; and there are also higher national training institutes and engineering schools. A continuing education university, created in the nineties, enables candidates who did not obtain the secondary school national diploma to enter into higher education through numerous continuing education centres spread throughout the national territory.

A specific feature of the Algerian higher education system is the existence, in addition to universities, of dispersed university campuses, which are decentralized components of universities. These campuses are focal points that enable higher education to flourish at the local level. The task of the eighteen tertiary schools and institutes is to train future engineers in specific fields that cover various professional activities. The role of teacher training colleges is to prepare educators and instructors for primary and secondary schools and vocational centres.

In the Maghreb region, the number of HEIs keeps on increasing every year, reaching 96 in Algeria), 390 in Morocco, and 198 in Tunisia, in 2016. The number of students attending institutions of higher education in 2013 was approximately 1,252,000 (the aggregate figure for all three cycles and continuing education in 2013) and this number increases every year. As shown in Table 5.1, in most Middle Eastern countries, parity between students could nearly be achieved.

3.2 Tempus Programme Partnership Structures and Requirements

Partnerships between the Maghreb and European HEIs are formed around the three Tempus programme themes or pillars: Curricular Reform, Governance Reform, and Higher Education and Society. Most Tempus programme themes

TABLE 5.1 Maghreb HEIs network (as of July 2012)

Higher education in country	Number of HEIS	Number of students (million)	Female students (%)
Algeria (EACEA, 2012b)	83	1.210	60
Morocco (EACEA, 2012g)	342	0.666	48
Tunisia (EACEA, 2012a)	193	0.362	61
Libya (EACEA, 2012f)	17	0.342	59
Egypt (EACEA, 2012c)	106	2.01	–
Jordan (EACEA, 2012d)	28	0.230	52
Lebanon (EACEA, 2012e)	42	0.195	53
Palestine (EACEA, 2012h)	49	0.213	–
Syria (EACEA, 2012i)	27	0.370	–

have been covered through the Tempus III and IV programmes. All project partnerships selected during the programme's different calls for proposals responded to the national priorities fixed by the partner countries' national authorities and responded to the regional priorities based on the EU's policy for cooperation with partner countries' regions, which are identified in the EU's strategic documents as concerning neighbouring countries.

In the Tempus programme, partnerships are discerned between national or multi-country joint and structural measures projects. They have to fulfill eligibility criteria, otherwise, they face automatic rejection. They also have to respect various requirements, including the formal submission of rules, compliance with national and regional priorities, compliance with grant size limits (€ 500,000 to € 1.500000) and duration (24 or 36 months), and, depending on the type of project applied for, consortium composition. Tempus programme fixes the conditions for eligible partnerships for each type of partnership, national and multinational (Joint or Structural Measures).

3.3 Tempus Programme Partnerships

Many multi-country projects, such as the Tempus Programme, are structural measures projects that must involve the Ministry of Education in each participating country. They cover topics such as leadership in higher education, internationalization of HEIs, and promotion of innovation. Through the Tempus Programme, the participation of Algerian HEIs in project consortia has improved and the average size of consortia has gone from 10 (under the Tempus III programme) to 16 (Tempus IV). This increase has been encouraged by the lessening of minimum requirements in consortia composition, which occurred between Tempus III and Tempus IV. An intensive information campaign was planned by the national Tempus office, through the use of modern tools of information (website, conferences, newsletters, emails) and advertisement of the benefits of the programmes, which enhanced the motivation of Algerian HEIs to contribute to and participate in Tempus programme.

Figure 5.1 shows the project's relationship to national priorities. An uneven distribution of projects around the programme themes is clearly noticed on the graph. While the Curricular Reform area of the programme was well developed in Tempus III and IV, the Higher Education and Society section is in need of more calls for proposals. Themes such as institutional financial autonomy and accountability and training of non-university teachers were areas that were not covered at all.

On the regional side, more than 66% of Tempus III projects in the region focused on curriculum reform compared to 40% of all projects in Tempus IV.

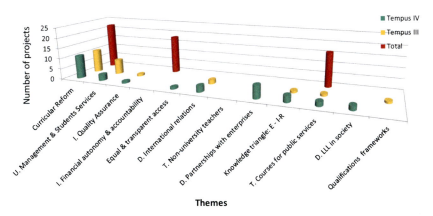

FIGURE 5.1   Partnership relationship to the priority themes (Benstaali, 2014)

24 % of Tempus IV projects in the SM region focused on the reform of higher education institutions' structures and processes. These reforms brought many HEIs to set up international relations offices or to improve the existing ones, and to set up career guidance offices and alumni associations as well. These Tempus programme impacts on HEIs in Algeria contributed in helping students find jobs immediately after graduation and in reducing youth unemployment, which is a widespread phenomenon in the region.

All projects required mobility of staff and students for activities, such as kickoffs, meetings, seminars, conferences, and case studies. Academic activities and scientific productions were disseminated through partners' websites connexions, improving visibility, attractiveness and international university ranking.

3.4   South Mediterranean Partners

The contribution of SM countries in projects involving Algerian HEIs is illustrated in Figure 5.2. Most SM countries participated as partners in project partnerships, with different rates of contribution. It is clear from Figure 5.2 that the EU's preferred partnerships are with French-speaking countries, such as Morocco, Tunisia, and Lebanon, with a higher frequency of participation within SM countries. Some of the reasons for the preference for same language partnerships could be related to communication facilities speaking the same language, and to the importance of tackling common regional issues and similar national challenges encountered from inherited colonial systems of education adapting to the Bologna Reform.

Tempus IV multi-country projects have been very popular, representing 52% of the total number of projects in higher education. They often include as many as eight countries from the region. Communication between national, regional

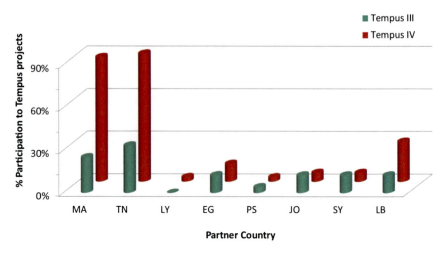

FIGURE 5.2 Contribution of South Mediterranean HEIs with Algerian counterparts to Tempus projects (Benstaali, 2014)

and European partners has improved during Tempus IV. Egypt, Jordan, Syria, and the Palestinian State were less active in partnerships involving Algerian institutions, and Libya only joined the programme in 2011.

When analyzing the trends in partnership composition, it is clear that both Mashriq and Maghreb countries tend to work on projects together. This could be related to common regional needs and objectives of the two sub-regions. Table 5.2 shows the number of partnerships projects involving HEIs of each country of the Maghreb and Mashriq regions.

National contribution in partnerships is limited to partner countries. Experienced HEIs tend to work together avoiding the involvement of new institutions and the sharing of good practices. The higher the percentage of HEI participation in a given country and region, the more involvement of HEIs in partnerships. It is noticed that the percentage of participation and the rate of involvement of HEIs in partnerships varies from one country to another as shown in Table 5.3.

Contributing as partners in Tempus projects helped HEIs build their management capacities of, which also facilitated their applications as partnership coordinators for the first time in Tempus IV. Approximately one-quarter of Tempus IV projects from that region have been managed by a local coordinator. Cooperation between countries in the region existed prior to the advent of the Tempus programme, however, certain pan-Arab higher education organizations, such as the "Arab Network for Quality Assurance in Higher Education" and the "Association of Arab Universities", have participated in Tempus regional projects to help boost and further fund their collaboration on certain topics.

TABLE 5.2 Tempus Programme partnerships for SM countries 2002–2012 (the main achievements of the Tempus programme in the Southern Mediterranean 2002–2013, 2013)

Region	Country	Tempus III	Tempus IV	
		2004–2006	2008–2013	2008–2014
Maghreb	Algeria	24	23	32
	Morocco	49	38	58
	Tunisia	31	31	47
	Libya		3	5
Mashriq	Lebanon	23	23	35
	Egypt	65	33	49
	Jordan	23	20	31
	Palestine	14	13	21
	Syria	32	13	15

TABLE 5.3 Rate of involvement of HEIs in partnerships (as of July 2012)

Region	Country	Number of projects	Number of HEIs participating	Ratio of HEIs participating/Total HEIs (%)
Maghreb	Algeria	32	31	37
	Morocco	58	27	8
	Tunisia	47	16	8
	Libya	5	8	47
Mashriq	Egypt	49	38	36
	Jordan	31	20	71
	Lebanon	35	20	48
	Palestine	21	12	24
	Syria	15	11	41

3.5   *European Partners*

HEIs from twenty European countries contributed to partnerships. As can be seen in Figure 5.3, France is present in almost all partnerships involving Algeria (85%). The reason for such a strong presence is related to history, language, and general proximities in communication. Most Algerian academics are

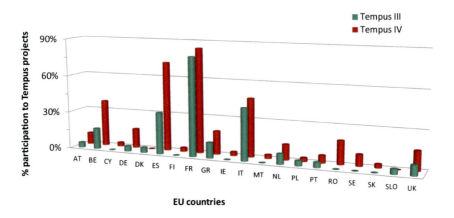

FIGURE 5.3   Partnership with European partners (Benstaali, 2014)

Alumni of French universities and still keep strong ties with their colleagues, supervisors and graduate institutions. Spain, Italy, and Belgium are also present in partnerships, while Greece, Germany, the Netherlands, and the United Kingdom contribute to projects. Other European countries have also been involved in partnership projects at least once.

Tempus partnerships in Europe were considered a useful support mechanism to help implement major reforms in higher education, through structural measures projects with Ministries of Education acting as effective partners and tackling national policy issues. The issues tackled included quality assurance, promotion of entrepreneurship in the education system, and improvement of curricula and studies. Constructive collaboration promoted the improvement of communication between HEIs and socio-economic partners as well as transparency in HEIs' governance through the participation of local enterprises and socio-economic partners in management committees.

Stakeholders' contribution using a "bottom-up approach" led to the implementation of new curricular reforms, improvement of courses and creation of new fields of study responding to the needs of local employers in the region.

3.6   *Erasmus Mundus Partnerships*

Student and staff mobility between North and South HEIs has been financed by the Erasmus Mundus programme, which is one of the main EU programmes for international mobility. Under this program, twenty European countries are involved in partnerships with Algerian institutions. As shown in Figure 5.4, France is in the first position with 49 participations, followed by Italy and Spain (21), Portugal and Belgium (7), and Germany (6). All HEI partners have made reasonable efforts to go beyond the minimum requirements of providing students with a series of documents aimed at the recognition of study abroad

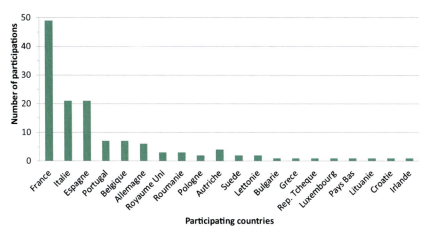

FIGURE 5.4   European universities' participation to Erasmus Mundus partnerships (Benstaali, 2014)

experiences (study contract, diploma supplement, and transcript), and have pushed for full recognition of either credits or degrees, further facilitating student mobility and exchange with European universities, and therefore allowing mutual institutional recognition upon returning home, after periods spent in Europe or another country in the region.

Excellent results have been achieved with the Averroes partnership in Lot 1 (Morocco, Tunisia, and Algeria), where credit and degree recognition was guaranteed at all levels and where 90% of students enrolled in a joint supervised research programme.

4   South-North Mobility

Fifteen mobility projects were implemented since 2004, with improving partnership size, leading to an annual increase of overall students and staff mobility reaching a total of 679 (67 Action 1 and 612 Action 2) in 2013. During the period between 2007 and 2013, Action 2 mobility, with 612 students and staff participating in the program, corresponds to a percentage of 13% of the SM region, which is relatively low behind Egypt (16%) and Morocco (14%). Considering Lot 1, the rate increases slightly for Algeria (23%) but remains lower than in Egypt (29%) and Morocco (25%). Table 5.4 illustrates the mobility resumes mobility of partner countries' HEIs in the framework of Action 1 and Action 2.

European students' mobility within the framework of the Erasmus Mundus partnerships is not as significant as that of Algerian students and this is due to the fact that Algerian institutions are not in high demand by European students. A small number of students chose Algerian HEIs, representing only

TABLE 5.4 Combined mobility for SM Nationals Action 1 & Action 2 (Erasmus Mundus in the Southern Mediterranean, 2013)

Region	Country	EMMC students 2004–2013	EMMC scholars 2004–2010	EMJD fellows 2010–2013	Total Action 1	Action 2 students 2007–2012	Action 2 staff 2007–2012	Total Action 2	Grand total	Grand total/ Sub-region
Maghreb	Algeria	50	16	1	67	526	86	612	679	2098
	Morocco	47	30	0	77	533	109	642	719	
	Tunisia	86	13	2	101	459	82	541	642	
	Libya	2	0	0	2	44	12	56	58	
Mashriq	Egypt	219	14	6	239	646	115	761	1000	2723
	Jordan	23	4	4	31	330	82	412	443	
	Lebanon	45	4	1	50	383	93	476	526	
	Palestine	27	2	0	29	313	46	359	388	
	Syria	39	8	0	47	267	52	319	366	
Total		538	91	14	643	3501	677	4178	4821	4821

7% of all European students (390) participating in the program, and only 13% compared to similar countries in Lot 1 (Algeria, Egypt, Morocco, and Tunisia). As shown in Table 5.5, only five Algerian universities welcomed European students. Morocco is the most popular destination in all of the Southern Neighbourhood (27%) and in Lot 1 (49%). European HEIs are interested in students' exchanges particularly for those students who are registered in Arabic language studies so that they can improve their speaking skills.

Half of the mobility in Averroes concerned academic staff while the other half was unevenly split between the student categories of Bachelor, Master's, Doctorate, and Postdoctoral. HEIs with lower rates of North-South student mobility should take the opportunity to foster the appeal of their country as a destination through the provision of better student services, facilities, and conditions of stay.

5   Impact of EU-SM Partnerships on Higher Education Systems

Tempus and Erasmus Mundus programmes have an outstanding and sustainable impact on HEIs, creating new dynamics among students, staff motivation,

TABLE 5.5   North-South student mobility within selected partnerships between 2007–2010

	2007	2008	2009	2010	Total	Share (%)
Algeria	4	4	10	10	28	13
Morocco	19	22	37	27	105	49
Tunisia	8	7	7	7	29	13
Egypt	13	1	10	29	53	25
Total	44	34	64	73	215	100

and competitiveness at national, regional and international levels. The programmes played an important role in upgrading curricula, enhancing capacity building of staff, improving HEIs' governance and management, and promoting links between HEIs and the labour market. Even though SM countries are not officially part of the Bologna process, participation in the Tempus programme with EU institutions has helped promote Bologna principles and tools and highlight their usefulness to the Maghreb and Mashriq regions as well. As a recent Tempus study showed, the Bologna Process is now officially embedded in the education systems of Algeria, Morocco, and Tunisia, and it has been implemented in a more ad-hoc manner in Egypt and Palestine (State of Play of the Bologna Process in the Tempus Partner Countries, a Tempus Study, 2012).

The implementation of curriculum reform following the three-cycle system structure (Bachelor, Master, and Doctorate) in the region is one of the main outcomes of the Tempus programme, with the introduction of new methods and skills for designing courses and structuring curricula, based on 'learning outcomes' and ECTS credits. New fields of study have also been developed in the region, such as environmental science, renewable energy, biotechnology, and others, meeting the needs of an evolving labour market in the region. New teaching methods, such as e-learning, blended learning and intensive on-site courses for students and professionals have been developed as well, breaking the more classical classroom-based learning. The programmes have encouraged the development of joint degrees and double-degrees with certain European HEIs, and the recognition of degrees from the region, for students who wish to pursue their post-graduate studies in Europe.

The Tempus programme provided HEI partners in the region with necessary laboratory equipment to implement curricular reforms in the areas of engineering, medicine, and sciences. Partnerships have been engaged in university governance and management reforms, challenging strict local hierarchies and policies previously existing in many HEIs in the region. University governance issues have been tackled through the creation of opportunities for university Presidents and Rectors in the Maghreb and Mashriq regions to meet their European counterparts in Europe. They had possibilities to exchange practices and learn from more democratic, transparent and effective ways of working while raising awareness on the importance of external representatives on governing bodies (EACEA, 2010).

Maghreb HEIs developed a quality-assurance standard, titled AQI-UMED, for the assessment and evaluation of the performance of programmes and institutions, which is a useful instrument that was either adopted or adapted from partner countries and led to accreditation and certification procedures (Tempus Project AQI-UMED, 2011). Lebanon is working on developing tools for its new Lebanese national quality assurance agency. The Arab Network for Quality Assurance in Higher Education and European accreditation, and quality assurance bodies are partners in many of these projects.

In the Maghred and Mashriq regions, HEIs have traditionally operated unconnected, far removed from the world of industry and commerce. Fostering links between HEIs and the labour market has encouraged the involvement of the private sector in partnerships, from multinationals to local small and medium enterprises, to NGOs and local institutions. The participation of local employers in the new curriculum design process and tailored courses has been encouraged in order to respond to the precise needs of the labour market. Concrete structures, such as career centres, technology transfer offices and entrepreneurship hubs, have been created on site in campuses, and have developed and maintained strategic and sustainable links with the labour market. Practical placements and graduate training programmes in companies for students have also been built into many new courses and have helped students secure jobs upon graduation, which is something particularly important in a region where youth unemployment is very high.

Tempus partnerships played an important role in the professional development of academic, administrative and technical staff in the region, allowing academics opportunities to meet other peers in their fields, in different countries. Tempus provided staff from the region the opportunity to develop intercultural skills by working together with staff from many other countries in multi-country partnerships, exchanging best practices, and learning and benchmarking from each other. Benchmarking reports have highlighted how professional development from these kinds of projects often motivates countries to achieve better results in a particular area while allowing them to take pride in their accomplishments.

Various issues were addressed through the Erasmus Mundus partnerships. Reassuring results regarding a balanced mobility programme of both sexes were encountered in partnerships covering the whole region of the European

Neighbourhood and Partnership Instrument (ENPI). It is particularly encouraging to note that partnerships for Palestine, Jordan, Syria, and Lebanon have managed to achieve a balanced scholarship distribution between men and women in an area that has generally been characterized by the low participation of women candidates. When there were unexpected levels of abandonment from female candidates, these were reported to derive from cultural reasons, especially in the Maghreb countries.

In most partnerships, measures were put in place to avoid brain drain and proved to be adequate and encouraging. A good example of this is the Averroes partnership, where students were encouraged to maintain links with their home universities and receive support to find jobs in their home countries.

Close cooperation was encouraged with partners and led to the implementation of measures to overcome potential obstacles to reach vulnerable groups (Target Group III) in politically/socially fragile and unstable situations in the region. All Target Group III scholarships were awarded in Lots 3 and 4 respectively, in Palestine, Jordan, Syria, and Lebanon.

Sustainability is often addressed through the establishment of academic bilateral agreements between the EU and third country partners, and through the investment of existing synergies participating in other programmes, such as Tempus. In most cases, the premises from the Ministry of Education regarding their own countries were consulted and raised awareness on the country's interests regarding the cooperation and student exchanges with EU universities.

Tempus and Erasmus Mundus programmes had a considerable impact on HEIs and systems on both shores of the Mediterranean Sea. Solid North-South HEI partnerships were maintained due to their successes in achieving their objectives and outcomes. They fostered the sharing of best practices with new inexperienced HEIs and the development of new international relationships. The following Erasmus+ (2014–2020) programme simultaneously combines capacity building (from the ex Tempus programme) and student mobility (from the ex Erasmus Mundus programme). While partnerships in previous programmes were limited to specific regions in the European neighbourhood, Erasmus+ widens the scope of previous programmes to other HEIs in other regions of the world, involving programs such as the Intra-Africa academic mobility scheme, which covers all HEIs of the five regions of the African continent.

6   Conclusion

The partnerships between HEIs in EU-SM countries that formed following the Tempus and Erasmus Mundus programmes were a key instrument for the improvement of higher education systems and institutions. They helped reinforce governance policies, upgrade curricula, improve staff capacities, and increase student competencies. Communication improved between HEIs at national levels, encouraging discussions, sharing of best practices and expertise with regards to course upgrades, curricula development, and governance, and providing the development of better services for students and society. Through the partnerships the economic sector is becoming a significant partner in the professionalization of curricula, promoting entrepreneurship, research development, innovation, and the creation of interfaces for graduates' insertion and employability enhancement.

New flexible methods of learning delivery (e-learning, blended, distance-learning platforms) enhanced students' and professionals' skills. Various networks (university libraries, higher education reform experts, regional and European) were formed for collaborating and exchanging good practices, and for benchmarking to improve the quality of higher education. While prior to Tempus IV, cooperation tended to be more 'North-South', multi-country partnerships under this programme eventually helped promote a more 'South-South' approach in the programme as well. HEI partnerships gained extensive experience throughout the past decade and can, therefore, compete in new cooperation programmes on a continental level, such as the Intra-Africa academic mobility scheme.

References

Benstaali, B. (2014). *The Tempus programme in Algeria 2002–2013.* Algiers: NTO Algeria Publications.

EACEA. (2010). *Changing rules: A review of Tempus support to University Governance, a Tempus Study.* Brussels: Education Audiovisual and Culture Executive Agency.

EACEA. (2012a). *Higher education in Tunisia.* Brussels: Education Audiovisual and Culture Executive Agency.

EACEA. (2012b). *Higher education in Algeria.* Brussels: Education Audiovisual and Culture Executive Agency.

EACEA. (2012c). *Higher education in Egypt.* Brussels: Education Audiovisual and Culture Executive Agency.

EACEA. (2012d). *Higher education in Jordan.* Brussels: Education Audiovisual and Culture Executive Agency.

EACEA. (2012e). *Higher education in Lebanon.* Brussels: Education Audiovisual and Culture Executive Agency.

EACEA. (2012f). *Higher education in Libya*. Brussels: Education Audiovisual and Culture Executive Agency.

EACEA. (2012g). *Higher education in Morocco*. Brussels: Education Audiovisual and Culture Executive Agency.

EACEA. (2012h). *Higher education in Palestine*. Brussels: Education Audiovisual and Culture Executive Agency.

EACEA. (2012i). *Higher education in Syria*. Brussels: Education Audiovisual and Culture Executive Agency.

EACEA. (2013). *Erasmus Mundus in the Southern Mediterranean*. Brussels: Education Audiovisual and Culture Executive Agency.

Project Tempus AQI-UMED. (2011). *Référentiel AQI-UMED, Version Finale, Reinforcement d'Assurance Qualité Interne dans des Universités de la Méditerranée*. Retrieved from http://www.univ-setif.dz/CAQ/documentations/REFERENTIEL%20AQI-UMED.pdf

Ruffio, P., Mc Cabe, R., & Xhaferri, E. (2012). State of play of the Bologna Process in the Tempus Partner Countries (2012). A Tempus Study. Issue 09. Education, Audiovisual and Culture Executive Agency, European Commission.

CHAPTER 6

Developing International Quality Assurance Standards in Africa: Reference to the Pan-African University as Institutional Partnership in the Framework of Bologna

Abbes Sebihi and Leonie Schoelen

1   Introduction

Since the end of the last decade, the issue of quality assurance has increasingly been put on international higher education policy agendas. On the African continent in particular, there have recently been promising initiatives and developments with the potential to rise to a future, unparalleled, all-comprehensive framework for the thematic complex of quality in higher education institutions and beyond. As a cross-cutting topic, the aspect of quality plays an important role in a variety of fields within higher education, and relates to admissions, research and development, innovation, international cooperation, curriculum development, academic staff recruitment, and information and communication technology (ICT), including e-learning.

With particular emphasis on the three points last-mentioned, the Pan-African University Institute of Water and Energy Sciences (including Climate Change) (PAUWES), serves as a case study to illustrate the various aspects and success factors of an Africa-European Union (EU) institutional cooperation project, within a framework that involves African higher education's leading role in the development of international quality assurance standards. The establishment of the Pan African Institute is an essential innovative project, the experience of which allows the identification of correlations and lessons learned for future initiatives.

After an introduction of the project, this chapter provides a spotlight on African Higher Education policy trends, including existing parallels with the European Bologna Process. The chapter also focuses on the Institute's curriculum development as a best-practice. Furthermore, the chapter deals with one of the main challenges observed in both the establishment and management of a new, pan-African, higher education institution, which is the demand of qualification harmonization in the recruitment of high-level professors, in order to teach excellence programmes. Subsequently, it addresses the role of new technologies in quality assurance and standardization processes, discussing the PAUWES Learning Management System (LMS) and the online networking platform Community of Practice (CoP), and finally concludes with a discussion on Africa-EU collaboration opportunities, in the form of successful institutional partnerships.

The PAU is a continental initiative of the African Union Commission (AUC) to revitalize higher education and research in Africa. It aims to exemplify excellence, nurture quality, enhance the attractiveness and global competitiveness of African higher education and research, and establish African Universities at the core of Africa's development. Five thematic institutes establish Master's and Ph.D. level programmes and engage in collaborative, development-oriented research programmes. The institutes that constitute the PAU work with satellite centres in other African regions as well, while also cooperating closely with the public and private sectors, and civil society.

The four institutes of the Pan-African University are hosted in different regions of Africa and are currently supported by the Key Thematic Partners. The different Institutes within the PAU are supposed to tackle challenges in their respective fields. Germany is the partner for the PAU Institute of Water and Energy Sciences (including Climate Change) (PAUWES) at the Abou Bakr Belkaid University of Tlemcen in Algeria, and, as stipulated by the African Union Agenda 2063, PAUWES is supposed to tackle challenges in the Energy and Water sector. The PAU Institute for Basic Sciences, Technology and Innovation (PAUSTI) is based in Kenya, the PAU Institute for Life and Earth Sciences (PAULESI) in Nigeria, the PAU Institute for Governance, Humanities and Social Sciences (PAUGHSS) in Cameroon, and, yet to be established, the PAU Institute for Space Sciences (PAUSS) is to be based in South Africa. In addition, satellite centres are connected to the five main hubs. According to the AUC, PAU Master's programmes should facilitate high-quality education for graduates who are sufficiently skilled and who can be retained on the continent to make significant contributions to Africa's development. Students are to be educated to perform as future leaders, entrepreneurs, decision-makers, change agents, and reformers, in the core areas relevant to the African continent. In addition, they are trained to become researchers and it is expected that a number of the graduates go into academia.

Based on the authors' observations during professional activities in the timeframe of duty assignments, it was observed that this expected future elite, which constitutes students from all parts of the African continent, sits together in the classroom where they discuss and learn to analyse, expose and solve problems. By doing so, they become accustomed to collaboration and teamwork and learn to appreciate the diversity of perspectives present in

Africa. Furthermore, analytic thinking to arrive at acceptable solutions is being learned when disagreements arise. This experience is new for most students and the soft skills acquired by living and learning in multi-national environments on a daily basis are meant to help them find solutions to issues and challenges in Africa with their colleagues at their future workplaces as well, and are meant to facilitate their individual contribution to Africa's advancement in their chosen field.

Integrating the pan-African aspect, this new set-up makes for an innovative approach that fosters skill development for existing competencies in Africa, which have so far not always been duly recognized due to challenges in implementation. As examples of this novelty, the joint learning experience, and common student activities are presented in the last section of the chapter.

The quantitative data presented is drawn from PAUWES Institute publications and co-authored working papers written during the authors' duty assignments in Tlemcen, Algeria, from 2014 to 2016, and refer to the first academic year, from October 2014 to July 2015.[1]

2   Spotlight on African Higher Education Policy Trends with Reference to the Bologna Process

Africa possesses a higher education tradition, which existed prior to colonization, and included centres of knowledge in (present-day) Mali, Ethiopia, and Egypt, among others, that, for long attracted scholars from all parts of Africa and the rest of the world (Tefera, 2008b). Colonial higher education policies in Africa were marked by limited access, colonizer language in instruction, limited freedom and limited curricula, all elements that must be taken into account in an analysis of the current higher education system in Africa (Teferra & Altbach, 2003). The continuing impacts of colonialism expose the need for advancement in African higher education policies.

Until recently, European policy-makers were not very interested in Africa. Indeed, it took ten years after the Declaration of Bologna, which, in 1999, had the objective to create a European Higher Education Area, until the Bologna Policy Forum eventually opened up to other regions as well, in 2009. The Arusha Convention that involved African Ministers of Education, which detailed the promotion of student mobility by mutual recognition of qualifications in Africa, took place in 1981, thus preceding the European Bologna Process, which aimed at streamlining, organization and unification. The more recent awareness of the African continent and its associated higher education landscape has contributed to the implementation of the European Bologna Process reform.

The novelty the Bologna process brought, which makes it unparalleled with past higher education reforms, is the link it created between European states, as well as between institutional, private and third-sector actors (Croché, 2009), which made it equal to "one of the greatest socio-economic reforms of the last decades" (Vögtle & Martens, 2014). Drawing on the rationale that international-level policies facilitate implementations or even impositions on the level of individual countries (Charlier & Croché, 2011), the significance of the Bologna process has been acknowledged in recent literature, which takes an interest in both an assessment as well as a critical reflection of the Bologna process (Boucher, 2014) and its on-going impact on the Maghreb region (Ghouati, 2011) and on sub-Saharan African higher education (Koehn & Obamba, 2014; Woldegiorgis, Jonck, & Goujon, 2015; Charlier, Croché, & Ndoye, 2009).

Defined as, "by far the best example of success in using regional integration to provide higher education" (Ogachi, 2009, p. 337), and "imposing a coherence on all the scattered elements which it comprised" (Charlier & Croché, 2011), the Bologna Process in Europe could potentially serve as an inspiration for other regions to contribute to and foster more international knowledge creation and use. However, it is only one of several – for example, North American, Chinese, Turkish, Brazilian – models of cooperation in higher education policy reform which Africa may consider. In fact, the European Commission became active in reaching out to Africa only after sub-Saharan countries commenced official partnerships with other regions in the world (Charlier & Croché, 2011). The EU has thus become anxious to keep up competitively and, at the same time, strives to be well-prepared for the increasing importance of African higher education policy options.

In 2006, in what is known as the Libreville Declaration, the heads of state of the Economic and Monetary Community of Central Africa (CEMAC) signed a document stating the creation of the *CEMAC Space for Higher Education, Research and Professional Training* (CEMAC, 2005). At this time, the Tarragona Declaration of Mediterranean countries, with 33 participating universities intending to create a *Euro-Mediterranean Area of Higher Education and Research,* had also come into creation (Meditteranean University Forum, 2005). In 2014, a revised version of the 1981 Arusha Convention was signed by more than a third of the 41 participating African countries, and this step was influenced by the Regional Conference on Higher Education of 2008, where an *African Higher Education Area* was declared as an objective for Africa (United Nations Education, Scientific and Cultural Organization (UNESCO), 2014).

In light of the rapid expansion of – especially private – African higher education institutions, since the early 2000s, the question of quality has increasingly received more attention (Tefera, 2008b). Both the African Union, in its harmonization strategy, and the African Association of Universities (AAU), supported by UNESCO and the World Bank, have been aiming at developing a quality assurance system for which the launch of an African Quality Assurance Network in 2009 marked an important milestone (Huisman et al., 2012). This initiative, among others, is also proof of an on-going dominating role played by international actors in African higher education development (Tefera, 2008a), which is perpetuated by the fact that "external forces, either through their own internal think-tanking or by alliances with powerful players [...] influence local institutions toward a favoured policy track [...] through their financial and technical muscle" (Tefera, 2008a).

3 From EU Models to New Concepts: The Case of the Pauwes Curriculum Development

As the Bologna process has constituted a 'European brand', with tools such as the European Credit Transfer System (ECTS), it is necessary to ask why and to what extent African higher education policy has chosen to develop "reliable instruments to help them have a good place in the world competition and the brains hunt" (Croché, 2009), not only with tools from models in different regions of the world.

The French-specific model of licence-master-doctorate (LMD), including the modularization and credit transfer system (ECTS), has been adopted by some countries in North and West Africa, with the French government, the EU and the World Bank playing an active role in its promotion (Huisman et al., 2012). In the example of Cameroon, this has been justified locally by both the need for international comparability and the international recognition of Cameroonian degrees and its graduates (Eta, 2015). In light of globalization and compelling factors to make one's degree structures compatible, other features that have been newly adopted in the African higher education landscape are two-semester academic years. The consequence of internationalization is an exchange between educational systems worldwide, in particular with regards to enhancing possibilities to draw on the experiences of others elsewhere (Eta, 2015), however, while adapting to internationalization requirements is something that is done to not be left behind, it must also be a conscious policy decision (Sall, Hamidou Nacuzon, & Ndjaye, 2007).

The European idea of student mobility, which lowers the barriers for students to spend part of their studies in another country, beyond providing international visibility, also ignites a consciousness for the continent (Charlier & Croché, 2011). When adopting Bologna-modelled higher education policy harmonization in Africa, intra-Africa student and staff mobility has similarly been proposed as an advantage and has been based on the assumption that aligned systems will facilitate mobility processes (Huisman et al., 2012), which is a presupposition that has proven true for Europe overall. However, as Ogachi (2009) points out, it is necessary to address the challenge which inevitably presents itself regarding "how to utilize imported curriculum for local knowledge and curricula requirements while being ready to share knowledge unique to regional imperatives" (Ogachi, 2009, p. 343). Cooperation agreements and partnerships are generally formed and based on previous and established relationships between countries, more than on a factual needs assessments (Charlier & Croché, 2011). Overall, the advancement of the Bologna process ideas in Africa, while voluntary, have also at times been coercive (Eta, 2015).

The development of internationalization processes in global higher education addresses the demand to meet expectations of high-quality teaching and research (Sall et al., 2007). The PAUWES curriculum has been developed in a process that included several workshops with a group of international experts from AU member states and leading academic institutions, who were invited to participate in a curriculum planning process that began in September 2012. Within one year, the curriculum was designed in a sequence of five workshops: Curriculum Development Workshop, Pre-Validation Curriculum Workshop, Validation Curriculum Workshop, Curriculum Refinement Workshop, and Curriculum Harmonization Workshop. In the initial working group phase, the topics "Learning Outcomes and Skills", "Programme structure, modules, courses", "Teaching methods", "Target groups, Admission Requirements, Recruiting, Marketing" were discussed, and this was followed by the second plenary phase, with an agenda addressing the topics of "Quality control and Continuing Development", "(African) Placement", and "Alumni Work" (African Union Commission, Direction Générale de la Recherche Scientifique et du Développement Technologique, University of Tlemcen, Deutsche Gesellschaft für Internationale Zusammenarbeit (GIZ) GmbH, 2012).

Through a follow-up, Lead Coordinators were responsible for finalizing the curricula and involving additional experts as coordinators of curriculum modules, drafting the course descriptions of the single modules. Two interlinked curricula for Master's programmes were developed in Water and Energy Sciences, consisting of a total of 120 ECTS (according to European credit standards), 30 ECTS per semester, plus 30 ECTS for the thesis. Both programmes contain an engineering track as well as a governance track. There are a number of common courses across all four programmes, which account for the sociopolitical aspects of the programme, and these include courses in 'Academic

Writing ', 'Communication', 'Marketing', 'Networking', 'Entrepreneurship and Intrapreneurship ', 'Project Design and Management ', 'African History ', 'Human Rights and Gender'. As can be seen from electives such as 'Rural Energy Supply', the curriculum has also been designed to address topics specific to the African context (PAUWES, 2013). The Algerian Ministry of Higher Education and Scientific Research has promptly accredited the two Master's programmes, with both engineering and policy/governance tracks.

The development of these programmes is a new concept that was a result of a joint harmonization effort; African scholars met and developed the curriculum as to work towards good and realistic outcomes, based on Africa-specific realities and challenges. European expertise was integrated as well but was only limited to methodological feedback, input on guidelines, and structural and organizational know-how. The intensive exchange on this occasion marks a new level of pan-African collaboration in higher education where the ownership and decision-making is conceptually entirely African, as well as innovative, and does not replicate European models designed for other contexts from the past. Five modules have been developed so far and an application to secondary school-level curriculum development is conceivable.

4   Demand for Qualification Harmonization in High-Level Recruitment for Excellence Programme Teaching

Drawing on extracts from amended reports covering the first academic year, including respective annexes (Sebihi & Schoelen, 2015b), the following section illustrates the issue of staff recruitment within the programme. In the establishment phase, the data presented is not relevant in terms of quantity, but in terms of quality because it allows an insight into an essential aspect of academic institution-building.

The first PAUWES Master's programmes in engineering (water and energy sciences specialization) commenced at the end of October 2014 with 26 students, ten specializing in Water, and sixteen in Energy. Until long-term academic staff will start working at PAUWES, following a recruitment process on the AU level, teaching at the Institute is being delivered by short-term academic staff, who usually teach block courses between two to six weeks' long. Teaching operations started in mid-November 2014 with two short-term professors initially, one for the water specialization and one for the specialization in energy.

Teaching has been delivered in a block format of two to six weeks depending on credit hours. Examinations have always taken place directly after the end of each course, as stipulated in the Canevas, with one day in between allowing for revision. Lecturers were contracted for two additional days in order to mark exams before departing. This 'flying faculty' model as a quick-fix innovative solution, is a model that is also used by international organizations such as the United Nations University Institutes. Duties of the short-term professors also include suggestions of adaptations to the curriculum.

Capacity-planning, including room planning, was achieved for twenty-six courses, and twenty-three short-term professors of fifteen different nationalities were recruited, both through a formal application process and head-hunting when necessary. Professors were recruited through a pre-screening and formal selection committee consisting of accomplished academics from the five geographical regions of Africa, who established a shortlist based on an evaluation sheet with candidates' best match to the position advertised. The recruitment recommendations were then forwarded to PAUWES, which communicated the selected academics to its Institute Board for final review. Subsequently, as per PAUWES policy, the Institute sent the shortlist to the PAU Rectorate for approval.

The call for applications for short-term academic staff was launched in mid-June 2014, with the deadline for application set for mid-July, 2014. Overall, 203 applications were received by more than 100 individuals, of which 87 passed the first round of screening. A total of 23 professors and lecturers were recruited in the first academic year, four of which were females, originating from the following countries: Algeria, France, Jordan, Cameroon, India, Togo, Germany, Ireland, Canada, Nigeria, Tanzania, Morocco, Egypt, and Tunisia. Consequently, most regions of the globe were represented and the African Diaspora contributed to University teaching as well. Several professors were recruited through head-hunting. The 7th, most recent call from November 2016, advertised 19 positions for the second semester of the third academic year at PAUWES, 2016/2017. Courses were paid as per contact hours – between 20 and 60 per course – where one credit equals 10 contact hours. Additionally, health insurance, visa costs, and travel expenses are covered according to PAUWES guidelines (PAUWES, 2016).

There are two mandatory requirements for all short-term positions. Firstly, a candidate must be a full-time Professor at a recognized University, with an earned Ph.D., or be an associate professor with minimum 5 years' experience at an institution of higher education in the thematic field, and secondly, a candidate must have excellent English language proficiency. Additional criteria are:

- Knowledge of national, regional and international accreditation and quality assurance standards and processes;
- Experience in higher education and research environments in Africa;

- Membership in academic and professional national and international networks;
- Experience in relevant areas of teaching and learning, in innovative programme design, and in academic/research development and support;
- Commitment to supporting institutional and programme development;
- Knowledge of French and/or Arabic are additional advantages (PAUWES, 2016).

Overall, operative and planning instruments for establishing a new administration were successfully implemented by adopting innovative measures in recruitment, such as the 'flying faculty' model and block course-teaching for capacity-planning. Recommendations from the experience thus far include starting the recruitment and capacity-planning process early and calculating a two-person full-time recruitment team, if necessary, with external expertise (e.g. consultants), for a period of approximately three to four months, to factor in and address last-minute cancellations by head-hunting, and to recruit long-term lecturers and avoid block courses with a heavy load of teaching hours (Sebihi & Schoelen, 2015a). These lessons learned to give crucial insights into the set-up of the University, with the conclusion that an establishment period over five years will be necessary to put well-organized Institute structures in place.

With regards to mechanisms of recruitment, the AUC is directly involved as, according to the regulations, PAUWES personnel are AU staff members. Special rules allowing the recruitment of international short-term professors have been applied until 2016. While guidelines exist for the process on the AU level, the universities that are a part of PAU have not been concerned so far. In addition, the fact that long-term recruitment is tied to the nationality of an AU member state – regardless of place of current or long-term residence – hinders possibilities to recruit members of the Diaspora. From a bureaucratic point of view, this process has proven to be somewhat complicated and lengthy, especially given the size of the AUC. As excellence in a competitive environment requires a certain degree of freedom, such as the freedom to recruit reputed academics from different parts of the world, it is recommended to have Pan-African University Institutes conduct their own staff selection process independently, by means of an Academic Steering Committee.

5 The Role of New Technologies in Quality Assurance and Standardization Processes – The Pauwes LMS as Best-Practice

In recent years, the development of Web 2.0 technologies has deeply affected education policies and pedagogies, leading to an increasing integration of curricular content, learning strategies, and technology practices. Internet-based technologies have a considerable impact on present-day issues in international higher education. They foster some of the main objectives of the Bologna reform, such as mobility – by means of digital learning and teaching modules, students' stay abroad is being integrated into their course more efficiently, intensely, and successfully – and international cooperation, which is stimulated by web-based, innovative forms of collaborations. On the individual level, institutions are able to enhance their marketing activities through digital media and thus become more visible on an international level. From an international development cooperation perspective, offering digital learning and e-learning elements can also contribute to the important goal of reducing the skilled workers gap in developing and transition countries and, most importantly, can build local know-how.

Information and Communication Technologies (ICT) are also being attributed a significant role in the ongoing internationalization of African higher education institutions. For the continent in particular, "eliminating chronic isolation means providing dependable ICT access to the marginalized academic and research communities, thus encouraging them to become engaged members of the larger global scholarly society" (Tefera, 2008a, 2008b). It is still not uncommon that the benefits of increasing globalization cannot be reaped when there is a lack of or insufficient institutional development and quality assurance, which need to match international standards. Consequently, the African challenge is, "how to design a quality assurance standard that addresses national, regional and global trends in higher education" (Ogachi, 2009). In this context, ICT has facilitated tapping into academic migrants' potential through facilitated connectivity in their host countries and could therefore effectively counteract brain drain by stimulating brain circulation (Tefera, 2008b).

As Botha (2012) points out, professional learning communities can overcome pre-existing differences in students' individual backgrounds. Dedicated systems are therefore ideal for bringing all members of the academic community together and for ensuring a balanced and equal level of participation. Likewise, academic staff benefit from assessment data generated for advancing teaching methods (Botha, 2012). Considering the active involvement of different types of users within the academic community, a Learning Management System (LMS) proposes an answer to the issue of theorising stakeholders' participation within an African higher education quality assurance system, a concept which is still novel to education, and, furthermore, should be specifically fitted to each institutional context (Jita, 2006). As Gomez-Ruis, Rodriguez-Gomez, and Ibarra-Saiz, (2013) have pointed out, learning-oriented e-Assessment, in particular, provides a means for an educational institution to keep up with present-day social and professional demands, and, furthermore, it allows for the development of several key academic and professional competencies, such as critical thinking, the application of knowledge in problem-solving, and the improvement of communication skills.

In line with the African Union's strategies for Science and Technology Innovation, PAUWES is keen on integrating a framework for technology-mediated learning within its existing academic practices. The main objective there has been to create a platform for sharing, enhancing and standardizing information, communication, and practices within the PAU network. It was decided to implement an LMS as a software system that encompasses tools designed to manage user learning interventions and provide access to online learning services for students, lecturers, and administrators. The software system allows the development and delivery of educational courses using the internet as a delivery system.

The PAUWES' own LMS[2] has been deployed in three phases. Firstly, a 'Design' phase, including a needs analysis for academic and administrative capabilities, open-source software featuring communication, course organization, time tabling and administrative components, didactical and instructional concepts for future training, and an information exchange platform for virtual activities and communication. Secondly, 'e-Learning Pedagogies' phase consists in the development of e-learning pedagogies founded on socio-cultural theories, training manuals, workshops, and training opportunities for staff and students, a needs assessment for further e-learning capacity development, theoretical concepts with practical activities and demonstrations, and assessment schemes based on collaborative values. Thirdly – yet to be accomplished – the 'PAU network integration and practice dissemination' phase, which is the integration of the PAUWES platform within the wider PAU network, encompasses strategies for networking and collaboration, including identification and mapping of stakeholders, monitoring and evaluation of e-learning provisions, sharing practices and theoretical foundations of e-learning, and the development of policies for cross-country and organization collaboration.

The LMS features a dedicated facility as functional for each of the following communication or learning administration activities: Announcement, Notes, Document, Forum, Multimedia, Learning Track, Links, References, News, Assignment, Assessment, Portfolio Management, and Learning Cube. The design, as well as the three-phase process, ensure a tailor-made software product oriented on PAUWES' needs, which also adapts to the implementation progress. So far, phases 1 and 2 have been realized. The local PAUWES IT Administrator has been trained in its utilization, all short-term lecturers receive an introduction to the system upon their arrival, and students are employing the

LMS on a daily basis for their course work. The LMS has proven to be a very helpful tool for quality assurance and standardization processes, as important documents such as course evaluation sheets are available online for students to submit. PAU is currently revising its e-learning strategy and it intends to upscale the PAUWES LMS to the PAU level.

Another important element in the PAUWES Institute's e-learning environment is the Community of Practice (CoP). The PAUWES CoP is an online social collaboration platform that connects PAUWES students and alumni, as well as researchers, practitioners and private-sector actors from PAUWES' larger network. It revolves around the four main pillars of its objectives, 'Networking and Interaction', 'Companies and Job Database', 'Knowledge-sharing and Discussion' and 'Online Events/Webinars', which all address the main functionality clusters of Profiles, News, Exchange and Discussion, Knowledge Factory, Organization/Company Database and Vacancies, and Events/Webinars. The Community's target group are its own stakeholders, namely PAUWES students and alumni, scientists and lecturers at PAUWES, affiliated researchers and lecturers, companies and start-ups, experts, managers and policy-makers, NGOs, Think Tanks and research organizations, International and Pan-African networks, organizations and institutions (Tambo, Schoelen, & Passelewitz, 2016).

The network is student-driven and managed by a leadership team and seven thematic groups with a specific focus such as 'Career Development'. The institute's administrative staff is closely involved in its coordination. The platform covers offline activity online. Students' individual commitment to it is voluntary, and this kind of extra-curricular activity constitutes a best-practice example of the innovative approach to learning at PAUWES, which is based on problem-solving and analyzing through joint collaboration efforts.

6 Cross-Border Collaboration Opportunities for the Internationalization of Higher Education with a Focus on Africa-EU Institutional Partnerships

The Higher Education Consortium supporting PAUWES during the first project phase, consisting of the Center for Development Research (ZEF), affiliated with the University of Bonn in Germany, the United Nations University Institute for Environment and Human Security (UNU-EHS), and the Institute for the Tropics and the Subtropics (ITT) at the Cologne University of Applied Sciences in Germany, was funded by the German Academic Exchange Service DAAD (Deutscher Akademischer Austauschdienst), and has been accompanying the implementation process and implementing a variety of activities at and in close collaboration with PAUWES (Zentrum für Entwicklungsforschung (ZEF)/Center for Development Research, University of Bonn, 2014); United Nations University Institute for Environment and Human Security [UNU-EHS], 2015). Some of the activities derived from this cooperation serve as an example of an institutional partnership in the Africa-EU context.

Most recently, in March 2016, the Africa-EU Renewable Energy Cooperation Programme (RECP), PAUWES, and the University of Tlemcen jointly organised the first Africa-EU Symposium on Renewable Energy Research and Innovation, with 135 international experts attending the event, including representing universities, research institutions, the public sector, industry associations, and international organizations from thirty countries in Africa and Europe. The event successfully achieved its goals, fostering the dialogue and exchange between renewable energy experts, promoting Africa-EU academic networking, research cooperation and sharing of information, and building capacities to access research funds and cooperation platforms. During a series of panel discussions, thematic sessions and workshops, the needs, challenges and potentials of renewable energy research and innovation in Africa were identified (Africa-EU Renewable Energy Cooperation Programme, the University of Tlemcen, the Pan-African University Institute of Water and Energy Sciences, 2016). The symposium greatly contributed to the PAUWES Institute's visibility as well as that of the University of Tlemcen, and it was the first of its kind on an international scale. PAUWES students were actively involved in the preparation and implementation of the symposium, by taking on registration, translation, and media coverage duties prior to and during the event, which gave them opportunities to interact informally with the experts present and helped them further develop required organizational and communicative soft skills.

The foundation of this joint venture was laid during the Consortium-facilitated first symposium at PAUWES in 2015, titled "International Symposium State of the Art – Challenges and Trends in Energy and Water in Africa". It aimed to kick off activities of the PAUWES Community of Practice by providing a platform for stakeholders, actors, and institutions, interested or already engaged in the cooperation with PAUWES, to discuss challenges, novel solutions, and trends in energy and water in Africa in general, and in the context of PAUWES specific activities. Furthermore, international experts and representatives of international institutions of development were able to use the event as a platform to learn about the institutional framework in German/African/Algerian science and technology cooperation, benefit from encounters with industry and education leaders and policy makers, and identify synergies to increase impact with regards to education and research at PAUWES (PAUWES, 2015). These two events constitute excellent examples of collaboration opportunities, with a focus on Africa-EU institutional partnerships and can be considered examples of best practices in higher education partnership. PAUWES has also been successfully practicing cooperation with African higher education institutions by involving professors from different countries – many of them former or current short-term lecturers at PAUWES – in Master's thesis supervision and defence processes of the first batch of graduates, who graduated in October 2016.

7   Conclusion

PAUWES can be considered a pilot model institution of two types of cooperation: bilateral cooperation, which allows new Africa-EU collaboration opportunities to be transferred to other parts of the continent and other regions in the world; and multilateral cooperation between individual African higher education institutions and partners. With regards to African higher education policy trends in relation to the Bologna Process, rather than playing a passive role in receiving or adopting pre-existing models, Africa has been significantly active in making its own conscious policy decisions, employing and advancing some concepts inspired by the Bologna process, among others. This has allowed for a two-way knowledge transfer/sharing between Africa and the EU, which shall be reinforced not at the detriment of cooperation within Africa.

As new intra-continental cooperation programmes are to be launched, with student and research exchanges and best-practice forums as tools, EU involvement in these strategies, if so wished, is yet to be determined. African countries' cultural identity should be the basis for higher education institutions' development, and this means drawing on the experiences of actors involved in academia so that curriculum and research development can eventually leave behind the colonial and neo-colonial impacts that are still present in some higher education policy elements.

Overall, Europe, in terms of the Bologna Process, has long overlooked the African continent. The Bologna process has taken a long time to come into shape and extend on to a global level, and this is also due to the complexity of the different national higher education systems, in different European countries such as in Germany, France or Italy. African countries are now in a position to evaluate some of these Bologna and post-Bologna experiences for their own continental system, taking into account their diversity in terms of culture, history, and existing structures, and they can, in fact, also create something new. The way forward for the African continent on a whole likely comprises policy-making for research and curriculum development and incorporating innovative concepts such as those already implemented in the Pan-African University Institutes. The case study of PAUWES features the first stage of this process in learning and teaching harmonization. The next step will be increased mobility.

In this context, simply taking on policies implemented in Europe will not be relevant, and, where applicable, outcomes of official political meetings might serve as an inspiration. Hesitations, doubts and bureaucratic mechanisms which in the past have slowed down the higher education harmonization process in Europe bear testimony to the fact that young, dynamic African economies have an advantage in advancing respective processes if and when these are sufficiently backed on an organizational level by strategic plans that include quality assurance, and when they are prioritized in political agendas.

Notes

1 Visit the Institute's website: http://www.pauwes.univ-tlemcen.dz and http://www.pau-au.org (accessed October 30, 2016).
2 Available online: http://www.pauwes-lms.univ-tlemcen.dz (accessed December 14, 2016).

References

Ajayi, J., Lameck, K., Goma, G., & Johnson, A. (1996). *The African experience with higher education*. Athens, OH: Ohio University Press, Scott Quadrangle.

Africa-EU Renewable Energy Cooperation Programme, the University of Tlemcen, the Pan African University Institute of Water and Energy Sciences. (2016). *Summary report Africa-EU Symposium on renewable energy research and innovation*. Tlemcen.

African Union Commission (AUC). (2017). *Pan African University (PAU) – Université Panafricaine: Admissions*. Addis Ababa. Retrieved from https://pau-au.net/en/admissions

African Union Commission, Direction Générale de la Recherche Scientifique et du Développement Technologique, University of Tlemcen, Deutsche Gesellschaft für Internationale Zusammenarbeit (GIZ) GmbH. (2012). *Regional Curriculum Development Workshop for the Launch of the PAU*. Tlemcen.

Altbach, P. G. (2007). Globalization and the university: Realities in an unequal world. In J. J. F. Forest & P. G. Altbach (Eds.), *International handbook of higher education* (pp. 121–139). Dordrecht: Springer.

Botha, E. M. (2012). Turning the tide: Creating Professional Learning Communities (PLC) to improve teaching practice and learning in South African public schools. *Africa Education Review, 9*(2), 395–411. https://doi.org/10.1080/18146627.2012.722405

Boucher, M. (2014). The gap between intention and results in the Bologna-based university system. In P. Hayes & J. El Gammal (Eds.), *Wissenschaft-, Technik- und Umweltsoziologie. Universitätskulturen – L'Université en perspective – The Future of the University* (1st ed., pp. 215–232). Bielefeld: Transcript.

Charlier, J.-E., & Croché, S. (2011). The Bologna process: A tool for Europe's hegemonic project on Africa. *Power and Education, 3*(3), 304–316. http://dx.doi.org/10.2304/power.2011.3.3.304

Charlier, J.-E., Croché, S., & Ndoye, A. K. (2009). *Les universités africaines francophones face au LMD: Les effets du processus de Bologne sur l'enseignement supérieur au-delà des frontières de l'Europe. Thélème: Vol. 1.* Louvain-La-Neuve: Bruylant Academia.

Croché, S. (2009). Bologna network: A new sociopolitical area in higher education. *Globalization, Societies, and Education, 7*(4), 489–503. http://dx.doi.org/10.1080/14767720903412317

Eta, E. A. (2015). Policy borrowing and transfer, and policy convergence: justifications for the adoption of the Bologna Process in the CEMAC region and the Cameroonian higher education system through the LMD reform. *Comparative Education, 51*(2), 161–178. https://doi.org/10.1080/03050068.2014.941174

Ghouati, A. (impr. 2011). *Processus de Bologne et enseignement supérieur au Maghreb. Europe Maghreb.* Paris: L'Harmattan.

Gomez-Ruis, M.-A., Rodriguez-Gomez, G., & Ibarra-Saiz, M. S. (2013). Development of basic competencies of students in higher education through learning oriented e-Assessment. *e-Journal of Educational Research, Assessment and Evaluation, 19*, 1–17. doi:10.7203/relieve.19.1.2609

Huisman, J., Adelman, C., Hsieh, C.-C., Shams, F., & Wilkins, S. (2012). Europe's Bologna process and its impact on global higher education. In D. K. Deardorff, H. d. Wit, & J. Heyl (Eds.), *The Sage handbook of international higher education* (pp. 81–100). Thousand Oaks, CA: Sage Publications.

Jita, L. C. (2006). Theorizing stakeholder participation within the higher education quality assurance system in South Africa. *South African Journal of Higher Education, 20*(6), 924–931.

Koehn, P. H., & Obamba, M. O. (2014). *The transnationally partnered university: Insights from research and sustainable development collaborations in Africa.* New York, NY: Palgrave Macmillan.

Ogachi, O. (2009). Internationalization vs regionalization of higher education in East Africa and the challenges of quality assurance and knowledge production. *Higher Education Policy, 22*, 331–347. Retrieved from http://www.palgrave-journals.com/hep/2009.9

Pan African University Institute of Water and Energy Sciences (including Climate Change) (PAUWES). (2013). *Curriculum master of science in energy*. Retrieved from http://pauwes.univ-tlemcen.dz/wp-content/uploads/2014/03/PAUWES_curriculum_MSc-Energy.pdf

Pan African University Institute of Water and Energy Sciences (including Climate Change) (PAUWES). (2015). *International Symposium State of the Art – Challenges and trends in energy and water in Africa: Report*. Tlemcen.

Pan African University Institute of Water and Energy Sciences (including Climate Change) (PAUWES). (2016). *Call for short-term academic staff: Academic positions and job descriptions*. Retrieved from http://pauwes.univ-tlemcen.dz/wp-content/uploads/2016/11/Call-for-Short-Term-Academic-Staff-Summer-2017-final1.pdf

Sall, H. N., & Ndjaye, B. D. (2007). Higher education in Africa: Between perspectives opened by the Bologna process and the commodification of education. *European Education, 39*(4), 43–57. https://doi.org/10.2753/EUE1056-4934390403

Sebihi, A., & Schoelen, L. (2015a). *Factsheet academic affairs first academic year 2014–2015*. Tlemcen.

Sebihi, A., & Schoelen, L. (2015b). *Report academic affairs first academic year 2014/2015*. Tlemcen.

Tambo, E., Schoelen, L., & Passelewitz, L. (2016). *PAUWES Community of Practice (CoP): Online platform for exchanging, networking and MORE...* Bonn, Tlemcen.

Tefera, D. (2008a). Internationalization of higher education: Legacy and journey in the African landscape. In D. Teferra & J. Knight (Eds.), *Higher education in Africa: The international dimension* (pp. 553–559). Chestnut Hill, MA/Accra: Boston College Center for International Higher Education; Association of African Universities.

Tefera, D. (2008b). The international dimension of higher education in Africa: Status, challenges, and prospects. In D. Teferra & J. Knight (Eds.), *Higher education in Africa: The international dimension* (pp. 44–79). Chestnut Hill, MA/Accra: Boston College Center for International Higher Education; Association of African Universities.

Tefera, D., & Altbach, P. G. (2003). Trends and perspectives in African higher education. In D. Teferra & P. G. Altbach (Eds.), *African higher education. An international reference handbook* (pp. 3–14). Bloomington, IN: Indiana University Press.

United Nations University Institute for Environment and Human Security (UNU-EHS). (2015). *UNU-EHS supports development of a Pan African University campus in Algeria*. Bonn. Retrieved from http://ehs.unu.edu/news/news/unu-ehs-supports-development-of-pan-african-university-campus-in-algeria.html

Vögtle, E. M., & Martens, K. (2014). The Bologna process as a template for transnational policy coordination. *Policy Studies, 35*(3), 246–263. https://doi.org/10.1080/01442872.2013.875147

Woldegiorgis, E., Jonck, P., & Goujon, A. (2015). Regional higher education initiatives in Africa: A comparative Analysis with the Bologna Process. *International Journal of Higher Education, 1*, 241–253.

Zentrum für Entwicklungsforschung (ZEF)/Center for Development Research, University of Bonn. (2014). *ZEF embarks on cooperation in higher education with the Pan African University*. Bonn. Retrieved from http://www.zef.de/index.php?id=2168&tx_ttnews%5Btt_news%5D=6206&cHash=21ad033fafb1489b39b658d4bdf80397

CHAPTER 7

Internationalizing Higher Education through Service Learning: The Case of the University for Development Studies, Ghana

Lydia Kwoyiga and Agnes Atia Apusigah

Internationalization processes are an integral part of the future of partnership in higher education. Through internalization processes, universities open up their national systems to international experiences, via academic mobility and other strategic alliances. This chapter highlights the role that service learning plays in internationalization of higher education.

Universities have long been associated with the concept of internationalization and in recent times there has been a drastic change in the conceptualization of internationalization, which had the tendency to take the form of universalization of knowledge and related research, and/or the mobility of students and scholars (de Wit et al., 2015). According to Hawawini (2011), the concept has been discussed and analyzed in several reports, articles, and books, with some universities initiating the analysis and discussion themselves. However, higher education internationalization processes remain connoted by a variety of diverse actions, tools, and motives, for different actors. While some see it as a means, others see it as an end in itself (Qiang, 2003). It is therefore not surprising when de Wit (2002) states that, "as the international dimension of higher education gains more attention and recognition, people tend to use it in the way that best suits their purpose" (de Wit, 2002, p. 14). The author further explains that the concept is multifaceted and complex in nature, which makes it difficult to conceptualize. It is not strange therefore that de Wit and associates (2015) see it as an umbrella term under which different dimensions, components, approaches and activities of education are sheltered.

One key and general trend that has been emerging from a variety of different higher education internationalization efforts is the extension of service learning (SL) to international students. This has often taken the form of students moving from their home countries to other destinations throughout the course of their studies or immediately after, in order to learn about the practical aspects of their study programmes, while also providing services to communities and organizations who are hosting them.

Some benefits of SL for students have been noted in a study conducted in Ghana by Boakye-Boaten (2011) entitled *"The Ghana Street Children Literacy Initiatives"*. These benefits found include: development of leadership skills and responsibilities, a better understanding of roles as global citizens, development of a high sense of moral and civic responsibility, and enhancement of students' international and intercultural competence. According to Boakye-Boaten, ethics, internationalism, and diversity are the key aspects and assets of SL.

In Ghana, the promotion of SL in higher education has been met with mixed reactions. While it has been generally embraced as a way of shifting higher education from a traditional "ivory tower" approach, with a highly theoretical focus on teaching and research that is disconnected from the realities of society to a practical and environmentally sensitive educational approach, its implementation has been fraught with challenges. As far back as the 1960s, a former vice-chancellor, Professor Kwapong, preempted the need to refocus higher education toward community service, highlighting the disjuncture between scholarship, community and the national development realities of Ghana.

Indeed, the use of the term SL has yet to gain currency, and it is more popularly used with the terms industrial attachment or practical experience. No matter what jargon is in vogue, the essence has been to create a platform for experiential learning, while giving back to society. However, the extent to which SL has inspired practical training programmes in Ghana is debatable. Undoubtedly, the UDS has been a pioneer in its attempt to model an approximation of SL by framing the experience in the context of joint learning and strategizing among multiple stakeholders, including students, faculty, local government authorities, traditional leaders, and communities. Indeed, apart from the UDS, which has a third-trimester system where students are sent to local communities to stay and learn, no other university in Ghana, particularly the public ones, fully runs such a programme as a formal part of its academic curriculum (Kaburise, 2006, cited in Tagoe, 2014). What comes close to a standardized SL programme in Ghanaian public universities are industry-based experiences, such as attachments and internships, which are also additional practical training requirements for UDS students.

There is thus a need for further analysis of SL implementation, particularly through an understanding of how the Third Trimester Field Practical Programme (TTFPP), as an SL programme, could be strategically packed for internationalization. The analysis that ensues in this chapter looks at the UDS TTFPP as a site for SL, with potential for international studies. This chapter examines trends in internationalization processes of higher education in Ghana, discussing its drivers and shapers while also examining SL as a tool for higher education internationalization, and the UDS TTFPP as an SL programme. This chapter highlights the strengths, benefits, challenges, and options for a sustainable improvement of the programme, for meeting both local and international needs.

1   Conceptualizing Internationalization

The currency of higher education internationalization has given rise to diverse efforts to define and confine the agenda and practices that are a part of internationalization processes, which has resulted in diverse conceptualizations of the phenomena. Notable among them is the definition given by Knight (2003), who sees internationalization as "the process of integrating an international/intercultural dimension into teaching, research and service functions of the institutions" (Knight, 2003, p. 21). However, this definition has been criticized by Hawawini (2011) for its failure to capture the importance of the process inherent to internationalization, which he links to globalization. However, there is more to internationalization than globalization. Literature has shown how movements in internationalization processes are often one-sided, going from the West to the rest of the world, with the reverse hardly happening. Beyond this, in internationalization processes, there is also the drive to promote intercultural and hands-on learning, which is central to any SL initiative.

The concept has also been seen as involving "systematic sustained efforts aimed at making higher education responsive to the requirements and challenges related to the globalization of societies, economy and labour markets" (Van der Wende, 1997, p. 19, cited in Qiang 2003). This perspective has tended to characterize many proactive efforts, especially by higher education institutions (HEIs) of developing countries, seeking to establish linkages with counterparts elsewhere. Through internationalization processes, the practical challenges of resource paucity and advancements in science and technology drive HEIs in developing countries to reach out to HEIs elsewhere in order to benefit from their experiences, while compensating for their limitations.

However, as indicated by Knight (2008, cited in de Wit et al., 2015), internationalization of higher education should take cognizance of two key components in policies and programmes, as these are constantly evolving and becoming increasingly intertwined. These components are *internationalization abroad*, which includes all forms of education across borders, and *internationalization at home*, which relates to curriculum and activities that shape international/global understanding and intercultural skills. Thus, higher education internationalization should make it possible to connect with HEIs outside one's local area, while allowing curricula to be broadened in order to enrich local learning.

1.1 Trends and Forms in Ghana

According to Effah and Senadzi (2008), within the Ghanaian context, internationalization of higher education is rolling out on a modest scale, with the country's public universities making giant strides to attract international students, as access to education abroad for Ghanaian students continues to improve. Various partnerships are being established and are resulting in curriculum exchanges, joint research and publication, and staff and student mobility across the border. Such efforts are also marked by the establishment of International Studies Centres on local campuses, as coordinating centres for both local and foreign students and staff.

Akplu (2016) explains that the process of higher education internationalization in Ghana is gaining grounds especially regarding the contributions of private participation. On the other hand, Effah and Senadzi (2008) sustain that private participation in higher education is a more recent issue. In the private sector, such partnerships exist amid the growing trend toward the establishment of overseas campuses in partnership with local actors. Examples include the University of Maastricht in the Suez Canal, Egypt, and the Sikkim Manipal University, in Accra, Ghana.

As the process has unfolded, the following features have tended to define the nature of higher education internationalization in Ghana. Firstly, it manifests in the form of actor mobility, whereby Ghanaian students get the opportunity to study abroad and international students enroll in Ghanaian universities as well. The University of Ghana and the Kwame Nkrumah University of Science and Technology are the net receivers of students who have undertaken this form of internationalization through a study abroad experience. In recent times, students from several West African countries, especially Nigeria, clamour for enrolment in Ghanaian universities. Another dimension of student mobility characterizing higher education internationalization in Ghana takes the form of Visitorship, Research, Joint or Double Degrees, and Language Studies programmes. Some other attributes of the internationalization process are: the offering of foreign curricula and awards in the form of certificates, diplomas and degrees through collaborations with other HEIs, the location of offshore campuses, the adoption of institutional governance systems from foreign HEIs, the recruitment of scholars as faculty members, and the E-education and Distance Education market.

1.2 Actors, Drivers, and Shapers of the Higher Education Internationalization Process

According to Effah and Senadzi (2008), the propelling factor driving the internationalization process is the desire to be part of the global knowledge process. In the case of Ghana, this includes the need to bridge the knowledge gap between Ghana and the rest of the world, and the impetus to open opportunities for Ghanaian HEIs to access new ideas that can lead to improvement in research, teaching, and learning. Another factor is the yearning of institutions to promote knowledge and understanding of international cultures, which occurs with students from diverse backgrounds meeting and interacting through learning. These kinds of learning exchanges have the tendency to inculcate in students understanding of one another, appreciation of cultural differences, and promotion of international peace and harmony. The need to increase the international patronage of Ghana's HEIs with students from the United States (USA) and West Africa is yet another stimulus driving the process, as this can not only market the potentials of these institutions but also contribute to generating income through the fees paid by international students.

In order for the process to unfold, some actors are required to fuel it. Effah and Senadzi (2008) have categorized three significant groups of actors in the process.

The first comprises actors at the national level, including the Government of Ghana, with the Ministries of Education, Finance and Foreign Affairs. These agencies go into bilateral agreements with other countries in specific areas of education cooperation, and the agreements are implemented directly by the government or given to public higher education institutions to execute. These agreements are formalized in the form of Memoranda of Understanding or working agreements. Scholarships for Ghanaian students to study abroad, research and publications collaborations and technical support often characterize them.

The second group of actors are universities who launch independent international efforts themselves in areas such as student and faculty exchanges, research collaboration, curricula development, and technical cooperation with higher education institutions abroad. For instance, in 2015, the University of Ghana took it upon itself to prepare a report detailing strategies to internationalize the entire university. The aspects targeted were the internationalization of the policies and strategies of the University to fall in line with the policies of its own colleges and schools. Other aspects included partnership strategies and implementation, governance structures, financial and human resources, research development, including research in internationalization processes, academic and administrative staff development, student recruitment strategies, language policies, having programmes be delivered in the English language, curriculum and pedagogy developments, and development of services and information for incoming international students and study abroad and/or exchange students.

The last category of actors comprises organizations or bodies who are international in their outlook and have special interests in education. These include organizations such as the Association of African Universities, the United States Agency for International Development (USAID), the United Kingdom's Department for International Development (DFID), the United Nations Education, Scientific and Cultural Organization, the British Council, the Government of The Netherlands, the Japan International Cooperation Agency (JICA), and the World Bank.

1.3 Policies and Practices

Though the country is witnessing various forms of higher education internationalization, policy development in this regard actually paints a gloomy picture. Effah and Senadzi (2008) lament the absence of clear and coherent internationalization strategies, at both national and institutional levels. They have also offered suggestions for the measures at policy and institution levels that could improve the situation. Effah and Senadzi (2008) state that it must be obligatory that five (5) percent of admission slots be given to international students. Further, they suggest that universities' International Programme offices be headed by deans or directors saddled with responsibilities of marketing the university abroad, coordinating existing student/staff exchanges, developing new exchanges, organizing orientation programmes for international students, and handling welfare issues/accommodation. Moreover, many universities in the country, such as the University of Ghana and the Kwame Nkrumah University of Science and Technology, have built hostels specifically for international students, and the facilities are well furnished and spacious.

Undoubtedly, against the backdrop of growing competition, each Ghanaian university has instituted its own local mechanisms, including policies, strategies, and structures, to regulate the process, as the case of the University of Ghana discussed above shows. Other public universities, such as the Kwame Nkrumah University of Science and Technology, the University for Development Studies, the University of Cape Coast and the University of Education have their own mechanisms in place as well for competing in the growing international market.

2 Service Learning and Higher Education Internationalization

2.1 Conceptualizing Service Learning

In considering some of the ways in which efforts to internationalize higher education, particularly in research, can be projected and implemented to meet both global and local needs, SL presents as a cohesive strategy for blending the academic world with a community of work and has increasingly become an important window. Indeed, this is how the UDS conceptualizes its TTFPP initiative. Researchers and students of development studies, political studies, political economy, empowerment studies, and social justice programmes, among many, are required to embark on service learning locally, nationally and internationally. According to Bringle and Hatcher (1996), SL should not be equated to voluntary service. SL is curriculum or course-based, involves credit earning and is a formal requirement built around practical and reflective activities of direct relevance to programme specialization, while voluntary service is extra-curricular and linked to social/moral callings. SL is therefore seen "as a credit-bearing educational experience in which students participate in an organized service activity that meets identified community needs and reflects on the service activity in such a way as to gain further understanding of course content, a broader appreciation of the discipline, and an enhanced sense of civic responsibility" (Bringle & Hart, 1996, p. 2).

A more elaborate definition of SL is the one offered by the USA National and Community Service Act of 1990 (cited in Waterman, 1997), which describes SL as a method (a) under which students learn and develop, through active participation, in thoughtfully organised service experiences that meet actual community needs and that are coordinated and collaborated with the school and community; (b) which is integrated into students' academic curriculum or provides structured time for students to think, talk or write about what the students did and saw during the actual service activity; (c) that provides students with opportunities to use newly acquired skills and knowledge in real life, in their own communities; and (d) that enhances what is taught in school by extending students' learning beyond the classroom and into the community, helping to foster the development of a sense of caring towards others. This definition is apt and more relevant to exploring the context of the TTFPP of UDS. It is worth examining the extent to which the UDS model addresses these prescriptions, with the aim of enriching and extending the learning and benefits to students, communities and staff, and to promote it to international audiences.

2.2 *Criteria for Service Learning*
There are a number of criteria for SL in higher education. The ones offered by the Bennion Community Service (BCS) and discussed by Crews (2002) relate well with the UDS TTFPP. Their criteria are the following:
1. Students in the class provide a needed service to individuals, organizations, schools or other entities.

2. The service experience relates to the subject matter of the course. Every course comes with its teaching and learning objectives, outcomes or expectations. The content of SL thus contributes to meeting the objectives of the courses offered.
3. Activities in the class provide a method or methods for students to think about what they learned through the service experience and how this learning relates to the subject of the class. That is, classroom work is organized around events or activities that necessitate students to connect their understanding with SL and vice versa.
4. The course offers a method to assess the learning derived from the services. Credits are given for the learning experience and its relation to the course, not for the service alone. Students under SL are obliged to spend some hours, days or months offering various services to the study communities.
5. Service interactions in the community recognize the needs of service recipients and offer an opportunity for recipients to be involved in the evaluation of the service. SL is structured towards meeting the needs of students and the improvement of the entire programme, and students are also given the opportunity to appraise the programme in order to determine their level of satisfaction.
6. The service opportunities are aimed at the development of the civic education of students, but can also be focused on career preparation. SL offers a window through which students deepen their civic awareness and engagement. This is because students learn to live on their own, interact with different people, and develop new relationships that come with rights and responsibilities.
7. Knowledge from the discipline informs the service experiences which students are involved in. The nature of SL offers students the opportunity to reflect on their experiences in the community in a well-structured manner, and activities are undertaken to enable students to reflect on their experiences, within a given time frame.
8. The class offers a way to learn from other class members as well as from the instructor. Students do not learn in isolation, but may be put in groups and assigned an instructor.
9. Course options ensure that no student is required to participate in a service placement that creates a religious, political and/or moral conflict for the student.

Limitations of the SL criteria in the BCS include the sole focus on student learning and students' relationships to their studies. There is hardly any mention of the benefits to the community in the process, and it tends to present

SL as a one-sided streak that focuses on the benefits for students and not the mutual benefits to both students and host organizations or communities.

2.3 Nature and form of the Third Trimester Field Practical Programme

Since its establishment, the UDS has adopted practically-oriented methodologies to teaching, learning, research, and outreach services, as a means to fulfil its mandate, spelled out by the PNDCL 279 Section 3, to blend "the academic world with that of the community in order to provide constructive interaction between the two for the total development of Northern Ghana in particular, and the country as a whole". An integral component of this approach is the TTFPP.

The TTFPP is an iterative process (with the work of each year building upon that of the preceding year, in a dynamic manner) and it is modelled as an integrated approach. This integrated approach offers students from various faculties/schools and programmes of the University the opportunity to have an early introduction to inter-professional learning by living and working together in selected communities. The integrated programme covers two phases of engaging students from the first year through to the second year in a single community. As an academic programme, it is mandatory for all students and carries a total of 6 credit hours.

In the first year, students are introduced to aspects of community studies. Students practice community entry and aspects of community diagnosis, using participatory approaches. Emphasis is placed on techniques for needs assessments, which culminate in the assessment of the problems and potentials of the community, through the use of a variety of complementary techniques, as well the suggestion of tentative/possible interventions.

The problems and potentials analysed during the first year serve as the starting point for the activities of the second year, where students are tasked to propose pragmatic interventions to the resolutions of the problems assessed. Students are also expected to demonstrate the use of the identified potentials of the community in their proposals or plans.

2.4 Preparation for the Third Trimester Field Practical Programme

As part of preparations for their fieldwork, first-year students undergo an orientation during the second trimester of the academic year on their respective campuses. The time allocated for the orientation during this time is estimated to one week and is deducted from the eight weeks of the TTFPP period, leaving actual field work to seven weeks. At the start of the third trimester, students go through pre-departure preparation and sensitization, at a venue determined by the TTFPP directorate. Students are required to make adequate preparation for their bedding and lodging while in the field. Essential items that students need to bring along include mattresses, lanterns, torch lights, mosquito nets, First Aid kits, and some protective clothing. Assessments are made during the orientation and in the field. Students who fail to participate in the orientation do not qualify to go to the field and are regarded as having failed in the TTFPP. Students must pass in all the assessment areas to be able to complete the Year One programme.

In the second year, students again are refreshed and oriented with the second-year tasks through an orientation programme like the one given in the first year, on their different campuses. When the third trimester begins, students are expected to follow again the procedure that they applied upon entering and exiting the communities during their first year. Supervision of students before and during the fieldwork follow the same format as in the first year.

2.5   General Objectives of the Third Trimester Field Practical Programme

The general objectives of the integrated TTFPP are to:
1. Help students develop favourable attitudes towards working in rural communities.
2. Expose students, practically, to the nature and dimensions of development problems plaguing rural communities.
3. Provide useful services to Ghanaian communities through the exchange of knowledge and its application to address the felt needs and aspirations of these communities.
4. Generate data for further research in problem-solving development issues, and other issues.

The specific objectives for year 1 are to:
1. Equip students with the basic tools, techniques, and skills required for community studies.
2. Introduce students to community studies through living in and working with communities.
3. Introduce students to the need to blend traditional knowledge with scientific knowledge, in their community studies.
4. Assist students to apply the methods and experiences acquired to collect relevant data, analyse the data and, on that basis, write a comprehensive community profile.

The specific objectives for year 2 are:
1. To assist students to apply methods and skills to the preparation of participatory development planning proposals/plans, as determined by the felt needs of communities/target groups.
2. To introduce students to the practice of the techniques and strategies of development problem-solving.

2.6 Preparation before Community Placement

Due to the fact that the field study communities are under the government's political authority before students enter their study communities, the responsible directorate for TTFPP contacts, informs and seeks permission from local government authorities in order to receive permission for and support towards the programme in the communities. Officials from the university normally meet with the regional minister (s) of the selected regions and their district assemblies to discuss the intentions and present their plans for discussion. After this exercise, field coordinators, who are always and usually lecturers drawn from all faculties, are appointed to supervise students on the field. The first task of these coordinators is community mapping, which is the identification of local communities in the various districts in which students will be dispatched to. The other tasks borne by these coordinators include the supervision of students while on the field, leading other lecturers in the field to assess students, and submitting students' field reports and assessment documents to the Directorate.

2.7 Community Placement

2.7.1 District/Municipal/Metropolitan Assemblies

Before the community mapping commences, various political leaders at the district, municipal and metropolitan levels are contacted by the University's field coordinators. This is done to inform/remind the leaders about the arrival of the students to the communities, and to obtain information regarding the profile of the district and other related information, which is important for the TTFPP so that field coordinators can start mapping the study communities. The meeting of the coordinators and the local assemblies is also done to solicit their support towards the students, while they do their fieldwork. For instance, as part of the report write-up, students may need secondary data about the study district and this can easily be obtained from the District Assembly and other local units. Another reason for the pre-fieldwork meetings is to canvas any other support, which the students may need while on the field.

2.7.2 Community Leaders (Chiefs, Elders/Assembly Persons/Unit Committee Members)

As far as the TTFPP is concerned, the local community plays a major role in the programme, as it is the place where students stay for the period of their fieldwork. During the community mapping process, the study community is often tasked to provide the students with accommodation at no fees. This task normally lies with the chief, elders, assembly person and other opinion leaders in the community. They liaise with community members to get students accommodations.

Some members of the community often willingly offer the students' places to stay and support them with feeding as well. Aside from supporting the students with accommodation, host community members play a major role in community entry and exit processes and also assist students to identify key informants or respondents in the community during their data collection process. Moreover, this caliber of people possesses special knowledge about the study community, which must be captured in the field report. Students, therefore are always advised to value and cherish their presence at all times.

2.7.3   Students Teams

As already mentioned, a team of students in a given study community normally comprises of students from all the faculties/departments in the University. This makes the TTFPP integrated by nature. A team is supposed to have between 10 and 13 students. Once in the community, students are required to conduct proper community entry and exit. Students on the field are expected to gather primary data about the problems, challenges, and potentials of the study communities, facilitate community members undertaking their own needs assessments, in relation to their development needs, and develop a proposal for development intervention.

While on the field, students are supplied with research materials for their studies. Attendance of students is taken daily and no student is allowed to leave the community without informing the group leader and the field coordinator. Each student is supposed to score at least 75% in attendance if not a student will be made to repeat the programme for that year. Students are expected to work as teams during data gathering and proposal writing. Each student has a field note book, which is used to document their daily learning activities in the community. These note books are marked twice by the field coordinator and scored over 50. On the final day of assessment, an assessor goes through the notebooks and scores each student's note book over 50 to bring the total to 100.

3   Situating the UDS TTFPP in Crew's (2002) Criteria of Service Learning

Drawing from the criteria spelled out above regarding service-learning (Crew, 2002), one can see how the UDS TTFPP permeates and covers all areas of the criteria.

Firstly, students are obliged to live and study in various deprived communities for at least five (5) weeks, both in the first year and in the second year. While on the field, through a primary data gathering process, students are expected to identify some development challenges and potentials in relation to their study communities. Aside from these, students also volunteer in community-based initiatives and services. They engage in the field of education through teaching in local schools, providing remedial classes to youth and adult literacy classes; in health and sanitation promotion, through clean-up campaigns, talks and durbars; in agricultural development through working on farms with community members and sharing their ideas; and in social events such as participating in festivals, funerals and anniversaries. This is normally an opportunity for students to share directly with communities what they have learned in their lecture halls, laboratories, and workshops classroom. In the process of this emersion learning, students do not only get to practice their learning, but also experience the real life of communities while they are learning. Copies of reports generated by students are made available to the districts of their fieldwork and become public documents. Through the District Coordinators, the communities and the District Assemblies have attested to the services that they received from these students.

Secondly, the programme provides students with the opportunity to put into practice what they have learned in the classroom. For instance, students are expected to apply participatory tools for community needs assessments, which are taught in campus-based courses, such as Introduction to Development Planning Process, Approaches to Community Development, Participatory Research Approaches, and Communication Dynamics for Participatory Development. The programme is integrated and covers a variety of areas such as health, education, agriculture, planning, politics, economics, mathematics, and business. It is required that each group has students from all the faculties of the university. The team of students of diverse disciplinary backgrounds brainstorm collectively and work together and with communities to propose and discuss appropriate tools for participatory community engagement in order to come up with interdisciplinary and trans-disciplinary solutions to real-life problems related to rural development constraints. In designing solutions to rural development challenges in the community, students become pragmatic and look for alternatives that solve problems rather than serving disciplinary egos.

Furthermore, the TTFPP draws on the mandate of using local resources to initiate and sustain community development by encouraging students to identify development niches in their learning communities, through the assessment of available resources. Students are taken through a series of practical activities in the classroom, which give them opportunities to apply their experiences from the community. For instance, aside from students producing reports about their study communities, they are often also given assignments and seminars upon their return, which require that they draw from the experiences and knowledge gained on the field. Also, questions for class assignments and end of trimester examinations may also require students to draw upon and use their TTFPP experience. Final year students who are expected to carry out project works are normally encouraged to select topics from their various study communities. In this process of integration of knowledge, science students have been found to be the ones who have had challenges in the field work aspect of their studies as it has been difficult for them to reproduce their theoretical learning on community development work.

As already noted, students are expected to produce group reports about the entire work conducted in and with the community. Each group of students is assigned a Field Coordinator who supervises students during their stay in the community. After the fifth week of fieldwork, as per the university academic calendar, the Field Coordinator and a multidisciplinary team of assessors (three other lecturers) assess the students through a group oral presentation and an individual oral assessment. Grades are then awarded. The TTFPP attracts six (6) credit points and no student in the UDS can graduate without participating in and passing the TTFPP.

Through the use of participatory tools in community needs assessments, the students usually engage the community in the identification and ranking of community needs. Students often observe that various groups in the communities hold divergent and competing needs, but their six-week stay allows them to continue to engage with communities in pruning down their needs list over a period of time, which is one of the major tasks of second-year students on the field. The TTFPP also allows service recipients in the community to partake in the students' evaluation, particularly in their final assessment. Students are required to invite community leaders, in particular, to be present on the day of assessment. This is to ensure that the reports produced actually reflect the views expressed by the community.

The TTFPP as a service programme enables students to voluntarily offer various services to their host community and improve community relations. As a result, during the period of stay, most students develop empathy with the community and begin to see themselves as part of the community. It has been reported that after completing school, graduates often refer to their service communities as "my community", indicating a bond between them and the community. Also, students learn through this programme to become development advocates, policy planners, development officers and some have been able to build a career out of this programme. Students gather experience of working, for instance, with development agencies and NGOs, and they develop skills and favourable attitudes towards working in rural areas in Ghana.

The programme is constantly being evaluated by both the Directorate and students. The Field Coordinator spends some hours with each group of students discussing their general concerns about the programme. As previously mentioned, the coordinator visits students on the field three times before they are assessed. When students return to school, they are given another opportunity in their lecture rooms to assess their activities in their communities (termed Community Feedback), with their various Faculty Coordinators. Their views are compiled by the Faculty Coordinator and forwarded to the Directorate.

Lastly, the primary and ultimate goal of TTFPP is an academic one. No student is allowed to participate in any religious and political activities in these communities, while on the field. Some of the criteria that guide Coordinators in the selection of communities for third-trimester placements are acceptability, welfare, and security. Coordinators assess the community beforehand to ascertain whether there are any existing religion or chieftaincy conflicts. On top of this, coordinators also make sure that community leaders are prepared and willing to host students from different religious and political backgrounds. During orientation, students are equipped to learn to live with others regardless of differences in ethnicity, religion, culture or other attributes within their group and their service community. They are also oriented not to engage in partisan political discussions while in the community. The community is also prepared to support and co-operate with students. These rules are also spelled out in the Students' Handbook and Field Practical Guide.

3.1 Factors Driving the Internationalization of the UDS

The programme's success is reflected in the type of graduates it has churned out yearly and, in the recognition, given to local communities in contributing to training graduates, while addressing local development challenges. These factors in the programme have been admired by many institutions, individuals, and students, locally and abroad, who have expressed wish to be part of the process. According to the UDS International Office, several institutions, and especially foreign ones, have requested that their students take part in the TTFPP. For instance, recently, the University of KwaZulu Natal in South Africa has expressed interest in the programme. In an interview with a dean, he revealed that the University of Aalborg of Denmark and Brandeis University in the USA have also expressed similar interests. The University of Applied Sciences in Dusseldorf, Germany has placed graduate students in communities with UDS undergraduate students for such joint learning experiences.

Another factor which is driving the internationalization of the UDS TTFPP as an SL programme is the desire of the UDS to showcase the university's unique programme on a global platform (marketing drive). As highlighted by Tagoe (2014), the UDS is the only university in Ghana which runs an integrated and mandatory third-trimester system, a module which has become a pinnacle of success that is reflected in the calibre of graduates produced. As a result, the university intends to share its success story globally, giving others the opportunity to participate, while also learning from the outside world that comes to participate. This is in line with Effah and Senadzi's (2008) analysis that HEIS in Ghana have seen the need to increase international patronage of their programmes and to also be part of global knowledge processes.

Another factor which is driving this process in the UDS is the need to expose foreigners to the unique structure and organization of Ghana's community systems, which relates to the internationalization of indigenous knowledge systems. The content of the TTFPP allows for the study of the profiles of local communities as the basis for understanding local development challenges and potentials, upon which development solutions and propositions are constructed. This reinforces the notion that local knowledge systems and participatory community appraisals are crucial, especially in considering and addressing the ills of development, particularly in the rural north of Ghana. By internationalizing the TTFPP, this kind of agenda can be sold to the rest of the world.

Furthermore, the UDS has seen the need to provide the opportunity for cross-cultural learning between communities and students, on local and international levels. The University intends to take its mandate further to promote local development through research and adding an international dimension to its efforts. Considering the dynamic, multiple and complex nature of development issues, the university deems it fit to integrate international students and researchers in its programme so as to share and acquire knowledge from people of different backgrounds.

Following the University's recent active participation in conferences, meetings and fora regarding higher education in Africa, and its involvement in the activities of organizations concerning higher education internationalization, such as the Association of Africa Universities (AAU), the UDS finds it necessary to open up more to the world as a way of implementing some of the ideas gathered thus far and to also showcase its potentials.

Financial attractions have also been motivating the UDS to internationalize, and mostly its flagship programme, the TTFPP. As state support for HEIS in Ghana dwindles, universities are pushed to seek alternative ways of generating funds internally. This situation has pushed many universities to design new and diverse programmes to attract a variety of students, including ones who pay fees. While engaging in study abroad and classroom-based services for generating resources, UDS has found how, the TTFPP, as a local initiative, has been targeted as a site for generating funds. By expanding its mandate to include international students, UDS hopes to generate additional income to support the growing community placement budget of the programme and to support its other initiatives as well.

4   Ways in Which Drivers Shape and Define Changes towards Internationalization

In an effort to give a broader perspective to the programme that can meet increasing numbers and more diverse backgrounds of students, the following preparations are taking place at UDS.

4.1   *Policy Document Preparation*

Firstly, an institutional document concerning the internationalization of the TTFPP was prepared by the directorates of International Relations and the TTFPP, and spells out the description of the programme, including the application process, duration, fees, and accommodation. As already mentioned previously, the TTFPP is mandatory for all students of the UDS. As part of the efforts to internationalize, applicants from NGOs, students from accredited tertiary institutions from Ghana, and foreign students/participants from accredited tertiary institutions and organizations working on a study abroad programmes are being encouraged to apply. Applications usually open on the 4th of January and the deadline for application is on the 1st of May or July each year. The UDS International Relations (UDSIR) office forwards all applications to the TTFPP Directorate for further processing and admissions. The list of applicants admitted to participate in the programme is given to the UDSIR office and made available on the University's Website. The UDSIR Office also writes to the applicants that are admitted to participate in the programme and those not admitted are also informed.

Admitted applicants must pay all of their fees, or 80% of fees, before the commencement of the programme. The annual cost of the programme for a foreign student, per academic year, has been set to include admission and registration, administrative charges, transportation from Accra to Tamale, accommodation on campus, orientation, transportation to fieldwork communities, monitoring and assessment, transportation from fieldwork communities to Accra, national health insurance coverage, certificate of participation, and accommodation in the field work community. In collaboration with stakeholders in the community, the University provides accommodation for all students during their stay and study in the various communities.

4.2 Continuous and Renewed University and Local Community Relations and Partnership Programmes

The UDS recognizes the important role that local communities play as far as the training of its graduates is concerned. The University is therefore constantly networking and participating effectively in development activities with local communities. For instance, some communities and their leaders are often invited to participate at important University events, such as matriculation and congregation. Also, the University has recognized and continues to recognize, prominent leaders, individuals, and communities who have indefatigably supported the university by presenting them with awards of honour or naming some structures of the university after them. These are all efforts that aim at strengthening the University and local community relations towards the realization of the goals of the TTFPP in particular, and of the university as a whole

4.3 Expansion of Student Learning to Include Giving Back to Community

Teams of students based in the communities are expected to get actively involved in community-based activities in order to lend their support. Rather than concentrating only on their learning from the communities, NGOs and local government authorities during their community placement, students are encouraged to initiate joint programmes with communities that enable them to draw from their studies to serve the community. For instance, for the many rural communities that the students are placed in, sanitation and hygiene, and education and health are popular challenges that students identify and propose mitigating interventions for. In communities such as Balungu and Tengzung in the Tongo District of the Upper East Region, Nsutem and Akokoaso in the Sekyere East District of the Ashanti Region, and Banda Nkwanta in the Band District of the Brong Ahafo Region, students embarked on educational campaigns to sensitize community members on the need to keep their environment clean. In all the communities visited over a three-year period, students also spent their spare time teaching in local schools and working in community health facilities. The services they rendered often helped agencies deliver their services better as they often face challenges with under-staffing.

5 The Strengths of the TTFPP

The programme has:
1. Helped students develop favourable attitudes towards working in rural and deprived communities.

2. Exposed students, on practical levels, to the nature of community-based development problems in Ghana.
3. Provided useful services to Ghanaian rural communities through the exchange of knowledge and its application to address the felt needs and aspirations of these communities.
4. Generated data for further research in problem-solving development issues, and other issues.
5. Equipped students with the basic tools, techniques, and skills required for community studies.
6. Introduced students to community studies through living in and working with communities.
7. Introduced students to the need to blend traditional knowledge with scientific knowledge, through their community studies.

6 Challenges of the Programme

The challenges listed here manifest on different programme levels.

1. Operational/Managerial level: On a financial level, the TTFPP is a very expensive exercise. Each year, the University deploys about three thousand students to various rural and peri-urban communities to undertake their fieldwork exercises. The orientation, transportation, coordination, monitoring, and examination aspects that are essential to the programme entail huge costs, which are hardly charged to students. Meanwhile, the state and ministry have been consistently failing to recognize the TTFPP as a special programme, so extra funds have not been allocated for its implementation. Such shortfalls are absorbed by the University, which is already starved of funds from the state. This situation affects services to staff and students involved in the programme. On a managerial level, the programme is organized during the period of time in which most tertiary students are on holiday vacation. Both students and staff have expressed how this scheduling does not allow enough time for students and teachers to rest before the resumption of the following academic year. Hence, both students and staff work throughout the year with very limited time for rest and recreation before the start of the next academic year.
2. Community level: Poor orientation of community members on the nature of the programme, the expected area of their participation and the nature of the interaction that should exist between them and the students have been found to occur. The UDS has not been able to establish a good rapport with most District Assemblies and communities in the TTFPP

process. What the university does is inform the Assemblies of the presence of the students, without putting mechanisms in place for the Assemblies and communities to actively participate. Also, the interest of communities in the programme is waning due to the frequency of student visits. Community members have said they do not see any practical benefit from the programme. Their expectations of converting the proposals into actual projects have remained unmet, even though the programme is not meant to deliver projects, but to equip communities to be able to do so on their own.

3. Student level: Due to the challenges associated with living and studying in rural areas, there is a low level of appreciation of the SL experience and the learning outcomes of fieldwork in the community. For instance, some students struggle to raise needed funds for their stay in the communities, especially when their home regions are far from the region/community of placement. The end result of this includes students reporting late to their communities, moving out of their communities frequently and leaving the assignments due to a few students to execute. In such situations, a lot of the students end the programme without actually learning and applying what they have learned in class.

4. Institutional level: While local government authorities have benefited from the reports produced from the TTFPP placements, there appears to be limited documentation on the actual community impact of the programme, such as the behaviours and social change impacts that the encounters and interactions are expected to generate. The UDS assessment has tended to focus on the documentation of student experiences in Reflective Journals, Community Profiles, and Needs Assessment reports rather than on assessments of students' impacts on the community and vice versa. The student reports are shared with districts and communities and submitted to the Directorate of TTFPP, where they are graded.

5. As expressed by many participants, UDS has tended to concentrate on the learning component, neglecting the service component of community field placements. Service to the community is not deliberate but expected to occur as students interact and learn with the community.

6. International Level: While the programme has been widely shared with various programmes, in view of spurring the interest of an international audience, neither the programme office nor University have been proactive in rebranding themselves to take on an international audience. So far international participation has been reactive. The few international students who have participated in the programme have arrived with expectations that have often not been met. Above all, as new students

in a new environment, international students need a lot of initial support that is often not available. When the students have come as a group, they have found companionship among themselves and sometimes arrived as a group earlier to take pleasure trips ahead of the community placement.

7   Options for Sustainable Improvement of the Programme

To promote effective and smooth running of the programme, the following options have been proposed by respondents and are worth considering:

1. It has been realized that there is a need for an overhauling of the programme to meet current realities, without unduly losing its original SL intent. According to one dean, before the integration of the programmes, there was stronger commitment from all, students, faculty and management alike. However, since the integration, science faculties have often felt that the programme is beneficial to the social and applied sciences and thus have not been very enthusiastic in their participation and commitment. They appear to be more enthusiastic about their own specialized industrial placement programmes compared to the TTFPP. An overhaul of the programme should enable faculties to make specific inputs of the programme's relevance to their disciplines and programmes. There should be effective dialogue and negotiations at the faculty and department levels, involving all, students, faculty and administrators.

2. The TTFPP Directorate, in conjunction with the Institute for Interdisciplinary Studies and Consultancy Services, could edit and compile students' work into user-friendly forms and post them on the University's online open access platform. In this way, both students and lecturers could refer to specific reports for practically oriented class room discussions. This is also important for helping curtail plagiarism among students when they are producing their community reports, as it has been noted that students sometimes pick old reports of communities which have been studied already and reproduce them verbatim, without acknowledging sources or updating the reports. Uploading the reports online would help coordinators and lecturers easily track these issues of copying and it would also give access to other universities who may be interested in these reports.

3. Re-organization of the programme to augment the level of community engagement is also necessary for the programme. Like the learning component, community engagement should be assessed and documented on

each occasion during fieldwork. Liaise with development partners in the delivery of projects to the community also needs to be improved. The Directorate has to also market the programme widely and attract interest in its services. For instance, in the past, the programme collaborated with the UNFPA to collect community-based data for its programmes. Through this collaboration, students learned from the exercise, while the University gained additional funds to support its programmes.

4. Increasing sustainable funding sources is also critical. The University needs to reconsider and recost the programme so that reasonable rates can be collected per student in order to support its effective delivery. A strong internationalization component could reel in much-needed funds. This would require actively identifying institutions with SL programmes abroad and entice them to enroll their students. This would also mean that the UDS would have to step up its student support services to international students who enroll in the programme.

5. There is the need to develop innovative ways of engaging and re-engaging with communities, on a continuous basis, and to provide them with proper orientation of the programme. This should include continuous engagement with not just the community leaders and host families, but with other members of the community, as well as local government authorities, for planning and monitoring purposes, and for accounting to communities and local authorities. One community respondent has suggested that after each round, the UDS/TTFFP Directorate should hold district level workshops to share the experiences and plans for the future that have come out of the fieldwork experience, to invite community input and enhance the spirit of collaboration and joint learning. Also, if involved in the process right from start, NGOs and donor development partners working in the districts could be further motivated to pick up the proposed interventions.

6. Participants (students) should be more formally required to offer their services to the communities, based on their disciplinary area of specialization. The exercise should move beyond integration and emphasize service to the community. The service component should be a part of the students' assessments for completion and graduation. Students should also demonstrate in their reports the services they have rendered and how they have impacted the communities.

7. There is a need for greater involvement of the UDSIR office in planning, especially with regards to international student involvement. They should work together to design additional activities for international students and improve student support services for them before, during and after

their involvement in the programme. This would reduce the pressure put on lecturers (coordinators) and would better help bring on board the new, different and relevant ideas and skills that come from international collaboration, which could enhance the quality of the programme. It would also help advertise and manage international experiences and interests in the programme.
8. There is a need for the TTFPP Directorate to be better equipped in terms of human, financial and other resources. Currently, the Directorate is managed by a Director and an administrative assistant, which is inadequate for the volume of work that is passing through the office. Other staff includes faculty coordinators, who come in around during peak times and for intermittent meetings. However, for the SL programme to be effective, faculty coordinators should be planning and organizing all year round. Also, provisions should be made for community support, including protocols to be respected by students and staff at all times.

8 Conclusion

The UDS, like any other universities in Ghana, has responded to the pressures of internationalization of its programmes. Through this process, its main focus has been on research, through the TTFPP. This focus and process has been a result of several requests made by other universities, researchers, and individuals, both in Ghana and abroad. As Effah and Senadzi (2005) have pointed out, the UDS has seen the need to be a part of the global knowledge process, and to further generate resources to support its development. The internationalization process has been rolled out and information regarding it can be found on the university's website (www.uds.edu.gh), with the TTFPP and the university's International Office championing this process.

Regarding SL, from start, the programme has captured almost all of the criteria highlighted by Crew (2002), and it has exhibited even more potential, well beyond the criteria. For instance, the programme is multidisciplinary, integrated and founded on team work. During the research process, students are taken out of the home and university community to rural settings, which enables them to connect and interact with key development officers, at the district and regional levels. One other feature of the programme, which places the TTFPP experience above the Crew (2002) criteria, is its ability to create lasting relations/ties between students and learning communities, long after the students have left the university and community. Students go back to these communities to conduct individual research after completion of the programme, and some, through proposal writing and other efforts, are able to lure development agencies to these communities and undertake development projects.

Despite inadequate financial support and other constraints characterizing the process, the UDS is poised to continuously fulfill its mandate of training undergraduate students through community learning, while addressing local development challenges, which the University is working on extending to the outside world. Considering the measures which have been put in place already, the programme has huge potentials for attracting international audiences. Overall, the programme has greatly equipped and enriched students, and it continues to do so, with skills and methods for working in rural communities in Ghana.

References

Akplu, F. H. (2016). Private participation in higher education in sub-Saharan Africa: Ghana's experience. *International Higher Education, 86,* summer.

Boakye-Boaten, A. (2011). From the classroom to the streets: Empowering 21st Century college students through the Ghana street children literacy initiative. In L. P. Lin (Ed.), *Service-learning in higher education.* Indianapolis, IN: University of Indiana Press.

Bringle, G. R., & Hatcher, A. J. (1996). Implementing service-learning in higher education. *The Journal of Higher Education, 69*(2), 221–239.

Crew, J. R. (2012). *Higher education service learning source book.* Westpost, CT: Greenwood Publishing Group.

De Wit, H. (2002). *Internationalization of higher education in the United States of America and Europe: A historical, comparative, and conceptual analysis.* Westport, CT: Greenwood Press.

De Wit, H., Hunter, F. Howard, L., & Egron, E. (2015). Internationalization of higher education. European Parliament [Online]. Retrieved June, 5, 2016, from http://www.europarl.europa.eu/RegData/etudes/STUD/2015/540370/IPOL_STU(2015)540370_EN.pdf

Effah, P., & Sednaza, B. (2008). Ghana. In D. Teffera & J. Knight (Eds.), *Higher education in Africa: The international dimension.* Accra: Association of Africa Universities.

Hawawini, G. (2011). *The internationalization of higher education institutions: A critical review and radical approach.* Faculty and Research Working Paper [Online]. Retrieved May 10, 2016, from http://sites.insead.edu/facultyresearch/research/doc.cfm?did=48726

Kaburise, J. (2006, September 3–5). Community engagement at the university for development studies. In *Proceedings of Conference on Community Engagement in Higher Education*. Cape Town, South Africa.

Knight, J. (2003). Updated internationalization definition. *International Higher Education, 33*, 2–3.

Knight, J. (2008). *Higher education in turmoil. The changing world of internationalization*. Rotterdam, The Netherlands: Sense Publishers.

Tagoe, A. M. (2014). Transforming teaching and learning at University of Ghana through community service learning: Listening to the voices of students. *Journal of Education and Training Studies, 2*(4), 85–96.

Qiang, Z. (2003). Internationalization of higher education: Towards a conceptual framework. *Policy Futures in Education, 1*(2), 248–270.

Van der Wende, M. (1997). Missing links: The relationship between national policies for internationalization and those for higher education in general. In T. Kälvemark & M. van der Wende (Eds.), *National policies for the internationalization of higher education in Europe*. Stockholm: National Agency for Higher Education.

CHAPTER 8

Prospects and Challenges in North-South Curriculum Development Partnerships: The Case of a Finnish-Cameroonian University Project in Higher Education Studies

Pascal Doh

1   Introduction

In the conceptual discussion of partnership, North-South joint curriculum development efforts have been taken as one of the integral parts of the process of both partnership and internationalization processes. The term North-South curriculum development partnership is used interchangeably with the term internationalization, and both have been employed to describe the conception of new academic programmes by partners from Northern regions for universities in the South. More specifically, this recent phenomena in the export of academic programmes to African universities have been a part of the internationalization processes that have taken shape in Africa.

Recently, many European donor countries have adopted this programme conception as a capacity building pathway for developing countries, especially for Africa. Internationalization is taking place in the form of joint or conventional degree programmes for African universities, with mentorship from European universities. Several postgraduate degree programmes in Africa today have been conceived from this kind of academic cooperation (see the European Programmes in Boeren et al., 2008). Interestingly, as suggested by the sources of funding for these programmes, the phenomenon seems to be captured more in the development cooperation literature than in the literature on internationalization in higher education. Although the often-cited OECD four dimensions of internationalization include capacity-building and mutual understanding (OECD, 2004), such academic programme development from abroad, especially in the not-for-profit field, has not been strongly articulated in the literature as a mutually beneficial process.

The development of institutional cooperation programmes in Africa has been mostly financed from development cooperation funds, which are most often lodged and evaluated under the respective Northern countries' development agencies and Ministries of Foreign Affairs. A survey of postgraduate programmes targeting developing countries indicates that almost all the programmes developed with and for the South have Northern countries' development orientation in the background (Boeren et al., 2008). Besides the development agenda within which these programmes are conceived, it has also been observed that internalization can also be seen as a mutually beneficial process for both North and South universities and countries alike, rather than one-sided development aid for universities in the South.

This chapter presents the operational dynamics and lessons from a three-year project between the University of Tampere in Finland and the University of Yaoundé 2 in Cameroon, which culminated in the conception of a Master's Programme in Higher Education Management in Cameroon, in the central African region. The issues discussed in the chapter are drawn from a longitudinal participatory observation with the author as central actor (scientific coordinator) in the project, and an analysis of proceedings and documents of the project. As part of the methodology, unstructured conversational phone interviews were conducted with five of the project actors. The chapter examines reasons for the involvement of the University of Tampere in the project, as well as the success and inhibiting factors that favoured the implementation of the project and affected its effectiveness.

1.1   *The Mentor University*

The Finnish University that was involved in the project with Cameroon is the University of Tampere (UTA), which is a ninety-one-year-old multidisciplinary university in Tampere, the third largest city in Finland, headquarter of the Pirkanmaa province, in Southern Finland. UTA was founded in 1925 as a civic university in Helsinki (current capital of Finland) and was moved to Tampere in 1966. UTA is composed of nine schools with 15,000 students. It is one of the most competitive universities in Finland, with strong programmes in social sciences, social studies, health, public administration, management, and governance. UTA is renowned for high-quality teaching and research, for being in the first half of many university rankings, and for its vision of becoming one of the most competitive international research universities. Its teachers and researchers are involved in various national and international networks. The University has a strong orientation to society in terms of the provision of public, private and professional services.

The main way in which UTA engages in internationalization is through the mobility of its students, researchers, and teachers. The English-taught Master's programmes at UTA include an important asset of student, teacher and researcher exchange and mobility, as well as connection to wider global networks. The Master's programmes and other capacity building programmes in higher education management aim at conceiving programmes to transform management capacities in higher education in sub-Saharan Africa and are hosted in the Higher Education Group (HEG). HEG is a research unit of the School of Management of the UTA, which is in charge of teaching, research and consultancy in the higher education management and governance fields.

1.2 The Mentee

The Cameroonian University, the University of Yaoundé 2 (UY2), is one of the second-generation state universities in Cameroon, Central Africa. UY2 was born from the split of the University of Yaoundé by decree No.93/026, on January 19th, 1993. Before 1993 there was only one state university in Cameroon, the University of Yaoundé, which began as the Federal University of Cameroon, on July 26th, 1962. Following the 1993 reform, five new state universities were created, with two in the capital city, Yaoundé 1 and Yaoundé 2.

UY2 is predominantly a French-speaking university. UY2 is defined as a public, scientific and cultural institution with a mission towards the production, organization and diffusion of scientific, cultural and professional knowledge, as well as ethics for national development and the progress of humanity (Decree No.93/026 of January 19th, 1993). With the two Faculties of Law and Political Science, and Economics and Management Sciences as its original building blocks, UY2 is profiled as a social, political and management science university. It offers no natural science programmes.

As of 2015, the University of Yaoundé 2 had a student population of 37,331 students, comprising 16.3 % of the entire state university student population in Cameroon (Ministry of Higher Education, 2015). The students are spread across five areas; the Faculty of Law and Political Science, the Advanced School of Information and Communication Studies, the Institute of International Relations, the Institute of Demographic Studies, and the Faculty of Economics and Management Sciences, where the UTA Master's programme is hosted. Another very important partner in the project is the *Institut de la Francophonie pour la Gouvernance Universitaire* (IFGU), a higher education governance capacity building Institute of the *Agence Universitaire de la Francophonie* (AUF), which acts as sponsoring partner in the curriculum development of the Higher Education Management programme. The IFGU-AUF partnership was justified by its vision to build governance and management capacity in Cameroon and Central Africa. IFGU is hosted on the main campus of UY2.

1.3 Peculiarity of the Higher Education Management Programme

The development and implementation of the Master's programme in Higher Education Management at the University of Yaoundé 2 by UTA is interestingly peculiar and significant mostly because of the linguistic incompatibility between the two universities. The University of Tampere runs its academic programmes in Finnish and English, and UY2 is a French-speaking university. The Master's programme is in English at the UTA and has been conceived in French for UY2. When the partnership was set up, apart from one Cameroonian alumnus in the Finnish team, who was proficient in both English and French, no staff in the Finnish team understood or spoke French. Similarly, only part of the team of the Local Focal point at the UY2 was proficient in French and English, and most of the staff were French-speaking (Cameroon is a bilingual French and English-speaking country so some staff could use basic English, for less technical activities).

The second reason making the project experience peculiar is the lack of institutional agreements between UTA and UY2, as well as the lack of bilateral diplomatic links between Cameroon and Finland. All the transaction and activities in the project were thus based on trust and the determination of each party to have the project succeed. Thirdly, at the time of implementation, there was also no stable source of funding for the project, which eventually received funding.

Aside from two focal points, one from UY2 and the other the alumni of Cameroonian origin from the UTA, who were appointed as Focal Point and Scientific Coordinators respectively, the project did not have formally designated head people, with institutional backing from both institutions. Within a broad consortium of partners called LMUU II (see 2.2), the status of UY2 at the time suggested weakness in its legitimate involvement in the partnership. Aside from the strong support of Finnish experts and of many of the African partners in the LMUU II consortium, who provided ad-hoc support to the development of the curriculum in Cameroon, the project was implemented on a voluntary basis, without having any legal basis. All these factors beg the question as to why the project was successfully developed and implemented.

2   International Trends

In recent publications on how Finnish higher education institutions partner for development and change in Southern regions of the world, Seppo et al. (2015) have highlighted how "the knowledge economy has come to add more emphasis on knowledge, research and hence higher education as a public developmental and social good" (Seppo et al., 2015, p. 9). This knowledge economy is justifying the old Chinese proverb, *"teach a man to fish rather than giving him a fish"*. There seems to be unanimity in the donor world that capacity development is a sustainable low-cost investment for partners in the South and that education remains the main pathway for sustainable human capacity development. Doh (2015) postulates that higher education is a catalyst for countries of the South to adapt to the knowledge-driven realities of development and that it plays a role in the development of the lower education subsectors as well. The days when social and economic rate of return analyses suggested that higher education was not productive and was insignificant in developing countries are in fact gone (Asworth, 1997; Becker, 1994; Blaug, 1965; Psacharoloulos, 1981; Psacharoloulos, 1994).

Over the past fifteen years, there have been a lot of joint academic programmes being developed between North and South partners and increasing convergence in the international arena, with the case of Africa highlighting the importance of capacity building for development. The recent design of academic programmes for African universities is leading to a new pattern of internationalization, which deviates from the traditional pattern that was tied to ex-colonial networks. Within the recent development models, this type of curricula internationalization has also brought forth South-initiated projects and not just traditional donor- and North-initiated projects, which were the more traditional pathways of North development policies in the South. This switch has come as North-initiated projects have often failed to reflect the shifting priorities of recipient countries (Doh, 2015).

In the same vein, ownership and leadership by South partners have been seen as increasingly important (Vierck & Dann, 2011). These new trends are leading to the emergence of networks of North and South Universities. Some schools of thought have also highlighted South-South collaborations within North-South collaborations as significant for ensuring continuity and sustainability of North development policies.

The transition has also been from aid to collaboration, and, in some cases, aid to business, which has influenced a change from education for development to for-profit making education that is being exported in the South. The trends also point to a transition from individual professorial and academic collaborations to more institutionalized and organized forms of collaboration between North and South universities. It has also been perceived that, for projects to be more contextually relevant, there is a need for engagement in student and staff mobility programmes and visiting schemes, especially of Northern partners visiting the South in order to better understand the realities they collaborate with and fund, and to help improve the teaching and research standards in the South. Recent analyses of North-South collaborations have also articulated how the design of such collaborative programmes in the South also strengthens Northern countries, with university internationalization agendas ultimately benefitting the North as well.

Finally, there has also been a shift from traditional patterns of "wholesale importation" of curriculums that did not involve African partners, which was a characteristic of the colonial or post-colonial pattern of curriculum development in Africa. Castells (2001) has analyzed the case of French-speaking African countries whose conception of higher education systems and programmes was a true cultural imposition from the ex-colonial power. The impact and birthmark of this wholesale and cultural importation of higher education, which do not reflect the local African realities, are still to be reversed (Sawyerr, 2004). Pekkola (2015) argues that although the requirements of higher education in the global market are similar, the local circumstances and needs differ in the North and South, and also between African countries. This calls for a new pattern of curricula development that addresses the needs, challenges and aspirations of African countries, in terms of higher education.

2.1 Finnish Higher Education Cooperation with Africa

The involvement of Finnish partners in the Master's programme project in Cameroon translated Finland's development policy through the Higher Education Cooperation Instrument HEI-ICI. Finland does not have a history of colonial dominance, which consequently leads to the post-colonial pattern of education development that has been observed since the 1960s in Africa. Finland has however been active in Africa beyond the HEI-ICI programme, which started in 2010. It has been for long engaged mostly with its long-term partners in African on education, science and technology, and in various "soft politics" tactics, such as playing a significant role in the independence of Namibia.

Pajala (2015) argues that cooperation between Finnish higher education institutions (HEIS) and universities in the South, in the case of African countries, was originally in the hands of "active pioneers", which kept it unorganized and not institutionalized, and largely characterized by an individual teacher or *Professor-to-Professor* relationships. Pajala points out a few programmes that have characterized the evolution to a more structured, organized and institutionalized higher education cooperation between Finnish institutions and those in developing countries of the South. This is illustrated in the case of the 1994 institutionalization, within the Academy of Finland, of a component called, *"Development Research".* Although this component was begun by individual researchers, it covered wide international research projects and, in certain cases, involved individual professors of developing countries.

Pajala has also observed other forms of collaboration between Finnish Universities of Applied Sciences and NGOs in Africa, and the beginning of a North-South Programme in 2004, for teacher and staff exchange, which supported a network cooperation between HEIS that continued on through to the

HEI-ICI programme. Finnish development policies, conveyed by the HEI-ICI programme, pay attention to supporting human development in the South, of which education and higher education are a critical part. According to this perspective, raising the quality of higher education is one of the important development targets in the education sector and can be supported by networking with Finnish institutions and know-how (Pulkkinen, 2013). An important new emphasis from the 2016 HEI-ICI programme document (as amended) is that institutional capacity building should focus on research as well, as it can further contribute to the development of society, build competence consistent with national development goals, and contribute to the goals of inclusive sustainable development and reduction of poverty (HEI-ICI, 2016). According to the Finnish perspective, higher education can thus generally play an active role in fostering socio-economic and cultural development in developing countries.

2.2 Framework of the Masters Degree Project

The Master's degree project was attached to a joint interuniversity capacity-building project comprised of the University of Tampere and University of Helsinki in Finland, Makerere University in Uganda, the Ugandan Management Institute, and the University of KwaZulu-Natal in South Africa, with the title, "Strengthening Institutional Capacity for Higher Education Leadership and Management in Sub-Saharan Africa". Because it was a second or follow up project to a previous one from the same funding sources called, "Leadership Management of Ugandan Universities (LMUU I)", this project bore the label LMUU II, with the same consortium of universities extending to involve the Cameroonian component. The overall aim was to build the responsive capacities of African universities for engagement in national development, through the development of higher education management capacity programmes (LMUU II Project Document, 2012). The coordinating partner and main funding applicant was the University of Tampere, which had the Masters and related programmes aimed at the African LMUU II partner countries. UY2, and therefore Cameroon, were simply "associate" partners to the main LMUU II consortium.

This consortium of Finnish and African Universities, known as the LMUU II, consequently applied for competitive funding sources from the HEI-ICI programme (among other applicants), with sponsorship from the Finnish Ministry of Foreign Affairs, and received the sum of 500,000 Euros for the period between January 2013 to December 2015. As an associate partner, the main possibility and benefit for UY2 were that its staff and focal points participating in the project could enhance their capacities through curriculum development seminars organized for LMUU II partners, and could be marginally funded for this. UY2 did not have any institutional links with any of the other core partners, South Africa, the two Ugandan universities, and the UTA itself. The relationship with UTA largely centred on the Cameroonian alumnus, who had been trained in Higher Education Management programmes at UTA and other European Universities, and was recruited into the project as a key expert. Being the liaison, the UTA alumnus of Cameroonian nationality was also designated as the Scientific Coordinator of the Cameroonian project component, and associate in the LMUU II.

It turned out that because UY2 started direct bilateral discussions on this capacity building project earlier with the UTA, in June 2012, before the LMUU II funding application was made, the main link UY2 had was the one with the UTA, and this occurred without any formal written agreements. A French-English bilingual focal point had been designated by the Rector of UY2, but the project was not also formally embedded in the UY2 because it was not yet validated by its council and because of lack of any cooperation agreement. The loose relationship was caused more by the associate status of the UY2 and Cameroon, which limited the level at which UY2 could benefit from the LMUU II funding, which brought the Cameroonian liaison to constantly turn to UTA for supplementary funding. In fact, when the budget limit stated for an Associate Member (UY2) in the LMUU II was attained, the Finnish Ministry of Foreign Affairs had to take extra-budgetary measures to supplement the funding for the Cameroonian project, which was not entirely a component of the LMUU II project. When the Finnish Ministry of Foreign Affairs' supplement was exhausted as the curricula development in Cameroon was still progressing, the UTA provided an extra supplement for the liaison to complete the project.

These incidents and developments highlight UTA and Finland's significant involvement in the program, on the basis of the internationalization policy that guided support for the development of the Master's programme in Higher Education Management at UY2, in Cameroon (see Table 8.1).

3 Methods and Operations in the Master's Project

The method adopted by the experts for the development of the Master's programme curriculum was participatory. This participatory method was based on the philosophy that the most robust curriculum would result from an appropriate reflection on the local reality of Cameroon and the sub-region, versus a whole curriculum importation from the University of Tampere, which has a highly Eurocentric focus. This participatory method suggested seminars

TABLE 8.1 The curriculum development seminars for the Master's programme in higher education management in Cameroon

Seminar	Date	Objective	No. in seminar	No. in workshop
1.	12–14 May 2013	Curriculum development	28	13
2.	5–7 May 2014	Curriculum development	42	22
3.	14–16 Jan 2015	Teacher initiation	Uncounted (above 70)	21

and workshops (in the form of Focus Groups) as inexpensive and direct approaches to receive input from local partners and stakeholders in curriculum development, including the Ministry, University administration, and academic staff. The curriculum development process was undertaken over three seminars. Two of the seminars were focussed on the curriculum development proper and the last one was focused on local teacher initiation processes. The seminars were typically constituted of main plenary sessions, which involved top administrators of the Ministries and Universities, and academic staff joining in later and participating in workshops with the Finnish partners for the curriculum design. Overall, the seminars and workshops drew the number of participants outlined in Table 8.1. The above three seminars that were held at the University of Yaoundé 2 were the ones that most determined the successful design of the curriculum. In addition, three other seminars and workshops were organized abroad in Uganda and South Africa by the LMUU II consortium, with sponsorship of the Finnish Ministry of Foreign Affairs through the HEI-ICI programme.

3.1 *The Yaoundé Focus Group Seminars*

In the first seminar of May 2013 at the UY2, the Cameroonian UTA alumnus travelled with Finnish experts to Cameroon. Prior to this seminar, the UTA alumnus had written a concept note explaining the rationale and objective of such a programme in Cameroon and Central Africa, and also presented a collection of different higher education management courses from Tampere and other universities in the rest of Europe. During this first seminar, the participants adopted some pre-existing courses for curriculum development.

The second seminar of May 2014 brought together staff and administrators of the University and Ministry of Higher Education and aimed at the actual contextualization of the courses of the Master's programme, which were adopted from the 2013 seminar. This second seminar was chaired by the Cameroon Minister of Higher Education, who outlined himself the management challenges and the needs of higher education in Cameroon, including the required training capacities and skills that could be sought through such a programme. At the end of this seminar, a sketch of the curriculum was developed along with a list of different criteria the curriculum should address; i. context ii. needs iii. objective iv. orientation v. justification vi. organization of the training vii. competencies viii. targeted students ix. teaching mode and x. possible employment markets. The courses outlined in Table 8.2 were adopted definitively and presently run at UY2.

The last seminar, which was held in January 2015, aimed at preparing and contextualizing the content of the courses, whose sketch had been prepared in the 2014 seminar, and to examine a teacher initiation process that had begun several months earlier, in September 2014. The teacher initiation processes entailed teachers of related disciplines handling the courses and being supported in the preparation of the content and course plans for the programme through their own research, with a specific focus on addressing the different management challenges faced by universities in the Central African region. The proposed course contents and plans were then presented to a panel of international experts from Finland, who commented on the possibilities and readiness of individual teachers to teach the course.

At the end of the exercise only five out of nineteen courses were judged to be sufficiently and appropriately ready to be taught without outside assistance, but experts agreed that the programme could be launched since the AUF was to sponsor the mobility of international experts to teach the programme while the local capacity building process continued in the first years after the launch of the programme. The curriculum of the programme was then presented to and approved by the Council of the UY2 on June 23rd, 2015. On December 1st, 2015, admission of the first cohort was launched and 40 students were admitted from three African Countries, Cameroon, Chad, and Cote d'Ivoire. In total, about 150.000 Euros were spent on the project, through the LMUU II-HEI ICI funding, the UTA's own funding, as well as the AUF funding, which covered the costs for the organization of the seminars and travels. A large part of the budget was Finnish.

4   Analysis and Discussions

This chapter has set out to present and analyse the conception of the Higher Education Management Master's programme at the University of Yaoundé 2,

TABLE 8.2 Courses of the Cameroon Master's programme in higher education management

First semester		Second semester	
Code	Title	Code	Title
MESDE 4001 (M)	Introduction to Higher Education Studies	MESDE 4006 (M)	Higher Education Governance
MESDE 4002 (M)	The Historical and Philosophical Foundation of Universities	MESDE 4007 (C)	Ethical and Legal Issues in HE
MESDE 4003 (M)	University Pedagogy	MESDE 4008 (M)	Quality Assurance in HE
MESDE 4004 (C)	Student and Professorial Career Issues in HE	ESDE 4009 (M)	Management and Leadership in HE
MESDE 4005 (M)	Globalization and Internationalization in HE	MESDE 4010 (C)	Strategic Planning in HE

Fifth semester		Fourth semester	
MESDE 4011 (C)	Financing of HE	MESDE 4016 (C)	HE and Intellectual Property Rights
MESDE 4012 (M)	Economics of HE	MESDE 4017 (C)	Research Management
MESDE 4013 (M)	HE and Economic Development and Poverty Reduction	MESDE 4018 (M)	Research Methodology and Statistics
MESDE 4014 (C)	HE and National and Regional Development	MESDE 4019 (M)	Thesis Writing and Supervision
MESDE 4015 (M)	Entrepreneurship in HE		

Note: M = Main Cources; C = Complementary Courses; HE = Higher Education

introduced by the University of Tampere in Finland, as part of Finland's internationalization policy, and to highlight the experience in terms of the successes and inhibiting factors in the effective export of the programme to Cameroon.

4.1 *Mutually Beneficial Internationalization*

The University of Tampere's involvement in the development of the Cameroonian Master's programme was backed by the University's Strategic Plan, which includes internationalization of the University of Tampere to position itself both in Finnish society and in a changing global world as a space for international science and education (University of Tampere, 2010–2015 Strategic Plan). The UTA's internationalization perspective requires that the University takes an active role in debates about society and "in promoting justice and equality in society, [to] enhance the well-being of citizens at home and abroad" (University of Tampere, 2010–2015 Strategic Plan). The perspective engages the University in active cooperation and partnerships, to bear its own share of global responsibility. In this sense, higher education management capacity is identified as crucial for the development of sub-Saharan African higher education systems and can involve the engagement of a Northern university such as UTA, which already has higher education management programmes. UTA's current strategic plan, 2016–2021, presents "internationality" as the second main agenda (UTA, 2016–2021 Strategic Plan). This internationality entails the strategic importance of the mobility of ideas and people, the increase in the international exchange of staff and students, and longer periods of working abroad.

Finland's increasing belief in the importance of mobility of people and ideas to enhance the quality of teaching and research translates into its local policy as well, where, for instance, mobility has been instituted as the main condition for eligibility for university funding from the Academy of Finland. According to the perspective and new measure, it is no longer possible for a post-doctoral researcher to obtain funding from the Academy of Finland to conduct research in the Finnish unit and university where the doctoral degree was obtained. It is believed that the wide range of experiences that result from working in different environments enables researchers to conduct excellent research, promote science renewal and advance their research careers. In a presentation, as to why Finland, through the University of Tampere, should build these curricular and research development partnerships with the rest of the world, Holtta (2014) points out how internationalization is important for the promotion of a multicultural society and for Finland's competitiveness (Holtta, 2014).

According to this perspective, although funding of internationalization processes through curricula and research partnership projects mostly comes from countries in the North who apparently do not have financial objectives, the goals and projects end up being pecuniary to them in other ways and forms. This perspective highlights how internationalization promotes academic cooperation and enhances the international visibility of the North partner, providing it with academic prestige and opening its academia up to partners in the South. In fact, it could be argued that Finland's and the University of Tampere's not-for-profit internationalization approach, by strengthening capacities in Africa and Asia through various instruments, tends to move towards a market steering process of its higher education sector, which can be seen particularly in the recent prominence of education export policies in recent years and in the introduction of tuition fees in 2015. Internationalization policies and instruments thus advertise universities in the North on an international level. The HEI-ICI programme in Finland is also meant to support the internationalization of Finnish Universities to take part in global responsibilities and to utilize their expertise in solving global problems and in consolidating competencies in developing countries (HEI-ICI Programme document, 2012).

4.2 The Success Factors

The *pertinence* of a project is the first factor for its successful implementation. The Master's curricula development project in Higher Education Management attracted stakeholders both from the North and the South. The previous discussion on the Minister of Higher Education in Cameroon presiding over the curriculum development seminar of the Master's programme highlights the importance the government attaches to higher education management capacity building. A participant in the project has also expressed how "everyone is aware that this project is indispensably important and cannot be over emphasized".

The importance of training for university administrators and managers of higher education is premised on various complexities that exist in higher education today, especially in sub-Saharan Africa, which suggests the need for more informed governance and management. There has generally been a transition from elite to mass higher education, which has been affecting the quality and funding sources of higher education, and the advent of the knowledge economy is requiring more responses from higher education institutions. Globalization is also greatly impacting the sector in sub-Saharan Africa, which is often in a victim position due to brain drain and other related challenges. There is also a general phenomenon of shrinking funding, which calls for the ability *to do more with little*. New challenges resulting from today's diversity of student bodies have also recently emerged.

Many African countries are still to use higher education to address traditional challenges related to their specific development contexts, such as poverty and generally low levels of literacy. Sub-Saharan African higher education registers the lowest participation rate of 6% in the world (UNESCO, 2009). Quality and relevance of the higher education systems can attract greater awareness than ever before. Internationalization becomes critical as one of the major strategies for dealing with the effects of globalization and for improving the state of higher education. An example of this is how, while the Mater's programme project in Cameroon was being sponsored and supported by Finnish Partners and the AUF, it also received calls from different international organizations who wanted to participate in building and sponsoring the project. It has also already been discussed how the Finnish Ministry, as well as the University of Tampere, decided to supplement the budget for the project, amidst a weak institutional basis, because of the pertinence of the project.

In these processes, funding is a key aspect. Although the funding from the Finnish partners and AUF were neither significant nor stable and did not have a strong institutional base, they were significant for paying the air tickets and accommodation of the Finnish partners for the curricula development seminars in Cameroon, and for the Cameroonian Focal Point and Representatives to South Africa and Uganda. The seminar per diems paid by AUF were also important for motivating the local participants.

Another significant factor in the Master's programme project was the presence of a competent and determined alumnus, with the required technical skills. Unlike before, many organizations are beginning to understand the importance of alumni in internationalization processes. Participants who were interviewed suggested that the Master's project was almost a "one man" project because much of its conception and many of its activities were centred on the Cameroonian UTA alumnus. This can also be explained by the weak institutional basis of the project, with the concept note written by the alumnus, and the contacts at home and in Finland made by the alumnus as well. The scientific steering of the curriculum development was equally bestowed on the Cameroonian alumnus. The main driving force behind this was the bilingual skill of the alumnus, the fact that the alumnus could mediate between the Finnish partners in English and the French-speaking partners in Cameroon, and that the curriculum, which was in English, could be written in French.

Local high-level support was very important in driving the success of the project. The involvement of the high-level officials (Minister, Rectors, Secretary General, and Inspectors) not only pointed to the legitimacy of the project but was also important for mobilizing subordinates to the various curriculum seminars. The presence of a willing team of three local teachers and educational scientists, who gave the technical touch to the curriculum in French, was also significant. The importance of the travel and physical presence of the Finnish team in Cameroon gave special legitimacy to the project and to the alumnus as well and increased their understanding of the ground realities. In an interview, one of the project participants expressed that, "if you come here alone and start singing this project, no one will listen to you, but when you come with your European colleagues, they listen to you better". The presence of the LMUU II consortium was also important and provided the platform for discussing the curricular development with international colleagues with different experiences. Local co-funding is also important for legitimizing a project and embedding it in the university, and in this project, UY2 was able to be co-financed by AUF, which enabled the university administrators to follow up on the project.

4.3 Challenges

The project was seriously marred by the absence of a joint agreement in the form of Memorandum of Understanding (MOU) both between the University of Tampere and the University of Yaoundé 2 and between the LMUU II partners. The general and dated agreement between AUF and UY2 was also not specifically for this project, and the involvement of the AUF was most generous and discretional. With an MOU, the Finnish partner institutions, who, by international standards and indices are committed to agreements, would certainly have been more engaged in and committed more resources to the project.

Although the management chain of UTA, from the faculty to Vice Rector for cooperation, recognized this project as highly important, very few at UTA knew about the project from an institutional point of view. There is no evidence that the project was embedded or recognized at UTA, more so due to its associate status within the LMUU II. Although the project received some newspaper and website publicity in Finland and at UTA-HEG, it was hardly gazetted and registered as one of the UTA cooperation activities. This experience suggests that the negotiation, agreements, drafting, and signing processes leading to an MOU are in themselves a learning process for the actors involved in the scientific and administrative chains of a project, as both parties can learn and assimilate more knowledge regarding the project. A proper understanding of the project facilitates further steps in progress and engagements.

Without a proper MOU and stable financial and remuneration base, the involvement of the different partners and actors of the project (UTA, Helsinki, the LMUU II partners, CIMO and Finnish Ministry of Foreign Affairs, Focal Point and local staff) was merely voluntary, which also became a stressful reality for the Scientific Coordinator to deal with. Without an MOU and a stable remuneration base, the Scientific Coordinator adopted a mechanism that involved co-opting different local staff as some became reluctant to participate, and having to rely on different administrators of the UY2.

Consequently, the involvement of many different people in the project affected the coherence and institutional understanding of the project, as "each individual has to learn anew of the project and bring his or her own ideas into it". The lack of an MOU that could have registered the governance of the project also rendered the Scientific Coordinator vulnerable to the two institutional partners (UTA and UY2), both of whom questioned the representativeness of the Scientific Coordinator of the project, who was the UTA alumnus. More so, the Scientific Coordinator (UTA alumnus) was not a full-time staff of any of the institutions.

The Finnish partners also expressed difficulties in compelling the receiving institution to comply with some of the agreements reached different meetings and seminars. This was the case with the local teacher training aspect of the project, which had been agreed upon as the exit strategy of the partners, the absence of which could also affect the effectiveness and efficiency of the project, as intended by the North partner.

Another example of lack of understanding between the partners was regarding the finances involved in the project. Although it was never intended by the North partners and AUF to finance the project, a significant differential fee was immediately instituted to the programme once it was launched by the UY2. Whereas the North partner's purpose for sponsoring the project (as agreed upon with UY2) was mostly developmental, through capacity-building, it turned out that, by virtue of its autonomy and local regulations, the receiving UY2 university introduced this income generating objective without consulting the other partners. The project would have actually received more resources and impetus from Finland if there was a bilateral diplomatic relationship with Finland. The attempts to discuss with the Finnish authorities about stable funding for this project received a lot of encouragements, but these were marred with regrets that Finland did not have a bilateral diplomatic relationship with Cameroon. This bilateral relationship would have been able to open many more funding avenues for the project and avoid UY2's introduction of an income generating fee.

Poor understanding of the governance pattern of the receiving University of Yaoundé 2 also affected the project. When the project discussion first started, the actors involved had not figured out the actual department or faculty that would host the Master's programme. In technical terms, the project started from the top layer of the higher education system before moving down to the hosting faculty, in ignorance of the *'bottom heavy'* or *'bottom-up'* theories which characterize higher education governance and authority (Clark, 1983). This could be explained by the fact that the project involved training administrators and their input was necessary for the curriculum development. Although there is no clear evidence that if the conception of the project started from the bottom-up (from the department or faculty) it could have moved more smoothly, and the various misunderstandings and resistances that occurred when the project was finally handed to the faculty suggests that it was important to start from the bottom. It is important to note that this approach does not neglect the involvement of the higher layer of officials with power and authority due to their having launched, legitimized and facilitated the project.

The University of Yaoundé 2 runs a typically French model of university governance, whereby the locus of power is situated in the faculty, with the deans. This is opposed to the European continental model, which has a weak middle authority and strong Professors at the bottom, the United States' model, which has a strong top administrative layer and a weak bottom, the Japanese model, which has power at the top levels, and the British model, where you find strong authority at the bottom that emphasizes collegiality (Clark, 1983). The UY2 deans are very powerful and pull their powers from the top layer down to themselves, as middle management, thus controlling the bottom layers. At UY2, the Rector merely validates the proceedings of the deans or negotiates in the event of differences in views. As many aspects of the project were discussed at the top level and later questioned at the level of the faculty, with some aspects changing and new ones being introduced, project actors expressed the feeling that the official power to start the project was in fact with the faculty, through the deans.

There is generally a lack of central internationalization and cooperation structures, cultures and practices, for example, in the form of an international office in universities. In the case of the University of Yaoundé 2, these structures exist but they are weak and marred by a poor understanding of internationalization, especially in the sense of handling and embedding such new projects from abroad. At the UY2, there is the office of the Vice Rector for Cooperation, central offices for international cooperation, and the Vice Dean for Cooperation. However, it was not clear to the project partners who were the key figures that were supposed to run the project, as the files sometimes vacillated between the Vice Rector for Cooperation and the Vice-Rector for Academics, or from the Vice Dean in charge of academics to the Vice Dean for Cooperation. Partners also observed the minor role of the Director of Academic Affairs and Cooperation as a central office played throughout the project implementation.

Another issue is local staff in countries of the South, such as Cameroon, having to adapt sufficiently to the use of international and communication technologies (ICT), related internet tools like Skype, video conferencing, and various other forms of social media, which can be used for project related discussions at a distance. A discipline time culture is also important.

The unstable sources of funding and parsimonious funding of such a project can hinder its evolution. This was one of the main reasons why the local staff capacity building and training of the future teachers of the programme was not as successful as it could have been, the reason being that it was not included in the LMUU II budget, which was, again, linked to the associate member status of the UY2 in the project.

The local culture of the people is also a highly important aspect of designing projects. In Cameroon, as in other countries of the South, no matter how important and developmental a project is, if individuals do not find their direct benefits and interests in the project, they will often be reluctant in engaging in it. Although per diems were paid at the seminars and daily allowance was paid to the Focal Points and representatives at the LMUU II seminars, the project could have been invigorated if the local Focal Point and staff, who were permanently involved in conceiving the project, received some statutory pecuniary benefits. This could have come from the local host institution, the UY2, or resulted from agreements written in an MOU. Finally, such a project raises the motivation of local staff working in a country of the South such as Cameroon, especially if it reflects local administrative practices as well. For instance, the terms of the HEI-ICI programme imposed the Finnish rate of daily allowance, which is only one-third of what is paid by the developing countries. This could be a cause for reluctance.

In further analyzing this particular case of internationalization and partnership it would also be interesting to investigate the implications of the project with regards to general trends in North-South HEI partnerships and to attempt to answer the question of what can be learned or inferred about these partnerships, beyond the specific case.

5   Conclusions

This chapter examined the mentorship of the University of Tampere of Finland in the development of the Cameroonian Master's programme in Higher Education Management, at the University of Yaoundé 2, and analysed the success factors that influenced the project and the inhibiting factors that could negatively affect similar projects by other partners elsewhere.

It is possible to conclude that the conception of the Cameroonian Master's Programme by the UTA, amidst no institutional, diplomatic or bilateral cooperation links, conveys Finland's and the University's extended internationalization policies, visions and strategies, which are beneficial to Finland as well. This has been suggested by many non-bilateral country partners who were in the HEI-ICI programme of 2013–2015, to which the Cameroonian project was attached, as a non-bilateral partner. Rather than leaning on traditional ideas that see development aid as only beneficial to the recipient country, in this particular case, it has been argued (and can also be seen in some of the strategic documents in Finland) that such an internationalization process has enabled the UTA and Finland to strategically position themselves in the international sphere, and this was at the expense of their international responsibility to fully and bilaterally institutionalize the partnership. The importance of mobility of ideas and people, the increase in international exchange of staff and students and the promotion of a multicultural society were factors that were mostly meant to promote Finland's competitiveness and to enhance its international visibility. These aspects have had indirect returns to Finland and can be captured in pecuniary and development terms for Finland.

When a project is pertinent it attracts several stakeholders, organizations and individuals, both from the North and South. This is the case of higher education management in sub-Saharan Africa, which is a concern and goal of international development agencies and bilateral partners. As can be seen from this particular project, the pertinence of a project in terms of development can render other factors, such as bilateral and diplomatic links or the necessity for written bilateral agreements (MOUs) less relevant. When a project is pertinent, many partners also want to finance it. When it addresses the local needs of the people, the level of engagement and enthusiasm of local partners is also high and projects receive high political support that legitimizes them. Co-funding by local universities is important for increasing the level of commitment of local partners.

This particular project highlights how an alumnus of the North partner university, who originates from and understands the targeted country of the project, and who has the required training and technical skills can be an important asset to the project. Alumni are important facilitators because they understand the cultures of the institutional partners, can be a part of the training process, and understand the landscape in the receiving country and in the North partner country.

Multilingual skills of the alumni and partners are important tools for the export of such a programme, between countries who speak different languages. The success of such a project also depends on the dynamism of the local Focal Point, which can include a strengthened corps of local teachers and specialists in the project. There is also the important aspect of travel and physical presence of partners from North to the South.

Written and well binding agreements are extremely important as institutional behaviours can often change during the life of the project. Understanding the governance and authority of the university in the South is important and not doing this can be an inhibiting factor to the development of the project. This also implies that the entry points where discussions and conception of projects start also matter. Although the involvement of the top layer of officials of the university can be important to legitimize the project and for mobilizing the university staff, a bottom-up approach, which involves conceiving a project with the direct institutional links at the level of the department or faculty, could be more effective.

Weak internationalization and cooperation cultures and structures in the South also account for some difficulties, and this includes sufficiently adapting to the use of ICT facilities and related long-distance communication tools, without which communication with partners in the North can be stressful.

Unstable sources of funding and parsimonious funding for such a project can also hinder its development. Although diverse funding sources are important, the multiplicity of funders in the event of unstable funding can also affect the coherence of the project. Finally, it is very important to provide stable and significant incentives to the individuals working permanently in the project in the South so that they can find their individual interests and benefits in the project, which increases the project's effectiveness. An imposition of the administrative culture of partners from the North could constitute a source of reluctance from staff in the South.

It is possible to speculate that some of the facilitating and inhibiting factors between European donor partners and African universities may often be identified through regular evaluations of projects, but the respective reports tend to remain in the archives of development agencies and Foreign Ministries. Since curricular development projects such as the one discussed in this chapter are increasingly taking place between European and African universities, it is important to have more influential forums that examine and make use of the inhibiting and facilitating factors that surface. In this regard, academics and universities in the North and South both seem to still have to embrace the fact that that they are agents of development policies and not just internationalization processes. Knowledge of this could perhaps strengthen their skills and sensitivities in the conception of such programmes.

References

Asworth, J. (1997). A waste of time? (Private rates of returns to higher education in the 1990s). *Higher Education Quarterly, 51*(2), 164–188.

Barker, R. (1995). *The social work dictionary.* Washington, DC: NASW Press.

Becker, G. (1994). *Human capital: A theoretical and empirical analysis, with special reference to education* (3rd ed.). New York, NY: Columbia University Press.

Blaug, M. (1965). Rate of return on investment in education in Great Britain. *Manchester School, 33*(3), 205–251. (Reprinted in Blaug, M. (1987). *The economics of education and the education of an economist.* Aldershot: Edward Elgar Publishing, pp. 3–49.)

Boeren, A., Bakhuisen, K., Christian-Mak, A. M., Musch, V., & Pettersen, K. (2008). *Donor policies and implementation modalities with regards to international postgraduate programmes targeting scholars from developing countries*. Belgium: Vlir-OUS.

Castells, M. (2001). Universities as dynamic systems of contradictory functions. In J. Muller, N. Cloete, & S. Badat (Ed.), *Challenges of globalization. South African debates with Manuel Castells* (pp. 206–223). Cape Town: Maskew Miller Longman.

CIMO. (2012). *HEI ICI – Higher Education Institutions Institutional Cooperation Instrument 2012–2014 Programme Document*.

CIMO. (2016). *HEI ICI – Higher Education Institutions Institutional Cooperation Instrument 2016–2018 Programme Document*.

Clark, B. R. (1983). *The higher education system: Academic organization in cross-national perspective*. Berkeley, CA: University of California Press.

Decree No.93/026 of 19 January 1993 Creating the State Universities in Cameroon.

Doh, P. S. (2012). *The responses of the higher education sector in the poverty reduction strategies in Africa: The case of Cameroon* (pp. 1–302, Doctoral dissertation). Tampere University Press.

Doh, P. S. (2015). In conclusion: Capacity development is the way: Sustainable impact of higher education development policy in the South. In S. Holtta et al. (Eds.), *Higher education institutions partnering for development and change: Reflections of the first round of the Finnish HEI ICI programme* (pp. 121–131). Helsinki: Centre for International Mobility CIMO & University of Tampere.

Holtta, S. (2014). *China-Finland education cooperation, potentials, and challenges* (Unpublished presentation at the University of Tampere). Retrieved from http://www.uta.fi/cerec/2014forum/Seppo%20presentation.pptx

Holtta, S., Pekkola, E., & Moore, A. (2015). Reflection on higher education institutions and capacity development. In S. Holtta et al. (Eds.), *Higher education institutions partnering for development and change: Reflections of the first round of the Finnish HEI ICI Programme* (pp. 9–14). Helsinki: Centre for International Mobility CIMO & University of Tampere.

OECD. (2004). *Internationalization and trade in higher education: Opportunities and challenges*. Paris: OECD Publishing. doi: 10.1787/9789264015067-en

Pajala, K. (2015). From Pioneering cooperation towards institutional change. In S. Holtta et al. (Eds.), *Higher education institutions partnering for development and change: Reflections of the first round of the Finnish HEI ICI programme* (pp. 15–16). Helsinki: Centre for International Mobility CIMO & University of Tampere.

Psacharopoulos, G. (1981). Returns to education: An updated international comparison. *Comparative Education, 17*(3), 321–341.

Psacharopoulos, G. (1994). Returns to investment in education: A global update. *World Development, 22*, 1325–1343.

Pulkkinen, J. (2013). *Preface: Evaluation of Finland's support for higher education institution, North-South-South and HEI-ICI programmes* (pp. 1–105). Finland: Ministry of Foreign Affairs.

Sawyerr, A. (2004). Challenges facing African universities. *African Studies Review, 47*(1), 1–59.

University of Tampere. (2012). *Strengthening institutional capacity for higher education Leadership and Management in sub-Saharan Africa (LMUU II) HEI-ICI programme (2013–2015)*. Finland: CIMO, Ministry of Foreign Affairs.

University of Tampere. (2016). *Towards a new university; Strategy of the University of Tampere 2016–2021*. Retrieved from http://www.uta.fi/esittely/strategia/index/strategia.pdf

Vierck, L., & Dann, P. (2011). Paris Declaration on Aid Effectiveness (2005)/Accra Agenda for Action (2008). *Max Planck Encyclopedia of Public International Law.*

CHAPTER 9

Prospects, Challenges, and Opportunities of International Exchange Programmes: The Case of a Double Degree Master's Programme

Thomas Asante and Agnes Atia Apusigah

1   Introduction

Partnership in higher education manifests in a number of ways, ranging from student mobility and exchange programmes to joint degree and research collaborations. This particular chapter highlights a case of a double degree Master's Programme established in partnership between the University for Development Studies in Ghana and the University of Applied Sciences in Dusseldorf, Germany. Through this case, this chapter provides an insight into the practical imperatives of partnership, along with the principles of mutuality, trust, transparency, and reciprocity, discussed in previous chapters of this book.

The growing trend towards internationalization of higher education institutions (HEIs) throughout the world has entailed a variety of things for participating or collaborating institutions. As Kabdiyeva and Dixon (2014) have pointed out, collaboration is a "process by which organizations with a stake in a social problem or issue see a mutually determined solution aiming at objectives they could not achieve by working alone" (Kabdiyeva & Dixon, 2014, p. 28), and it can have benefits as well as challenges. In the context of the internationalization of higher education (HE), collaboration gives institutions opportunities to offer their faculty and students cross-border experiences that are otherwise not available to either partner. Such international academic exchanges are carefully planned by the collaborating institutions.

Students in International Academic Exchange Programmes (IAEPs) often undergo such programmes as international experiences in institutions outside their national borders. As Shayo (2014) has pointed out:

> For many decades, IAEPs have been promoted as a strategic component for strengthening academic curricula of most northern and southern universities. These supposedly, mutually-beneficial academic exchange programmes have been motivated by several factors including cultural,

> social, economic, and technological. First, in terms of promoting culture, international academic exchange programmes offer unique opportunities for beneficiaries to explore, appreciate and understand different academic and non-academic cultures both within and across universities in northern and southern countries respectively. Such social and cultural knowledge is necessary for eliminating, minimizing and demystifying misconceptions, fears, and prejudices among students and staff, especially those from the northern countries regarding the real-life conditions of people (including fellow students and staff) in universities located in southern countries. On the other hand, at an individual level, most academic staff and students exchange programmes especially those from universities located in southern countries get opportunities to broaden not only their own personal academic competencies and qualifications but to also contribute to building strong institutional academic links and social networks with their northern counterparts. By so doing, these international academic links and networks tend to be beneficial to respective universities and countries in many diverse ways. (Shayo, 2014, p. 114)

Undoubtedly, there are good reasons for embarking on IAEP collaborations. Many times, curricula, publicity, ethical and even financial imperatives inspire such initiatives, and all collaborators are expected to be winners in the process. However, as Shayo (2014) has also noted, African universities, with the exception of Stellenbosch University in South Africa, have had tendencies to be recipients of IAEPs, with the tendency of their academic staff and students ì to be more on the receiving end of the process.

Under various collaborations, students may move from one institution to another for course work, research studies or practical exposure, for lengths of stay, ranging from a few days, weeks, months or even years. Institutions in the North tend to receive students from Southern and other Northern destinations for course work and research. Graduate students are more likely to move to different destinations for research work. Southern students often seek technical support (i.e., through the use of laboratories and libraries) from Northern institutions, while Northern students tend to seek opportunities for empirical studies in communities, agencies, and organizations in the South. Development Studies, Social Sciences and Humanities students of institutions in the North have tended to dominate the process by taking time off during their studies, or immediately after, in order to gain some practical experience. Institutions, organizations, and communities in the South have often been the recipients of these programmes. On occasion, students from Southern countries enrol on similar/parallel programmes that take them to Northern destinations, often for course work and/or research experiences rather than practical exposure.

IAEPS contribute tremendously to the progress of collaborating institutions' academic quality and global citizenship, but not without challenges. The shift from being local to international already adds value to the collaborators involved in partnership. Depending on the context and terms of the collaboration, benefits can be equitably shared. However, there can also be challenges that collaborating institutions need to consider when designing their partnership options.

In 2012, the University for Development Studies (UDS) in Ghana and its partner, the University of Applied Sciences Dusseldorf (UASD)[1] in Germany embarked on a double degree Master's programme aimed at deepening an existing partnership that brought together faculty and students for various intercultural learning experiences (UDS, 2014). As a new initiative between the two partners, a lot of negotiation, research and consultations were initiated as part of the design, legitimatization, and implementation of the programme. After four years of implementation, it has been necessary to assess the initiative for its successes and failures as part of a learning process, and this chapter aims at such an evaluation effort. It focuses on the prospects, challenges, and options for promoting international exchange.

The programme documents for the double degree Master's programme set up by UDS and UASD reveal that the establishment of the partnership programme was to foster inter-university partnership for institutional strengthening and for the promotion of innovative teaching and learning in the field of Development Studies. This chapter attempts to evaluate if these claims are being achieved or not. According to the partnership programme document, the project has three specific objectives: (a) strengthening of curriculum development (b) enhancement of the teaching/learning experiences of the partner institutions (c) establishment of joint learning environments and the synergetic effects of cross-border teaching and learning.

This chapter intends to reflect on how these objectives are being operationalized and seeks to generate insights for improving upon and institutionalizing the initiative as an avenue for internationalizing higher education in the two institutions. The chapter discusses the conceptualization of International Academic Exchange Programmes, the case study and the implications on partnership processes, and conclusions.

2 Overview of International Academic Exchange Programmes (IAEPS)

The practice of hosting students from other countries can be traced as far back as to the second and fifth centuries (Bevis & Lucas, 2007). According to Bevis and Lucas (2007) "as early as the second century BCE, the attendance rolls of the city-state's schools of philosophy and rhetoric attest to the admission of foreign students in comparatively large numbers" (Bevis & Lucas, 2007, p. 15). Also, in the fifth century, in Ancient Greece, Sophists (teachers of wisdom) arrived in Athens and were accompanied by protégées, who were youths from distant regions who travelled with their masters as they moved from one city to another, in search of new students (Bevis & Lucas, 2007). In tracing the development of the practice of hosting international students in an institution, Bevis and Lucas (2007) have referred to the significance of Socrates' statement about foreigners who followed Protagoras from city to city, in order to learn from his wisdom and philosophy.

It is a historical fact that students and scholars have always sought educational opportunities in countries other than their own, with the intention of getting an advanced education that distinguishes them from among their peers. This assertion is reinforced by Hegarty's (2014) observation that international students study in other countries "for the simple reason that they can get a better education abroad which will differentiate them from their peers upon returning home" (Hegarty's, 2014, p. 228). Even though international immigration laws in countries like the United States (USA) did not put international students on record until the late 18th century (Bevis & Lucas, 2007) and the Chinese Act of 1888 prohibited migration (Bevis & Lucas, 2007), Becker and Kolster (2012) have documented remarkable improvements in immigration policies as qualified students can be registered everywhere through the Students and Exchange Visitor Programme (SEVIS) system and obtain students visas for the duration of their various study experiences abroad.

The Middle Ages experienced an unprecedented increase in student migration as students from various regions moved to attend medieval institutions such as universities in Bologna and Paris (Altbach, 1998; Guruz, 2011; Haskins, 1957, as cited in Garcia & Villarreal, 2014). The reason for this movement was to satisfy a quest for advanced education. As the number of universities increased over time, migration of students in search of knowledge and education became rampant. This assertion aligns with Bevis and Lucas' (2007) observation that, "whenever a centre of scholarship and learning arose in ancient times, the gathering of scholars it drew invariably included 'foreigners' – that is, students not native to the immediate local area" (Bevis & Lucas, 2007, p. 13). This means that ancient universities embraced international students and provided them with opportunities for learning and development. Since then, international students have remained an important aspect of higher education and they continue to be in contemporary times.

During the medieval period, two of the oldest universities – Bologna and Paris – clearly showed the international character of Medieval universities and the degree of international mobility that existed centuries ago (Guru, 2011). At that time, it was characteristic of the two oldest universities to accept and admit international students. In the same manner, international education increased student mobility. Fortunately, this tradition has been sustained by contemporary universities in the sense that international students have come to represent an important demographic in higher education (Becker & Kolster, 2012).

In the 19th century, Germany had a record of international student migration since German universities opened their doors to a teeming population of students in search of scholarship and research (Altbach, 1998). German higher education was highly prestigious at the time and scholars educated in Germany tended to obtain faculty positions in major American universities (Altbach, 1998; Thelin, 2004). The historical trend of international student flows to universities in Europe and other parts of the world continued over the centuries to the present time. Currently, the tide of international student mobility has shifted to the USA, United Kingdom (UK), Australia and Canada, among other destinations. American universities enjoy contemporary prominence and fame, which can be attributed to the Second World War when American government heads and policy makers began to fund scientific research projects in different universities (Graham & Diamond, 1997, as cited in Garcia & Villarreal, 2014). After World War II, the USA invested a large amount of money in research and scholarship, and subsequently, these research funds attracted international students to their institutions of higher learning.

In recent times, IAEPs exist in diverse ways. According to Shayo (2014), IAEPs in the USA have given students opportunities to study abroad, including opportunities to pursue business-related studies in France, Spanish studies in South America, field research in Ireland, student internship programmes in Switzerland, and volunteer work in Honduras. Since 2008, approximately 65 percent of the third-year undergraduate students at Queen's University in Kingston Canada have participated in various study abroad programmes. Since the 1990s, the International Exchanges Programme at Douglas College in the USA has supported more than 1,000 students from over 60 different countries worldwide to participate in various overseas programmes, such as teaching programmes, academic research projects, cultural exchange programmes, and attending high profile international symposia (Carol, 2008). Interestingly, available records show that the majority of these foreign students came from China, Thailand, Japan and other Asian countries.

1.2 Factors Shaping IAEP

IAEPs have been moved by several factors, including interests towards cultural, social, and technological exchanges (Shayo, 2014; Mohamoud, 2003; Zeleza, 2012; Steenkamp, 2008; Irving, 2008). Shayo (2014) explains how, culturally, IAEPs offer

> Unique opportunities for beneficiaries to explore, appreciate and understand different academic and non-academic cultures both within and across universities in northern and southern countries, respectively. Such social and cultural knowledge is necessary for eliminating, minimizing, and demystifying misconceptions, fears, and prejudices among students and staff. (p. 114)

Shayo explains the cultural factor behind IAEPs by citing the former American First Lady, Michelle Obama, who, in a speech at Howard University, in Washington, DC, on December 19th, 2010, encouraged American students to register for courses in other regions as follows: "[g]etting ahead in today's workplace isn't just about the skills you bring from the classroom. It is also about the experiences you have with the world beyond our borders, with people and language and culture that are different from our own" (p. 115).

Such cross-border experiences offer rare opportunities to go beyond just reading about (i.e., through books, journals, bulletins, or websites), and listening to or watching (i.e., through radio, television, or videos) other cultures. Real life experiences in other cultural contexts help diffuse prejudices and biases and thus break class, racial and ethnic barriers. As has been the case for the UDS and UASD partnership, through joint programmes involving exchange and mobility, there is often the emphasis on intercultural learning and on social benefits. Cultural and social encounters might not transform people overnight, but, over time, strangers ease out, let down their guards and this results in more open and genuine interactions and relations.

Several authors have also highlighted the strong economic benefits involved in these processes as well (Shayo, 2014; Irving, 2008; Zeleza, 2012). Businesses of host countries receive benefits such as collection of visa fees, travel tickets, insurance plans, and accommodation charges. According to Steenkamp (2008), for the Province of Ontario in Canada, IAEPs have ensured huge economic benefits and "each international student was estimated to contribute more than $25,000 to the economy-thus making education for international students a $900 million industry in Ontario" (Steenkamp, 2008, p. 117).

Indeed, IAEPs are big budget enterprises, with various multilateral agencies, such as the Commonwealth of Nations and the United Nations, bilateral agencies, such as the German Academic Exchange Service of Ghana, the Dutch

Foreign Ministry and the International Development Research Centre of Canada, and philanthropies, such as the Carnegie Foundation and Ford Foundation, investing millions of dollars. In Ghana, almost all public universities have benefited from such investments. The UDS, University of Ghana (UG) and University of Education, Winneba (UEW) have benefited from Carnegie and Ford Foundation scholarships for staff development, gender equity programming, research chairs, and curriculum development. Regional entities, such as the Association of African Universities (AAU) and the Council for the Development of Social Science Research in Africa (CODESRIA) have also benefited in similar ways.

The ease of communication, with the explosion of the internet and investments in computerized technologies, has been very beneficial to collaborating institutions, especially those in the South, in terms of skills and knowledge development, and curriculum innovations. A World Bank funding initiative for Ghanaian tertiary education dubbed Teaching and Learning Innovations, resulted in the establishment of research laboratories, training programmes, communities of learning, video conferencing facilities, and automation of libraries.

Not only have competition and contest propelled internationalization of HEIs, but socio-cultural imperatives and scientific advancements as well.

3 IAEP between UDS and UASD

Project reports and proposals explain how the collaboration between the UDS and UASD has grown out of mutual interests in promoting academic exchanges that support intercultural learning. The project documents trace the collaboration to 2006, when two academics[2] met in Bolgatanga, in the Upper East Region of Ghana, to share ideas on poverty reduction efforts in Ghana. Several informal face to face and electronic meetings and internal and cross-border consultations eventually resulted in the UDS and UASD signing a Memorandum of Understanding (MoU) in 2008. The initiative resulted in two phases of collaboration (2009 to 2012 and 2013 to 2016) between two specific institutions, faculties and programmes: The Development Education Studies (DES) programme, now in the Faculty of Education of the UDS, and the Empowerment Studies programme of the Faculty of Social and Cultural Studies at UASD. With German funding support from DAAD, GTZ, now GIZ, and the State of North Rhine Westphalia, as well as from the two institutions, the programme was rolled out in its two phases. The initiative includes four main aspects: term abroad, summer school, community experience, organizational experience, and double degree programme.

3.1   Term Abroad

The term abroad programme was a Phase One programme that targeted undergraduate students. It entailed the enrolment of locally registered undergraduate students[3] in UDS for a term abroad at UASD. There they took relevant courses, predetermined ahead of their travel, after which credits were transferred back to UDS. The transferred credits replaced those missed in UDS due to the term abroad and as such counted toward the students' graduation in UDS. A total of 19 students participated in that programme and all graduated. The Ghanaian students left Ghana in September, at the start of their third-year first trimester, and returned in December of the same year, early enough to go for Christmas break and later join their counterparts in the second trimester at UDS in January. The Ghanaian students who enrolled in the courses with their counterparts at UASD were taught by German Professors. Thus, they were exposed to international study experiences in a German classroom and higher education context. The students also learned to quickly adapt, live and learn in the broader German context as well.

3.2   Summer School

Also, under Phase One, Summer School was organized for Master's students of UDS and UASD in Tamale, Ghana (one) and in Dusseldorf, Germany (two). The Summer schools were held in March over a three period and involved students and faculty of the two institutions. The summer schools took the form of joint programming of workshops, field trips, and research papers. A total of 60 Master's students, 30 from UDS and 30 from UASD, enrolled in the programme. In addition, six academic faculties (three from each side) facilitated thematic sessions in Tamale, Ghana and in Dusseldorf, Germany. For the staff as well, opportunities were offered for joint programming, theoretical and empirical learning, and intercultural exchanges. There was also an e-learning phase through a Moodle platform for all of the participating students, which enabled improvement of computer knowledge and skills and connection between colleague students for projects and workshops, as well as for facilitators for course materials and learning guides.

3.3   Community Experience

Community experience is a huge part of the UDS mandate. Each year, the UDS deploys over four thousand undergraduate students to deprived communities in selected districts of Ghana to live and learn with them. As an institutional mandate, it enables students to blend their theoretical campus-based learning with community experiences. Hence, the third trimester of the UDS academic calendar has been devoted to such community experiences, during the first two years of their programme. As part of the partnership, about 20 Master's students of UASD participated in such placement in the Northern region of Ghana, in Brong-Ahafo, and in the Upper West regions of Ghana. The students, who were placed in rural, resource-deprived communities, with undergraduate students of UDS, did not only learn about the difficulties of rural living and lack of development but also built relationships with the communities and among themselves. Like the UDS students, some of them maintained these relationships over time as well.

3.4   Organizational Experience

Also, as part of Phase One, Master's students of UASD were placed with non-governmental organization (NGOs) partners of UDS to learn about organized civil society work in Ghana. A total of eight students enrolled and undertook such experiences with the NGO CENSUDI in Bolgatanga, in the Upper East Region of Ghana, and with Pronet North and Plan Ghana in the Upper West Region. Five of the German students, undertook the experience with the NGOs as well, after their community experience, while three spent three to six months solely in the NGO experience.

3.5   Double Degree Programme

The double degree programme was initiated out of a need to institutionalize the benefits of the initial Phase One. It is the main pillar of the Phase Two collaboration and targets master's students of both our institutions. Details of the double degree programme are presented below.

3.6   History

The Double Degree Master's initiative developed as a second phase of partnership and collaboration between UDS and UASD, from 2013 to 2016, as a follow-up to the initial four-year Phase One, from 2009 to 2012. Viewed as a means to deepen the achievements of Phase One, the new initiative was introduced as a way of institutionalizing the existing partnership between the two universities, through the issuance of a joint degree programme. Unlike Phase One, which benefited both Master's and Bachelor's level students, phase two focused on Master's students only.

3.7   Nature of the Programme

– Like Phase One, the programme developed in Phase Two was anchored on the already existing and accredited programmes of the two collaborators: the MA Empowerment Studies programme at UASD and the MA Development Education Studies programme at UDS.

- It was estimated to benefit 80 Master's students, forty from each side, over the four-year period, from 2013 to 2016.
- Students were expected to spend two months together in "sandwich sessions" in Tamale, Ghana, from July to August and in the Spring Programme in FHD/HSD, in March of each year.
- The joint curriculum included six courses; three to be taken in Dusseldorf, Germany, and three in Tamale, Ghana. The courses in Dusseldorf comprised Theories and Approaches to Community Development, International Development Politics, and Democratic Governance and Development. Courses in Tamale were Advanced Methodologies for Community Education and Research, Gender, Citizenship and Development, and Human Rights and Development.
- E-Learning platforms for students and faculty to connect and engage ahead of the face to face meeting in Dusseldorf were arranged. Course descriptions and reading materials were shared on this platform and participating students worked together on preparatory assignments that facilitators required of them.
- Orientation of the faculties of each of the two institutions on the curriculum and institutional cultures of each university were organized in Tamale and Dusseldorf.
- Support to UDS in curriculum development, through the upgrading of library resources for research and course work, was offered.
- Students paid fees to their registered institutions while tuition fees were waived in the partner institution and counted as institutional contributions.
- Students from each university completed and met their institutional admission, graduation and certification requirements, such as entry qualifications, continuous registration throughout study duration, completion of all courses, and practical and research requirements, as stipulated by the institution and local regulations.
- Only after students graduated from their home institution could they qualify to be awarded a conjoint degree from the collaborating institution, upon submission of evidence of graduation.
- Students obtained two conjoint degrees (UDS) or diplomas (UASD) that tended together and not in isolation.

3.8 Process and Procedure of the Establishment of the Double Degree Programme

Preparatory stage: Following an end of project assessment involving the stakeholders of the two institutions, a second post-assessment phase was proposed to deepen the gains of the previous Phase One and attempt to create a more institutionalized form of the programme. Initial discussions were held over a period of time, online, between the two lead persons in UDS and UASD, regarding how to translate the proposal/recommendation into action. Consultations and discussions with funders in Germany were also conducted to assess what was feasible as a second phase (Phase Two), according to the agreement, and to initiate the double degree programme. The idea of instituting the double degree programme was presented among key faculty and managers in both institutions for buy-in. In UDS, the Academic Board, which is the highest academic decision body of the University, constituted a special subcommittee to study not a just the proposal for the double degree collaboration, but also a review of and advice on all requests for international collaborations. These internal/local activities paved the way for institutional recognition and acceptance.

The two lead persons of each university ultimately met together in Ghana to draw up the model for the programme, which was a new, one of a kind model in Ghana, except for the programme at the Kwame Nkrumah University of Science and Technology (KNUST), which, under its Spring Programme in partnership with the University of Dortmund in Germany, already initiated a similar conjoint degree programme (Abagre, 2013; UDS Executive Sub-Committee of on Double Degree Programme, 2013). While awaiting clearance, the two lead persons got together to prepare a funding proposal, which was submitted for funding to DAAD and approved. After obtaining the funds, the initiative was moved to the next level.

Confirmation and Legitimation Stage: In this stage, institutional mechanisms were put in place for implementation, with the first step of developing and endorsing a working agreement. Because there was already an MOU between the two institutions, a working agreement was developed based on Phase Two, and it was endorsed by the two institutional heads, the President of UASD and the Vice Chancellor (VC) of UDS. Institutional engagements for approval were also conducted for UDS. Since the institution of a double degree initiative was new to UDS, a formal request was made to the VC/Academic Board of UDS for approval to start implementation. The VC referred the request to the Executive Committee of the Academic Board, which set up a subcommittee with an expanded mandate to study all requests for collaboration and to make recommendations to the university. The subcommittee contracted a UDS graduate assistant who conducted a scoping study on various international collaborations which resulted in the drafting of a report. In Dusseldorf, similar scoping was done by the desk officer, who also contributed to the two reports, Abagre, 2013 and UDS Executive Committee Subcommittee, 2013. After several months of work, a report was submitted and approved by the Executive Committee for executive approval and later endorsed by the Academic Board. This cleared the way for implementation.

Design Stage: Since the initiative was being built out of the two already existing programmes in the two universities, the design of the joint curriculum was easy to do. The two curricula were juxtaposed to align areas that both student bodies could benefit from. This was possible because the two programmes, Empowerment Studies of UASD and DES of UDS, bore close similarities in terms of their goals and outcomes of preparing highly qualified professionals who could lead and facilitate social change through advocacy. In that process, six well-aligned courses were identified from the UDS curriculum to form the joint curriculum to be taken by both students. The agreed joint curriculum was then used by the team of facilitators on each side to develop course descriptions to guide teaching schedules and reading materials for the courses.

Implementation Stage: Each year, the programme is advertised in each institution for applicants who are processed, shortlisted and admitted into the programme. Qualified students are offered study scholarships that cover travel and stay in Dusseldorf and Tamale. Orientation workshops for students in both universities outline programme details and requirements, including an introduction to the E-Learning Platform (the Moodle), and these are conducted ahead of the overseas experience. The desk officer of UASD worked with the UDS lead to acquiring tickets, visas, travel insurance and other travel documents for students. Each institution, through its internal system, worked on student registration, accommodation, teaching, assessments, research, and community exposure, ahead of the arrival of students.

Pedagogical practices were not defined in the agreement but emerged during the design phase. The practices that were recommended were interactive, experience-based and self-directed ones involving multi-media teaching, field trips, group work, brainstorming, critical reflections, and take-home assignments. Use of guest lecturers was also encouraged. Whether in Dusseldorf or Tamale, students in the programme underwent intensive course work, which was often interlaced with field experiences. Both institutions used the systems of formative and summative assessments, comprising of class reflections and discussions, individual and group presentations, term papers, and critical reviews. In UDS, course facilitators have the flexibility of conducting end of course examinations or term papers. While the students of UASD found UDS courses too demanding, the Ghanaian students asked for additional stay time in UASD.

3.9   Outputs of the Double Degree Programme

From various project documents, such as reports, proposal and minutes, the following can be said to be true about the project outcome.

- The two institutions embraced the novelty of offering a double degree Master's programme and issuing conjoint degrees to qualified students. UDS students were yet to benefit from these degrees at the time of this evaluation and paper.
- So far 40 Master's students from MPhil Development Studies and MA/M.Phil. Development Education Studies have been enrolled in the programme.
- Over 1000 book titles have been acquired for the UDS Faculty of Education Library to boost the level of teaching and research resources there. The books are serving not just the enrolled students but the entire student body at the undergraduate and graduate levels, supporting academic staff preparation for lectures, research reviews and researchers at the University and beyond.
- Participating academic faculties have been connected to professional development through the programme, although language barriers have limited the extent of the exchange. The programme has created spaces for joint conferences, guest lecturing, and support for student learning experiences.
- The innovative curricula and methodologies have been shared and utilized by participating faculty and are being diffused in other programmes in the collaborating institutions. It is expected that other faculty members can be affected by the innovations introduced by the programme, such as the use of multimedia teaching techniques, field trips, participatory action learning, and self-directed learning.

4   Implications of International Academic Exchange Programmes

This chapter includes analyses and discussions from an evaluation study of the double degree exchange programme partnership between UDS and HHD/HSD. The objective of the study was to examine the prospects, challenges, opportunities, and options of the double degree programme. The analyses shared at this stage are from the empirical component of the study.

4.1   Socio-Cultural and Academic Experiences of the Double Degree Master's Programme

This section discusses prospects for strengthening IAEPS between UDS and FHD, including socio-cultural adjustments and academic restructuring.

On a socio-cultural level, both students from UDS and UASD indicated that there was the need for sociocultural adjustment as they crossed borders either to Ghana or Germany. In terms of interpersonal adjustments, the study revealed that the UASD students were more independent in organizing their experience abroad than the UDS students, some reporting weeks ahead of schedule to their host university or organizing their own accommodation. UDS students expressed that they felt they arrived in a completely different sociocultural setting with very little time to adjust. For the majority of students who were travelling to Europe for the first time, the new environment was both exciting yet challenging. UDS students tended to depend entirely on their host families, while UASD students tended to arrive independently and make their own arrangements. Indeed, the 2016 batch questioned the motives for not returning similar courtesies to the UASD students on arrival and it took a lot of effort for them to understand the differences in the dynamics.

The study also showed differences in time dedicated to socializing and leisure. Some students reported there was not enough time to engage in social activities in Germany, as compared to students who travelled to Ghana. Students who travelled from Ghana to Germany explained that in Germany people seemed busy all the time, while Ghanaians are more laid back.

Social norms, like handshaking and long greetings, seemed commonplace in Ghana and German students expressed not being sure when they were supposed to shake hands in Ghana. Ghanaian students expressed interactions with host families in Germany were different from what they were used to, for example, people in Germany were used to hugging and saying "I love you", which left Ghanaian students confused as to what to do in return.

Academically, almost all the students in the exchange programme (both Germans and Ghanaians), indicated that the length of the courses (two weeks per course) was too short and course contents were too loaded. Students expressed that class discussions were, however, prominent and that a lot of time was devoted to students sharing their ideas and perspectives. German students expressed they felt they could have more of a peer relationship with lecturers. Lecturers in Germany expressed they were more focused on helping students uncover their own interests (i.e. through guided explorations), rather than telling the students what to study.

Economically, donor and institutional funds have spared the students and faculty the cost of having to pay for the mobility piece of the programme. In addition, additional resources from donors have helped improve internal resources in each university. For UDS in particular, the new books acquired helped enrich the newly established Faculty of Education, which has been financially constrained. Also, as pointed out by Shayo (2014) and Zeleza (2012), students overseas spent money in the local industries, including in tour attractions, especially the UASD students in Ghana.

Technologically, participating students and faculty at UDS, in particular, expressed they gained skills and knowledge from the innovative knowledge share platform, Moodle. The platform allowed both faculty and students to interact at all times throughout the course of study. The skills and knowledge can be further scaled up, but the fact that they exist makes it easier to harness them when the possibility to scale up presents itself. A pioneer student of the programme, who is now a faculty member, has, over the past four years of the programme, trained UDS students ahead of their overseas experience.

4.2   Challenges of the Double Degree Master's Programme

The following challenges or barriers to the success of the exchange programme have been highlighted:

- Cross-cultural adjustments across both contexts, including differences in language, communication styles, customs, help-seeking behaviours and academic protocols, have created situations where students have felt lonely, overwhelmed and in ill-health, with difficulties accessing institutional and community resources.
- Procedural and accreditation challenges in Ghana delayed initial implementation, which caused the first batch of students to not be enrolled in the DES programme of UDS. Also, students did not appear to be at the same level of their programmes.
- Student subscriptions to the programme have wavered for both UDS and UASD. For UDS, only 24 students were able to be admitted into the programme. The first batch of 4 students did not all make it as two of them could not meet the required standards. In the case of UASD, five students have already graduated and have been awarded their degrees.
- Due to internal and external accountability requirements of their government and institution, by design, the German partners have controlled the most aspects of the programme and have tended to have final say in decision-making processes. While the process has led to the smoothness of accountability, the spirit of collegiality that should have characterized the entire process has been at times lacking.

4.3   Opportunities of the Double Degree Master's Programme

In spite of the challenges unearthed in the study, there were opportunities as well.

These include:
- The programme has allowed students to experience a new culture. Both UDS and UASD students have expressed that they have come to realize that the best way of finding out about another culture is by immersing yourself in it and that this can be done only by living in a different country.

- The programme has allowed opportunities to make friends from around the world.
- The programme has supported students in becoming truly independent.
- The programme has offered students opportunities to change ways of thinking. Students who participated in the exchange programme have expressed having different attitudes and perceptions towards people from other cultures.
- The programme has provided students with opportunities to prepare for international workplaces.
- The programme has offered opportunities for studying in a global context. With the world gradually becoming a global village, exchange programmes such as this one bring people closer.

4.4   Alternatives for the Double Degree Master's Programme

In spite of the challenges raised above, there are also options for the two universities (UDS and UASD) to remain partners in their efforts to promote quality education across borders.

First, administrators and faculty need to deepen their understanding of the difference and uniqueness of international exchange students as a population that is entirely different from domestic students. Such an understanding should be reflected in the ways in which facilitators and administrators relate to and work with international students. With such an understanding, classroom practices, field experiences, and social activities can be tailored to the international exchange students' needs and aspirations.

Second, faculty members should ensure they give international students additional attention and support by encouraging them to ask questions, take advantage of office hours, submit multiple drafts for instructional comments, by pairing them up with domestic students in class projects or group work, by providing them with language and social integration supports, and by having regular informal conversations with them to build good teacher-student relationships.

Third, international exchange students should be better integrated into campus activities. Some international students have expressed being passionate about events around campus but not getting involved in them because they perceive the activities to be for domestic students only, or because they are not made aware of the events.

Fourth, international students should be informed of the various support services and academic routines on campus for their use and benefit. This could include access to health services, basic language, and social integration support. Also, information on funding options for them to present their research at conferences, as well as opportunities for them to apply for scholarships and awards, should be made available to them. An effective orientation ahead of the overseas experience would be useful as well.

5 Conclusion

The key issues of concern highlighted in this chapter relate to the prospects, challenges, opportunities, and options that exist in this Double Degree Master's programme, in partnership processes in particular, and in internationalizing processes in HEIs in general. The case study shows how this collaboration has met the basic standards of an international collaboration, but not without challenges. The benefits intended in the proposal and supported by literature have been fulfilled through the programme implementation. The outcomes presented above, as well as the prospects and opportunities, paint a strong picture for not only continuing but also improving and scaling up. In order for partnership programmes to remain attractive to students and faculty seeking international experiences, while prospects and opportunities are celebrated, it is also important to take serious steps to mitigate the challenges that students and programmes bring up, such as the ones that surfaced in this particular case study.

Notes

1 Translated from German, the university is called Hochschule Dusseldorf (HSD).
2 One from Germany, the other from Ghana.
3 At the time, the DES programme was just starting. Over a period of three years, students from its cognate faculty, the Faculty of Integrated Studies, benefited from the term abroad. It was only in the fourth and final year of the programme that DES students benefited from the programme and have since graduated from UDS, with some returning to undertake postgraduate studies.

References

Abagre, C. (2013). *Report of scoping studies on international programmes* (unpublished). Submitted to the UDS Executive Committee Subcommittee on Double Degree Programmes, Tamale, Ghana.

Altbach, P. G. (1998). *Comparative higher education: Knowledge, the university, and development*. Greenwich, CT: Ablex Publishing.

Becker, R., & Kolster, R. (2012). *International students recruitment. Policies and developments in selected countries.* Retrieved from http://www.nuffic.nl/en/library/international-student-recruitment.pdf

Bevis, T. B., & Lucas, C. J. (2007). *International students in American colleges and universities: A history.* New York, NY: Palgrave MacMillan.

Cheng, R., & Erben, A. (2012). Language anxiety experiences of Chinese graduate students at U.S. higher institutions. *Journal of Studies in International Education, 16*(5), 477–497.

Garcia, H. A., & Villareal, M. D. (2014). The "redirecting" of international students: American higher education policy hindrances and implications. *Journal of International Students, 4*(2), 126–136.

Graham, H. D., & Diamond, N. (1997). *The rise of American research universities: Elites and challenges in the postwar era.* Baltimore, MD: JHU Press.

Guruz, K. (2011). *Higher education and international student mobility in the global knowledge economy.* Albany, NY: SUNY Press.

Hegarty, N. (2014). Where we are now-the presence and importance of international students to universities in the United States. *Journal of International Students, 4*(3), 223–235.

Kabdiyeva, A., & Dixon, J. (2014). Collaboration between the state and NGOs in Kazakhstan. *International Journal of Community and Cooperative Studies, 1*(2), 27–41.

Li, G., Chen, W., & Duanmu, J. (2010). Determinants of international students' academic performance: A comparison between Chinese and other international students. *Journal of Studies in International Education, 14*(4), 389–405.

Reinties, B., Nanclares, N. H., Jindal-Snape, D., & Alcott, P. (2013). The role of cultural background and team divisions in developing social learning relations in the classroom. *Journal of Studies in International Education, 17*(4), 332–353.

Ryder, A. G., Alden, L. E., Paulhus, D. L., & Dere, J. (2013). Does acculturation predict interpersonal adjustment? It depends on who you talk to. *International Journal of Intercultural Relations, 37*(4), 502–506.

Shayo, R. (2014). Prospects and challenges of international academic exchange programmes between universities in northern and southern countries. *Nokoko, 4,* 109–144.

Stoll, L., Bolam, R., McMahon, A., Wallace, M., & Thomas, S. (2006). Professional learning communities: A review of the literature. *Journal of Educational Change, 7,* 221–258.

UDS Executive Committee Subcommittee on Double Degree Programme. (2013). *Report submitted to Executive Committee of Academic Board, Tamale, Ghana* (unpublished) UDS-FHD (2012). Funding Proposal, UDS/FHD, Tamale and Dusseldorf.

UDS-FHD. (2014). *Report of mid-term evaluation.* Dusseldorf, Germany.

CHAPTER 10

Challenges and Prospects for Higher Education Partnership in Africa: Concluding Remarks

Emnet Tadesse Woldegiorgis and Christine Scherer

Higher education cooperation between Africa and Europe is not a new phenomenon. It is as old as the African university itself and it is reflected in Africa's colonial legacy. Its long history dates back to colonial times when it was introduced through colonial interventions that shaped the African higher education structure, curricula, and languages of instruction along European models. This has made cooperation and partnerships between the two continents easier than other collaborations.

Higher education partnership schemes today are reflected through the provision of scholarship programmes, joint degree programmes, institutional and programme accreditation processes, joint quality assurance and evaluation schemes, collaborative research endeavours, curriculum developments, and capacity building projects.

Historical legacies between Africa and Europe have persisted in shaping the trend of African higher education partnerships, which have generally been segregated along colonial lines, as Anglophone, Francophone, and Lusophone, until end of the 1980s. However, since the mid-1980s, we have been witnessing diversification in terms of higher education partnerships, which are occurring with institutions in regions that do not have colonial ties with Africa, for instance, China and India, and also with Latin American countries and among countries and institutions in Africa.

The current debate sheds light on the characteristics, challenges, and opportunities of partnership schemes. What are the models and approaches to successful higher education partnership? Under what circumstances are institutional linkages most likely to succeed—or fail? What are some of the strategies involved? What kinds of organizational structures are needed? This chapter, as a concluding remark, highlights some of these issues, within the framework of the various cases discussed in the chapters of this book. The first part discusses the problematic nature of the conceptualization of partnership itself in the African context, and it is followed by a discussion on the challenges of higher education partnership in Africa. The chapter then concludes with prospects for partnership in the future.

1   Conceptual and Practical Challenges of Higher Education Partnership in/with Africa

It is still challenging to clearly demarcate partnership processes with other related joint endeavours, such as cooperation and collaboration among actors in higher education since all can co-exist in a single project reflected at its different stages.

In principle, cooperation and collaboration are the early processes or stages of partnership, and act as prerequisites to constitute any kind of partnership in higher education. Partnership, on the other hand, is a more mature, solid, long-term, and institutionalized form of collaboration. This process of transition from collaboration to partnership is not necessarily linear but goes back and forth, based on the different imputes inherent to the process, such as funding, administration, time, capacity, political commitment, administrative efficiency, mutual trust, valid and shared interests. Thus, partnership is not a static status but it is rather a dynamic process that evolves and strengthens over time. The cases in the chapters of this book consolidate this argument as they adopt the various notions of partnership, cooperation and/or collaboration that co-exist in every single project in a broader sense. Therefore, even though partnership, cooperation, and collaborations can be theoretically discussed and distinctly based on their characteristics, it is challenging to clearly differentiate them on a practical level.

Moreover, higher education partnership is initiated to facilitate a sustainable, long-term and strategic collaboration among different higher education institutions, which operate in different settings, to boost both human and institutional capacity building. This assumption is based on the prerequisite that the process of partnership should be based on principles of mutuality, reciprocity, equality, accountability, and shared responsibility. Otherwise, instead of being a partnership on a mutual basis, it can assume a development assistance kind of model through which the roles of the parties involved are defined along the lines of donor and recipient, with latter holding a passive role. As the case studies in the chapters of this book reveal, this phenomenon has in fact been noticed in many higher education partnership schemes between African and European institutions.

As projects are initiated, funded, and in most cases, process-owned by partners in the North, with passive and/or strategic engagement from the partners in the South, most higher education partnership schemes between African and European institutions are characterized by a donor-recipient model Thus, if we take only monetary elements as the main resource for partnership, it is challenging to qualify the different collaboration schemes between African and European universities as partnership since the money, in most cases, comes only from European institutions. The prevailing dependency and difference in the balance of power when it comes to funding thus compromises the principles of mutuality, reciprocity, equality, accountability, and shared responsibility.

One can, however, argue that resources in partnerships should be defined in a broader sense, including non-monetary elements, such as research settings, expertise, experience, and other aspects. There is usually a tendency to reduce the challenge of higher education partnership to the scarcity of financial resources, citing the increasing cost of research and growing competition over funding schemes, but, in reality, the challenge goes beyond that. From the very outset, partnerships are happening among institutions that have skewed differences in terms of accumulated experience throughout their institutional histories, infrastructures, and knowledge management. It is challenging to expect equitable partnership schemes between a higher education system that has thousands of years of experience, such as the University of Bologna for instance, which was established in 1088, and a higher education system that started to emerge in the late 1930s in Africa.

Conceptualizing partnership in higher education in and with Africa, and taking its theoretical characteristics of forming mature, solid, long-term, and institutionalized forms of collaboration that operate within the principles of mutuality, reciprocity, equality, accountability and shared responsibility, is thus challenging. Furthermore, many South-South partnership schemes among African institutions have also been funded by European, Western or Northern institutions and agencies, which highlights the necessity to make a new conceptual trajectory that reflects this merge as well.

The conceptual distinction between cooperation and partnership is nevertheless important since it implies that partnership goes beyond a single project or operation that is based on current mutual interest. Partnership involves both development and delivery of sustainable strategies. Even though partnership involves cooperation, i.e. "to work or act together", it is not an isolated merge of interests, but a process that facilitates potentials for long-term synergies that live up to the motto, the sum is greater than the parts.

On a practical level, even though there are a growing number of partnership schemes, ranging from bilateral cooperation to multilateral engagements in higher education in Africa, most of them are not sustainable and phase-out after a certain period of time. The main reason for lack of sustainability has been the continued reliance of the projects on external/non-African funding.

From this perspective, the questions on the role and type of donors dominate too much of the current discussion on the suitability of partnership projects. Behind most of these discourses, there is still an assumption that external funding is the key to a suitable partnership process.

The most important challenge for the suitability of partnership schemes in Africa is actually how to ensure the political commitments of leaders and the mobilization of local funding and local constituency for science. In the face of increasing costs of research and growing competition for funding, it is challenging to totally rely on external funding in order to keep addressing critical issues.

Because of limited resources, so far, partnerships with African higher education intuitions in most cases are not comprehensive as only a few higher education institutions from certain parts of Africa have been able to participate in specific schemes, for a limited period of time. Having a sustainable higher education partnership scheme and bringing a lasting impact on the quality and quantity of knowledge production and dissemination has in fact always been a challenge in most African universities, and joint degree programmes, academic mobility schemes, capacity building and internationalization efforts are mostly donor dependent. It is thus important to work on designing institutional mechanisms that can sustain successful partnership projects.

Regional initiatives through the African Union (AU) to facilitate close collaboration and partnership among African higher education systems have also faced a number of challenges. From the very outset, the AU has kicked off the higher education harmonization strategy in 2007, with the objective of creating a regional higher education area that facilitates mutual recognition of academic qualifications, promotes student and staff mobility within Africa, ensures effective quality assurance mechanisms, and creates a mechanism of transferability of credits. The AU has also set up different functional processes for the realization of the above objectives, including the Mwalimu Nyerere programme, which promotes student and academic mobility; Tuning Africa, which works towards the harmonization of curriculums; the Pan-African University Network, which established joint degree programmes and centres of excellence; and quality assurance and rating mechanisms.

Despite all the efforts to enhance aspects of cooperation and partnership on all sides and all levels, and despite the success within the field in the past ten years, the progress seen on the ground in terms of implementing a harmonization strategy has been slow. The various components of the strategy have either not been implemented or their impacts have not been felt yet. This is because the process of the AU higher education harmonization strategy has been facing political, functional and organizational challenges since the time of its inception.

An example of an organizational challenge is the Arusha Convention (now Addis Ababa Convention), which is taken as the legal framework of the harmonization process and has not yet been fully ratified and implemented by its member states. The AU commission, which is now in charge of the harmonization process, is also underfunded and most of the functional processes of the harmonization strategy are dependent on external funding. The AU as a continental organization has also not yet been able to bring together the fragmented sub-regional initiatives of higher education. Moreover, the regional university associations, like the Association of African Universities (AAU), have also been institutionally challenged in terms of mobilizing stakeholders in the process to achieve the intended goals. Other enabling factors of higher education harmonization, such as visa regulations, harmonized tuition policies, qualification recognition frameworks, and credit transfer systems, are also not yet fully implemented in Africa.

One of the impetus of higher education partnership is creating a favourable research environment that mobilizes both a diverse set of funding sources and a pool of expertise. Partnership in higher education among African universities enables institutions and researchers to put resources together and achieve common goals, such as generating and disseminating knowledge to the wider community. Even though there has been increasing interest among higher education institutions and researchers to learn more about the different modalities of research collaborations over the past decades, there is still a prevailing neo-colonial conception that research collaboration that exists between the global North and South, in most cases, is dictated by those who supply the sources of funding.

In some cases, those who provide funding have also had the power to manoeuvre the priorities of the research conducted in partnerships. Partners from the North, in most cases, dictate the scientific agenda and its implementations processes because they have to serve their interests in the money they invest. Thus, even though there are many research collaboration programmes between institutions in the North and South on an international research agenda, it is still challenging to generate and mobilize funding and other resources for local research agendas in Africa.

In explaining the case of Health Research in the Tropics, Wollfers et al. (1995) have touched upon this issue and illustrated its dynamics;

> Lack of funds can be misunderstood as lack of funds for local research initiatives. There are funds for northern initiatives, and consultancies

within the framework of northern research programmes are well paid […] we have to accept their priorities and interests. (p. 1653)

However, time has also brought changes. Europe's and Germany's efforts, since the new millennium, to deal with some of these issues, indicates that there is a shift of paradigm happening in the set-up of research-cooperation, and it is supported by the quest for a broader view of Africa's potentials. When it comes to setting up priorities in regional research agendas, these potentials include integrating the perspectives of the South.

2   Prospects of Higher Education Partnership in Africa

The higher education partnership schemes between African and European universities have not yet fully developed enough to qualify and meet all the fundamental requirements discussed above. However, this does not mean that partnership projects that have been put in place do not also bear fruits. As many cases have already proved, there are successful partnership project approaches that are funded by external donors and that have brought positive higher education engagements in Africa.

Higher education partnerships between Africa and the EU have recently become more institutionalized within the general framework of Africa-EU cooperation, which was launched after the first Africa-EU summit held in Cairo, Egypt in 2000. The cooperation took the EU commission and the AUC as agents of negotiation on a broad scale of issues, including energy, climate change, migration, mobility, and employment issues. The higher education partnerships have mostly touched on the *"employment, mobility and migration"* piece, extending their dialogue to the areas of capacity building, networking, mobility, institutional support, and innovation in higher education.

There are positive prospects, which have already started to consolidate and sustain higher education partnership between and among African and European universities. As stated in the strategic document, the compressive Africa-EU strategic cooperation document, which was launched in 2007, has committed to take the partnership schemes to a strategic level;

> The purpose of this Joint Strategy is to take the Africa-EU relationship to a new, strategic level with a strengthened partnership and enhanced cooperation at all levels. The partnership will be based on a Euro-African consensus on values, common interests, and common strategic

objectives [...] which will provide an overarching long-term framework for Africa EU relations, will be implemented through successive short-term Action Plans and enhanced political dialogue at all levels, resulting in concrete and measurable outcomes in all areas of the partnership. (European Union, 2017, p. 2)

Despite many challenges, the Africa-EU partnership scheme has contributed to strengthening institutional partnerships in the field of higher education through networking, student mobility, and the promotion of institutional support and innovation. As highlighted in the chapters of this book, significant achievements have already been made through respective partnership schemes. Since 2007, more than 15 higher education networks, involving more than 120 partners from 37 African countries, organized different collaboration schemes and academic mobility programmes across the continent, in the framework of the Nyerere Programme (European Union, 2017). Other programmes such as Erasmus Mundus, Tempus, Edulink, and Erasmus+ have also contributed to enhanced academic collaboration between African and European universities.

The Africa-EU partnership has also been supporting South-South partnership among African universities in the area of academic mobility since 2016. Based on the experience of the Intra-ACP Academic Mobility Scheme of 2016, the European Union has launched the Intra-Africa Academic Mobility Scheme under the Pan-African Programme. The aim of the programme is to promote higher education cooperation among African Universities so as to improve the quality of African higher education through partnership, mobility, institutional support, and innovation. In the two selections in 2016 and 2017, 14 projects were selected for a total budget of 20 million Euros. Despite constant support from European partners, most African governments have not yet shown conceit commitment, allocating funding for both intra and intercontinental higher education partnership schemes.

It is therefore important to craft compressive, balanced clear and robust partnership arrangements and strategies, with good communication among and between different institutions that can bring forth sustainable political commitments, clear and agreed on purposes and objectives, shared commitment and ownership, and trust between partners. Even though partnership processes have often been taken as a capacity building process for the African institution, it is important to acknowledge that it is a two-way process that involves exchanging experiences and engaging in collaborative knowledge production and dissemination processes. Therefore, crafting compressive partnership strategies needs to ensure not only the establishment and maintenance of mutual benefits for all partners but also the development of systems to monitor, measure and document learning outcomes.

It is important to acknowledge the fact that partnership in higher education is an integral part of the future of internationalization processes through which universities will open up their national systems to international experiences, not only via academic mobility but also through different strategic alliances. As indicated in the chapters of this book, different partnership processes in higher education have managed to boost the institutional visibility and capacity of African universities.

In the process of developing a strategic approach to implement a sustainable partnership, it is important to constantly reflect on mutual interests, rationales, challenges, risks, and implications, to minimize the unintended consequences that can come out of partnerships. For a long time, African higher education institutions have been looking for partners outside of Africa, in Europe and beyond, and African universities have more partnership projects with European universities than with universities within Africa. Among the reasons for this skewed trend are the long historical relationships with European institutions, the desire to partner with more experienced and resourceful institutions, and the relative funding possibilities in the global North.

In recent years, however, there is a growing trend of higher education partnership processes among African universities on different levels. The African Union has been leading a set of processes to "harmonize" degree structures, courses, credits, and quality assurance mechanisms at different levels. There are also national, sub-regional, and regional initiatives already put in place to realize harmonization processes. These initiatives will promote and further facilitate higher education partnership within and among African universities.

This book has attempted to highlight some of the main trends of higher education partnership, not only between African and European institutions but also between institutions within Africa. The conceptual debate on higher education partnership or cooperation is still young and needs to be discussed further. Since partnership and its conceptions are constructed in the context of specific projects, the discussions in the chapters of this book lead to the conclusion that there is no single authentic model of partnership in higher education. The notion of partnership covers greatly differing concepts and practices, and it is used to describe a wide variety of types of relationship, in a multitude of circumstances and contexts.

There are, however, different factors that play an important role in the success of partnership in higher education. Among others, it is most crucial to have a clear objective on what exactly the partnership is seeking to do, in terms of its purpose, and whether it is strategic or project driven.

Many successful partnership processes are strategically driven, covering broad aims, with the objectives of arriving at sustainable and comprehensive mergers of interests. Moreover, it is important to define the changing relationship and roles of key actors involved in the partnership processes. It is imperative to clearly define interests and expectations and clearly state the resources that each party is going to commit to the partnership process. This is important to minimize confusion and grievances when implementation mechanisms are formulated and activities are carried out.

References

European Union. (2017). *The Africa-EU strategic partnership: A joint Africa-EU strategy*. Retrieved from http://www.africa-eu-partnership.org/sites/default/files/documents/eas2007_joint_strategy_en.pdf

Wollfers, I., Adjei, S., & van der Drift, R. (1995). Health research in the tropics. *Lancet, 351*, 1652–1654.

Index

academic exchange 18, 93, 94, 131, 185, 187, 190
Africa-EU 18, 24, 25, 81, 82, 84, 88, 90, 121, 132, 133, 208, 209
Africa-EU summits 84
Algeria 7, 103–105, 107–114, 126, 132

Bologna process 8, 115, 120, 122, 123, 133

challenges 9–11, 89, 104, 132, 177, 199
collaboration 2, 6, 62, 76, 78, 87, 90, 92, 93
colonial 5, 12, 17, 29, 33, 34, 46, 47, 53, 62, 79, 109, 133, 167, 168, 203, 207
cooperation 1, 2, 4, 8, 9, 13, 15–19, 31, 32, 46, 78–82, 88–93, 96, 98, 100, 104, 106, 108, 117, 120, 123, 125, 132, 133, 142, 163, 168, 170, 174, 177, 179, 180, 182, 203–206, 208–210

donor 5, 12, 18, 19, 22, 26, 45, 46, 77, 79, 82, 92, 159, 163, 166, 167, 182, 198, 204, 206
double degree 10, 141, 185, 193–197, 201

Erasmus Mundus 7, 38, 104, 112–114, 116, 117, 209
European Union 8, 13, 22, 23, 44, 66, 72, 79, 80, 81, 85, 87, 90–92, 95, 103, 120, 209

Ghana 8, 10, 38, 39, 92, 139, 141–143, 146, 151, 153, 154, 156, 160, 161, 185, 187, 190–193, 195, 197–199, 201
global south 5, 9

harmonization 1, 13, 16, 83, 120, 125, 126, 134, 206, 210
higher education xiv–xvi, 1, 4–9, 11, 16, 18, 23, 33, 71, 76, 83, 84, 103, 105–108, 110, 116, 120, 122, 123, 126, 131, 141, 163–165, 168, 169, 171, 173, 175, 180
higher education policies 6

internationalization 5, 29, 31, 32, 35, 37, 40, 41, 52–54, 138, 141, 152, 175

Intra-ACP 25, 209

knowledge xiii, xiv, 1, 5, 6, 7, 12, 13, 16, 19, 22, 29, 30, 31, 34, 36, 37, 40, 43, 44, 46, 52, 54, 55, 62–65, 67, 69, 72, 76, 77, 80, 83, 90, 91, 97, 103, 104, 122, 123, 125, 133, 138, 141, 144, 147, 149, 153, 156, 160, 165, 166, 175, 177, 186, 188, 190–192, 198, 205–207, 209

Maghreb 7, 47, 49, 104–107, 110, 111, 114, 116, 117, 123
mobility 4, 7, 12, 25, 67, 82, 114, 115, 209
Mwalimu Nyerere Mobility Programme 4, 12

network 4, 12, 48, 55, 88, 106, 107, 110, 116, 124, 206
North-South 9, 16, 26, 114, 115, 117, 163, 167, 168, 180

Pan-African University xvi, 4, 8, 12, 19, 21, 26, 83, 93, 97, 120, 121, 132, 134, 206
partnership 2, 4, 6–8, 11, 13, 15, 16, 18, 26, 62, 71, 76, 80, 81, 84, 112, 117, 120, 138, 155, 185, 203, 207

quality assurance xiv, xvi, 8, 110, 116, 124, 173

regional comparison 52
research xiv, xv, 6, 18, 35, 41, 46–48, 50–53, 62, 64, 66, 68, 70, 72, 85, 87, 88, 91, 92, 94–96, 98, 99, 106, 123, 126, 132, 141, 150, 168, 173, 191, 194, 207
research and development 6, 62, 64, 65, 69, 72, 73, 78, 85, 86, 88–91, 97, 120

service learning 138, 144, 197
sub-Saharan Africa 5, 29, 33, 39, 52, 79, 88, 165, 169, 175, 181
sustainability 3, 14, 15, 22, 43, 51, 80, 94, 97, 167, 205

Tempus programme 108, 111

Printed in the United States
By Bookmasters